BPS MANUAL OF PSYCHOLOGY PRACTICALS

Experiment, Observation and Correlation

compiled by

Rob McIlveen, Louise Higgins
and Alison Wadeley

with

Prefaces by
Paul Humphreys

BPS
BOOKS

Published by The British Psychological Society

BPS Manual of Practicals

THE EDITORS

Rob McIlveen is a Senior Coursework Moderator and examiner for schools A-level psychology, and teaches at Springwood High School, King's Lynn.

Louise T. Higgins is Head of the Department of Psychology at Chester College, and a former Chair of the Association for the Teaching of Psychology.

Alison Wadeley is Chief Coursework Moderator for A/S and A-level psychology, and a Senior Lecturer at Filton College, Bristol.

Paul Humphreys is the Chief Examiner and a Senior Coursework Moderator for A-level psychology. He is a Senior Lecturer in Social and Developmental Psychology at Worcester College of Higher Education.

For Gill and P.W.P. R.M.

First published in 1992 by BPS Books (The British Psychological Society), St. Andrews House, 48 Princess Road East, Leicester LE1 7DR.

Reprinted 1993, 1994, 1996, 1998

ISBN   1 85433 074 8

Printed and bound by Antony Rowe Ltd.
Whilst every effort has been made to ensure the accuracy of the contents of this publication, the publishers and authors expressly disclaim responsibility in law for negligence or any other cause of action whatsoever.

CONTENTS

INTRODUCTION

The aim of the BPS *Manual of Psychology Practicals* is to provide students and teachers with a range of practical exercises, in an engaging and stimulating way. The *Manual* is primarily intended for those students following an A- or A/S level course in psychology, or who are in the first year of an undergraduate course. However, there is no reason why the manual should not be used by students on other courses in which psychology is studied, since each of the exercises lends itself well to modification. Students following a GCSE course could, for example, conduct simplified versions of the exercises and analyse the resultant data in a way suitable to the requirements of the course. Equally, advanced undergraduates could take an exercise as the basis for devising an independently conducted research project. In short, we hope that the *Manual* will be a useful aid to anyone with an interest in conducting practical exercises in psychology.

The *Manual* has been divided into three sections representing the core psychological research methods of experiment, observation and correlation. Each section has a preface describing and evaluating the method, and contains five exercises drawn from different areas of psychological concern. The experimental exercises examine experimenter bias effects, parapsychology, laterality, intelligence and human memory. In the observation section there are exercises on sex-role stereotyping in the media, attribution theory, pedestrian behaviour, conservatism and aggression in children. The exercises in the correlation section look at attitudes to mental illness, fear of animals, aesthetics, locus of control and academic achievement.

The selection of contributions was based on three criteria. First and foremost, the exercise had to be interesting to conduct, and enjoyable to write up. As all practising teachers of psychology will acknowledge, ourselves included, there are few things more frustrating than having to guide students through, for example, yet another exercise based on the Müller-Lyer illusion. From the student's perspective, there can be few duller ways to spend a practical session than in conducting such an exercise. As a result, the enthusiasm for writing up the exercise is often non-existent, and thus our contributors had to convince us that an exercise would stimulate interest and be an enjoyable experience for students.

Next, an exercise had to be workable. To assess this, all of the contributions were initially 'road-tested' by our own students, to whom we owe a debt of gratitude. We asked them to comment on the readability, clarity and procedural simplicity of each exercise. In many cases, our students were able to offer suggestions about things which we, as editors, had taken for granted. For example, although many institutions follow the same syllabus, the facilities at their disposal vary widely: some have suites of computers, others have none. We have therefore concentrated on exercises that do not rely on technology. We are also aware that a growing number of students are studying psychology through distance or open learning courses. The exercises have, therefore, been 'fine-tuned' and written in such a way as to enable students following such courses to conduct a practical exercise with the very minimum of input from a teacher. However, we do advise students following open or distance learning courses to always check procedures first with their tutor who may be able to offer additional advice.

Our third consideration was the method by which the data resulting from an exercise were analysed. As our students reminded us, some methods of analysis are more familiar than others, and some are certainly more straightforward to conduct. Consequently all of the exercises suggest the simplest and most appropriate method of data analysis. All of the correlational exercises, for example, suggest either Spearman's or Pearson's method to analyse the data, as both of these methods are likely to be familiar to students following an A-level or higher level course. In those cases where a statistical procedure is unlikely to be familiar to most students, the method of analysis has been described in detail.

Each of the exercises uses the following headings: *Abstract, Materials and Equipment, Introduction and Hypotheses, Procedure, Results, Discussion,* and *Bibliography*.

The *Abstract* section provides an indication of both the broad and specific concerns of the exercise and the sorts of issues to which the resultant data are likely to give rise. The reader can thus see at a glance whether or not an exercise is likely to be appropriate to his or her needs.

In the *Materials and Equipment* section, advice is given as to the number of participants that will be needed for the exercise and, in some cases, the number of investigators necessary to conduct the exercise with maximum ease. Although most of the exercises have appendices supplying the material needed (such as questionnaires, stimulus material, and data recording sheets), some exercises require equipment that cannot be included in the manual (one of the exercises, for example, requires a number of yoghurt cartons!). In such cases, however, the necessary equipment should be easy to obtain. **It should be noted that copyright has been waived for the materials that are presented in the Appendices. Thus, investigators can copy as much of the material as necessary to conduct the exercises. Please remember, though, that the exercises themselves are subject to normal copyright restrictions.**

The *Introduction and Hypotheses* section provides theoretical background to the exercise and the formal hypothesis or hypotheses that will be tested. We have deliberately steered away from providing a detailed review of the relevant background literature, and have instead given a broad outline of the area under investigation. The background information thus provides a foundation, but we feel that students should be encouraged to search for detailed information themselves. To this end, the Introduction section also suggests sources that students could usefully employ. Although some exercises test more than one hypothesis, there is no obligation for students to test all of the hypotheses suggested. Instead students should aim to select an aspect of the exercise that most interests them.

The purpose of the *Procedure* section is to provide sufficient information to enable an exercise to be conducted with little or no assistance from the teacher. Great care has been taken to ensure that procedural details are presented in a clear and accessible style. Any procedural problems that might arise are also presented in this section.

The importance of clarity has not been neglected in the *Results* section. Detailed and specific guidance on how to summarize and present the data produced in an exercise is given, as well as appropriate methods for statistical analysis of the data.

In the *Discussion* section the original aims and hypotheses of the exercise are examined in light of the findings obtained and students are encouraged to examine their data in relation to wider theoretical issues. Additionally, interesting points for discussion such as the limitations of the exercise, possible modifications and extensions are also presented.

The *Bibliography* is sub-divided into the following three areas: *General Background References* (such as textbooks that contain information relevant to the exercise), *Specific Background References* (such as books devoted to the area of the exercise) and *Journal Articles* (empirical or review articles concerned with the area of the exercise). We have used this division to reflect the interests and resources of the different levels of readership. Thus, we would anticipate that A-level students would primarily use *General* and *Specific Background References*, whereas undergraduates would also incorporate *Journal Articles* into their consideration of the issues raised by the exercises.

In addition to the fifteen exercises, the Manual contains two very important appendices. The first concerns ethical issues in psychology. Ethical issues arise whenever psychological research is conducted, and in recent years there has been a growing emphasis on ethical considerations in psychological research. *Appendix 1* to this manual addresses these issues in the form of a checklist for students' own research in keeping with the idea of this publication as a manual. *Appendix 2* contains information on the writing up of practical exercises. Although there is no single correct way of writing a report, there are widely accepted standards and conventions which should be followed. *Appendix 2* outlines these and, by way of illustration, includes a model write-up of a research exercise annotated to show how guidance notes for writing up relate to the report itself (though it should be noted that the write-up is not of an exercise presented in this *Manual*).

This *Manual* is intended as a workbook, and the editors hope that teachers and students will feel free to adapt and modify the exercises presented, and to investigate the wide number of variations suggested throughout the *Manual* as well as conducting the exercises themselves. We have enjoyed compiling the manual, and hope that students and teachers will enjoy conducting the exercises.

ACKNOWLEDGEMENTS

Practical exercises are an integral part of psychology. Devising exercises that are interesting to students can, however, be a difficult task. In this *Manual*, teachers of psychology in both further and higher education have provided 15 exercises using the core psychological methods of experiment, observation and correlation.

The *Manual* could not have been prepared without the aid of Sandra Cadwallader and, especially, Joyce Collins and Susan Pacitti at the British Psychological Society. Joyce and Susan have worked tirelessly in the production of this *Manual* and they, as much as the editors, deserve any credit for it. We thank them both.

PREFACE TO THE EXPERIMENTAL METHOD

Paul Humphreys
Worcester College of Higher Education

An examination of the history of psychology (for example Wertheimer, 1970) reveals that early psychologists defined their discipline in terms of a science of mind and experience. William James (1890) defined psychology as 'the science of mental life'. Later on, and largely as a result of John B. Watson's (1919) influence, a concentration upon *behaviour* as the object of investigation came to prominence. Much of this emphasis resulted from the efforts of the pioneer psychologists – Wilhelm Wundt as well as James and Watson – to establish psychology as an empirical, research-based discipline separate from philosophy.

This was largely achieved by the adoption of one of the chief research methods of the natural sciences: the experiment. The use of the experimental method confirmed the establishment of 'mainstream' psychology firmly within the boundaries of a 'positivist' philosophy ('positivism' was founded by Auguste Comte who contended that human and societal experience should be studied utilizing the objective methods of the natural sciences such as physics and chemistry).

The emphasis on the use of 'the scientific method' remained strong and in fact became ever more central until the relative decline, in the late 1950s, of what has been called "Watsonian Behaviourism' as the principal model of psychology.

Hypotheses: one-tailed and two-tailed

The process of experimentation begins with the formulation of a *hypothesis* which, it is hoped, the results of the experiment will either confirm or reject. A hypothesis is an unambiguously-phrased prediction of the outcome of an experiment. One of the exercises in this section (*Evaluating a technique to aid the learning of people's names*), for example, hypothesizes that the use of mnemonic devices aids the recall from memory of verbal information. This hypothesis can be called an *experimental hypothesis*.

On some occasions experimenters are unable to specify precisely what the outcome of an experiment will be. For example, an experimenter might hypothesize that a certain drug will cause a change in a person's behaviour but be unable to specify precisely the way in which behaviour will change. On other occasions, it might be easier to hypothesize the way in which behaviour will change. An experimenter might predict that a certain drug will not only affect people's ability to, say, perform arithmetical tasks, but will affect their ability in a detrimental way. Any hypothesis that leaves open the possibility of how a given behaviour will change is called a *bidirectional* (or *two-tailed*) *hypothesis*, whereas a hypothesis that specifies the direction of behavioural change is called a *uni-directional* (or *one-tailed*) *hypothesis*. If a researcher were investigating gender differences in cognitive styles, he or she might use a uni-directional hypothesis such as 'females will perform better than males on verbal items in a given IQ test', or a bi-directional hypothesis: 'there will be a difference in the performance of males and females on verbal items in a given IQ test'.

The logic of the experimental method is delightfully simple. It is based upon abstraction, control and manipulation. The experimenter rarely studies events or phenomena as they occur in real life; rather, he or she 'pulls out' one facet (or variable) for close scrutiny and manipulation. Having abstracted the behaviour (variable) to be studied, the experimenter then works according to the following piece of simple logic, which J.S. Mill called 'the rule of one variable': if two groups of participants are equal in all respects save one and are not similar with respect to a behaviour that is being measured, then the difference between them *must* be attributable to the one way in which they were different.

Take, for example, an experiment conducted by Bell (1981) in which participants attempted to solve various problems within the laboratory. For some participants normal room temperature was maintained; for others, the temperature of the laboratory was raised quite substantially. Bell reported that the first group were much more efficient at solving the various problems than were the second group and, on the basis of this, it was concluded that heat reduces the efficiency with which people can perform problem-solving tasks. It should be noted that this sort of approach to experimentation has not been without its critics who contend that the experimental method is artificial and fails to recognize context and the interaction of factors. This point will be considered in more detail later.

Variables: independent and dependent

The one factor which is different between the conditions is called the *independent variable* (which is usually abbreviated to IV). The name derives from the fact that the variable is independently in the control of the experimenter. The aspect of behaviour that is measured in the experiment is called the *dependent variable* (usually abbreviated to DV). This term derives from the fact that it cannot be manipulated since it is the outcome of the manipulation of the independent variable and dependent upon it.

To return to the experiment conducted by Bell (1981), we can see that the difference in room temperature between the two groups of participants constitutes the independent variable whilst the measurement of efficiency in solving problems is the dependent variable. The purpose of the experiment is clear: to determine whether one factor (such as Bell's experimentally-induced difference in temperature level) has an effect upon another factor (people's problem-solving efficiency).

Experimental design

Three basic experimental designs can be identified:

(1) the *independent groups design* (sometimes referred to as the *unrelated groups design* or the *between subjects design*)

2

(2) the *repeated measures design* (sometimes referred to as the *within subjects design*)
(3) the *matched groups design* (sometimes referred to as the *related groups design*).

In the independent groups design, participants are allocated to the different conditions on a purely random basis (such as tossing a coin). The logic of this design is that if allocation to conditions is made on a purely random basis then any differences among participants that might influence results will tend to be distributed evenly across the various conditions.

In the repeated measures design each participant is tested in all of the conditions. The logic here is that since the same individuals are appearing in all conditions, individual differences between participants do not affect the outcome (each participant acts as his or her own 'control').

Finally, in the matched groups design, participants in the different groups are individually matched according to some variable or variables that the experimenter suspects may influence the experiment (such as age, intelligence or level of education) and therefore wishes to hold constant.

Standardizing procedures

A further strategy that experimenters employ to maximize comparability between groups or conditions is to *standardize experimental procedures and instructions*. This means that exactly the same instructions as to how to perform the task are given to all of the participants. Additionally, all participants are studied in identical or highly similar environments, at comparable times, using the same apparatus, and are assessed under the same criteria. In other words, experimenters do everything possible to ensure the uniformity of experience and assessment. In so doing they try to eliminate or control for any possible confounding or extraneous variables (that is, factors other than the independent variable) which may operate across the conditions.

But psychologists are not physicists or chemists and their subject matter cannot (and some would say will not) be controlled in exactly the same way. Consequently, experimental psychologists are forced to accept that there always will be some random fluctuations between the experiences of the participants in the different conditions, though the hope is that these will be minor and unimportant. As long as these minor differences between the conditions are random and not systematic (that is, consistently favouring participants in one condition and disadvantaging those in the other), there are ways of determining whether any differences found are due to the operation of the independent variable.

Statistical tests

Such ways involve the use of what are called *tests of statistical significance*. These tests determine the likelihood of obtaining the observed results (or more extreme results) if the independent variable has no effect and chance factors alone are operating. You will recall that experimenters advance an experimental hypothesis which predicts that some change in behaviour will be observed in an experiment: that is, that the independent variable will affect the dependent variable. Another type of hypothesis, termed the *null hypothesis*, predicts that the independent variable will *not* affect the dependent variable and that any observed differences between the groups can be attributed to the operation of chance factors alone.

By convention, psychologists accept that, if the likelihood of obtaining the observed results or more extreme results under the hypothesis that chance factors alone are operating is sufficiently small (typically, less than 5%), then it is reasonable to reject that null hypothesis in favour of the experimental hypothesis. Note that psychologists do not, and because of what they study cannot, talk in terms of absolutes or certainties – only probabilities. When the result of a statistical test indicates that it is extremely unlikely that a difference between the conditions as large as that actually observed would arise from the operation of chance factors alone, the effect is said to be *statistically significant* and the experimenter concludes that the independent variable has had an effect on the dependent variable.

Cause and effect

It is important to emphasize that the experimental method (and only this method) permits psychologists to talk in terms of cause and effect; that is, one factor causing an effect in another. This is an extremely powerful reason for the use of the experimental method in any discipline. The degree of control afforded by the experimental method, and its usage by the so-called natural sciences has given the experiment an academic respectability not found in other methods. This is significant when we view psychology as a young discipline trying to gain academic and scientific credibility and acceptance.

The experimental method

In terms of its actual usage, the experiment comes in many forms. These are usually defined by the following criteria:

the number of conditions used,

the setting in which the experiment takes place,

and the amount of control the experimenter is able to exert.

These will now be explored in more detail.

Number of conditions

The simplest version of the experiment has just two conditions. In one of these participants are exposed to the independent variable. For example, suppose that an experimenter hypothesizes that memories decay with the passage of time unless they are maintained by repetition or rehearsal (the *passive* or *trace decay* theory of forgetting). In order to test this hypothesis, the experimenter reads out loud four consonants (such as XMPT) followed by a three digit number. The participant has been previously instructed, on hearing the three digit number, to count backwards in threes from this number and to do so out loud. After a certain period of time, say 10 seconds, the participant is instructed to recall as many of the consonants as possible, in their correct order of presentation.

Suppose that a number of participants tested in this way had managed to recall an average of 2 consonants correctly. Is the experimenter in a position to claim that the hypothesis has been confirmed? Of course, the answer is 'no' since there is nothing against which to *compare* the performance. In order to be able to make some meaningful comparison the experimenter needs to know something about people's performance when recall is immediate. Thus, the experimenter must also test a group of participants who attempt to recall the list of consonants *immediately* after they have been presented (that is, after 0 seconds delay). This group of participants, who have *not* been exposed to the experimental treatment, are termed the *control group*, in contrast to those participants who *were* exposed to the experimental treatment, who are termed the *experimental group*.

More complex experimental designs have three or more conditions rather than just the two. In the case of the example given, recall ability following a 5, 15, 20, or 30 second delay could also be investigated and, as a result of the data generated, something could be said about the passive decay theory of forgetting.

The laboratory experiment

When lay people think of a psychological experiment they probably picture a room with an array of electronic equipment any of which can be attached to an unfortunate individual's head in order to 'read their mind'. The experimenter, usually a white coated, bearded and bespectacled individual carries a clipboard and pen and paces around the room nervously, muttering to himself. This picture is completely misleading.

A large proportion of psychologists are female and, therefore, unlikely to possess beards. Few (be they male or female) are shortsighted, and even fewer mutter to themselves. More importantly, most psychology laboratories do not contain a plethora of technologically advanced equipment. The psychology laboratory is very often little other than a room with a few chairs, a table and (on occasion) a portable computer.

In most cases, psychologists conduct their experiments in laboratories in order to *control* for the possibility of extraneous and confounding variables influencing the outcome of an experiment. For example, presenting a participant with a list of four consonants in a room in which other people were talking and laughing would not constitute a fair test of the passive decay theory of forgetting. The laboratory setting minimizes the influence of confounding variables and allows a much more confident claim to be made about the effect (if any) of the independent variable being investigated.

The psychology laboratory is not, however, the exclusive preserve of the experimental method. Many observational studies are carried out in psychology laboratories. Perhaps the best illustrations come from developmental psychology. In some cases, developmental psychologists interested in mother–child interactions invite parents and their young children to a 'play room' located within a psychology department. As the mother and child play, the psychologist, perhaps observing from behind a one way mirror, will observe and record patterns of interaction. Or, social psychologists interested in the development of social skills behaviour, might observe and video-record individuals interacting within the context of a laboratory setting.

Many of the advantages of the laboratory method are self-evident. As discussed, they facilitate experimental control, the reduction of confounding environmental variables (such as extraneous noise or variations in temperature and light), and the easier use of specialized apparatus. However, these important strengths also contribute direct-ly to the principal weakness of the laboratory as a setting for psycho-logical research – its artificiality. Heather (1976), amongst others, has argued that psychologists should not be surprised if humans studied in artificial and contrived environments display artificial and con-trived behaviour.

This exemplifies one of the most frequently articulated criticisms of the experimental method – that the very processes of abstraction and manipulation upon which it is based induces perceptions and expecta-tions in participants which create biases in their responses and be-haviours. Orne (1962) has termed such biases *demand characteristics*. In some situations, participants behave in a way which they believe will confirm the experimenter's hypothesis. In other situations, they will behave in such a way as to try and disconfirm the experimenter's hypothesis, a behaviour which Masling (1966) has termed the 'screw you' effect.

The behaviour of participants in the psychology laboratory has been well documented in an article entitled 'On the Social Psychology of the Psychological Experiment' (Rosenthal, 1963). As well as de-mand characteristics, Rosenthal's research has revealed the existence of *experimenter effects*. By this he means unintentional behaviours on the part of the experimenter towards the participants that might influence their behaviour on the task in question. The practical by Rostron and Hoyes tests the effects of experimenter bias.

Silverman and Shulman (1970) have argued that the psychology laboratory experiment is analogous to a chemist carrying out research with dirty test tubes: the histories, perceptions, expectations and motivations, that all participants carry with them will colour and distort the spontaneity and truthfulness of their responses. In Silver-man and Shulman's view no participant can ever be the equivalent of the clean, untainted test tube. It is probably fair to say that these effects will be most pronounced in the artificial setting of the labora-tory experiment.

The field experiment

As its name suggests, the field experiment is conducted outside the setting of the psychology laboratory. This gives the method a much higher degree of 'ecological validity', that is, relevance and applica-bility to the real world in which people live. An example will serve to illustrate this point. In a classic series of experiments, Feshbach and Singer (1971) investigated television and violence using boys in a residential setting as participants. In this natural environment the boys were randomly divided into two groups. In the experimental situation one group of boys watched non-violent television programmes whilst the other group watched television programmes with a high aggression content.

It is important to note that, although the experiment was not carried out in the controlled environment of the psychology laboratory, the experimenter still manipulated the independent variable, since it was Feshbach who decided how the boys would be allocated to the two conditions and what programmes they would watch. Feshbach and Singer reported data that was inconsistent with data previously obtained under controlled laboratory conditions, but their data were at least gathered in 'real-life' conditions and have high ecological validity.

The naturalistic experiment

Many students new to psychology confuse the field experiment and the naturalistic experiment. The distinction is clear. Although both use the general principles of the experimental method, they share one important similarity whilst at the same time possessing one important difference. They are similar in that they are both carried out in a real-world setting as opposed to a laboratory setting; but unlike the field experiment the experimenter conducting a natural experiment does not control or manipulate the independent variable, but takes advantage of a fortuitous and naturally occurring division.

The naturalistic experiment divides participants into various groups who are differentially exposed to the independent variable but the division is not made by the experimenter. An example will illustrate this. Like Feshbach and Singer (1971), Williams (1978) was interested in the influence of television viewing on the aggressive behaviour of children. Williams was able to locate a small town in the United States which did not receive television transmission but was about to do so. Williams then matched this town against a comparable town which did receive television transmission. The behaviour of the children in both towns was then compared, as also was the behaviour of the children in the first town before and after the introduction of television. Note that, although an independent variable can clearly be identified (television viewing), it is not under the control of the experimenter.

As with the field experiment, the naturalistic experiment has the advantage over the laboratory experiment of ecological validity (and is probably more ethically sound). However, the advantage is offset by the loss of control over potential confounding variables.

Summary

We have seen that the experimental method has been the dominant methodology and paradigm during the relatively brief period (by general consent just over 100 years) that psychology has existed as a discipline independent from philosophy. The main reasons for its

7

prominence include its precision, and its use of manipulation and abstraction. Most importantly, it enables researchers to infer cause and effect relationships between the variables they are studying. Although the experimental method may take a variety of forms, determined by the degree of control, the setting, and the number of conditions created, it is always based on the logic of the rule of one variable. This means that there will be only one factor which is allowed to differ between the control and experimental conditions; this is the independent variable. The effect of the independent variable is measured by the dependent variable. In the light of this outcome the experimental or the null hypothesis is accepted or refuted. Critics of the experimental method argue that its artificiality ensures that it cannot measure 'real' human behaviour and experience, and that its prominence was due to political rather than methodological advantages.

References

BELL, P.A. (1981) Physiological, comfort, performance, and social effects of heat stress. *Social Issues, 37*, 71–94.

COOLICAN, H. (1990) *Research Methods and Statistics in Psychology*. London: Hodder and Stoughton.

FESHBACH, S. and SINGER, R. (1971) *Television and Aggression: An experimental field study*. San Francisco: Jossey Bass.

HEATHER, N. (1976) *Radical Perspectives in Psychology*. London: Methuen.

JAMES, W. (1890) *Principles of Psychology*. New York: Holt.

MASLING, J. (1966) Role-related behaviour of the subject and psychologist and its effects upon psychological data. In D. Levine (Ed.), *Nebraska Symposium on Motivation*. Lincoln, Nebraska: University of Nebraska Press. (67–103)

ORNE, M.T. (1962) On the social psychology of the psychological experiment: with particular reference to demand characteristics and their implications. *American Psychologist, 17*, 776–783.

ROSENTHAL, R. (1963) On the social psychology of the psychological experiment: The experimenter's hypothesis as unintended determinant of experimental results. *American Scientist, 51*, 268–283.

SILVERMAN, I. and SHULMAN, A.D. (1970) A conceptual model of artifact in attitude change studies. *Sociometry, 33*, 97–107.

WATSON, J.B. (1919) *Psychology from the Standpoint of a Behaviourist*. Philadelphia: Lippincott.

WERTHEIMER, M. (1970) *A Brief History of Psychology.* New York: Holt, Rinehart & Winston.

WILLIAMS, T.M. (1978) Differential impact of TV on children: A natural experiment in communities with and without television. Unpublished paper presented at the meeting of the International Society for Research on Aggression, Washington D.C..

Experimenter bias effects: unintentional versus intentional factors

Andrew Rostron
University of Hull
and
Tom Hoyes
University of Aston in Birmingham

Abstract

The aim of this practical exercise is to investigate experimenter bias effects (EBEs). These refer to the ways in which experimenters can consciously or unconsciously influence experimental data. The original work of Rosenthal (1963) suggested that such effects were largely unintentional, and that the consequences of this for the behavioural sciences were, therefore, rather serious. In a subsequent review of EBE studies, however, Barber and Silver (1968) indicated that these effects were not as widespread as had originally been thought. This exercise examines a situation in which EBEs might occur and aims to establish whether any such effects do occur.

The general theoretical issue at stake is whether EBEs can be eliminated by a rigorous determination to be objective or if, as Rosenthal has suggested, they are the result of more subtle processes which are essentially unintentional and beyond the investigator's control. The discussion of the results looks at some of the reasons which might explain both the presence and absence of EBEs and examines the extent to which any observed biases have been intentionally or unintentionally produced. Some other methods of investigating EBEs are also suggested and the methodological problems involved in this area of research considered.

Materials and Equipment

This practical is best conducted by a single investigator who has access to about 40 participants. The participants should be randomly assigned to one of two groups, and within each group, participants should be put into pairs. Thus, about ten pairs of participants for each of the two groups should be available for the exercise. The investigator will supervise the exercise, and one member of each pair of participants will assume the role of experimenter whilst the other acts as the person to be experimented upon. (Along with the difference between the two groups, this methodological approach is described fully in the Procedure section.)

It may be that a single investigator does not have access to 40 or so participants. In this case, several investigators should each use a smaller number of participants and then pool their data for subsequent analysis. This approach will require some co-ordination and so it is suggested that one member of the investigative team assumes responsibility for the organization of the others.

The apparatus needed for the exercise consists of a 30 cm (12 inch) ruler and a pen to record the data. The data should be recorded on photocopies of Appendix 1. The remaining apparatus consists of a questionnaire (see Appendix 2). The data for each pair of participants can be collected within 15–20 minutes and the whole exercise, including data analyses, can be conducted within three hours. If several investigators conduct the exercise the time will be considerably reduced.

Introduction and Hypotheses

Psychologists have long suspected that experimental data can be influenced by the beliefs and expectations of the experimenters themselves and, when Robert Rosenthal (1963) first demonstrated an experimenter bias effect (EBE), it seemed that similar effects might pervade the whole of the behavioural sciences. Rosenthal's findings are described in a number of textbooks, especially those concerned with experimental design and methodology. Useful accounts can be found in Matheson *et al.* (1978), Calfee (1985), and Coolican (1990).

If the effects reported by Rosenthal were genuine, this would have had a profound effect on the whole discipline of psychology, particularly if certain theories had been unjustifiably accepted or rejected. However, by 1968, the universal nature and magnitude of EBEs were being questioned. In a review of the available literature Barber and Silver (1968) re-examined 31 studies purporting to have shown the EBE. Of these, they rejected no less than 19 on the grounds that they failed to clearly demonstrate the bias. In some cases, after initial analyses had failed to identify an EBE, *post hoc* procedures had been employed. Moreover, Barber and Silver accused the authors of these articles of not pointing out the limitations of such postmortem analyses. Some authors were also accused of going to extreme lengths to achieve a statistically significant EBE, in some cases accepting a 0.1 level of significance.

In addition, Barber and Silver reported that some researchers actually excluded from their analyses data which did not demonstrate an EBE! Perhaps even more importantly, Barber and Silver pointed out that, in the 12 studies in which the existence of the EBE was not disputed, participants were not only told to expect certain results, but also informed that they should find those results. Thus, the participant's desire to achieve results in line with the hypothesis under test could arguably be said to have confounded the expectancy effect. After Barber and Silver's review, the whole concept of the EBE received a general re-examination. Barber himself had repeatedly failed to observe any bias and others, such as Compton (1970) and Jacob (1971), reported experiencing similar difficulties.

The purpose of the present exercise is to create a situation in which it is possible for an EBE to be manifested and then, if an effect is observed, to determine whether it is intentional or unintentional. The absence of any EBE would be encouraging from the point of view of objectivity in experimentation, but if an effect does emerge it is important to ascertain where it comes from. In particular, the issue which must be addressed is whether, as Rosenthal suggests, EBEs are due to subtle and unintentional biases and therefore very difficult to eliminate, or whether they derive from things like the intentional cueing of participants or outright data fabrication.

It is worth mentioning that Rosenthal's unintentional EBE explanation was a far from naïve or unwarranted assertion. In fact it was based on careful analysis of film recordings of experimental sessions made while participants and experimenters were unaware they were being observed and in which the EBE was visible. Rosenthal (1966/1976; 1967) emphasizes the subtle, unintentional and covert mechanisms in his EBE account, but not on the basis of any theorizing; his label of 'unintentional' comes from his own experimental findings.

The possibility that the EBE may have an intentional basis is, however, a very real one. As Barber and Silver (1968) point out, it may not be easy to observe intentional biases, particularly if experimenters deliberately aim to conceal them. There is also a body of research which indicates that some experimenters are guilty of fabricating data. Indeed Rosenthal (reported in Rosenthal and Fode, 1963) had to exclude the data of five of his own experimenters who were discovered to be cheating.

A further example of fabrication was reported by Azrin *et al.*, (1961). These researchers inadvertently designed an experiment which was inherently impossible to carry out. However, such a technicality did not prevent 15 of the 16 graduate student experimenters from returning to Azrin and his colleagues with the 'results'. Other illustrations are provided by O'Leary and Kent (1973) who observed experimenters cheating by calculating falsely high correlation coefficients. Hyman (1954) was interested in the behaviour of interviewers and reported that, where interviewees were difficult to communicate with, half the interviewers fabricated a large proportion of their data, whilst all interviewers fabricated at least some.

In this practical exercise the situation to be examined for an EBE is one in which a fairly strong suggestion is made about the outcome of an experiment. The task that will be used to test for EBE is reaction time, something which at first sight should not be susceptible to bias effects. However, the method of measurement, where one individual drops a ruler and another attempts to catch it as quickly as possible, provides a more ready opportunity for biases to intrude.

An important feature of the design is the use of two groups of participants, each of whom is given a different expectation for the outcome of the experiment. After the data have been collected an attempt will be made to determine whether an EBE is present and to identify its source as either intentional or unintentional. Even if no bias is observed, there may still be evidence of an attempt to produce data conforming to the suggestion made about the outcome of the experiment.

Hypotheses

The exact wording of the hypothesis will, of course, vary depending on the conditions chosen. Given the aims of this exercise it may be hypothesized that if participants are given certain expectations about the outcome of the reaction time task, the data they produce will be in accord with these expectations. An appropriate null hypothesis would be that expectations given to participants will not affect reaction time data produced by participants. It may also be predicted that if any bias does occur, it is attributable, at least in part, to intentional factors.

Procedure

Prior to the exercise, investigators should photocopy a sufficient number of the data recording sheets shown in Appendix 1. The next task is to locate pairs of participants willing to take part in the exercise. Each pair of participants should be tested individually, and the procedure for each pair of participants is as follows.

First of all participants should decide which one of them will act as the experimenter and which as the person to be experimented upon. Once this decision has been made, investigators should provide a brief outline of the experiment. Each pair should be told that the investigation is a correlational study investigating the relationship between reaction time (RT) and the amount of sleep obtained the previous night.

The declared purpose should only be briefly spelled out at this stage, but it should be indicated to pairs of participants that further details will be made available later. In order to maintain the credibility of this cover story, investigators should then ask the person whose RT will be tested to indicate the length of time they slept the previous night, and the extent to which this time was longer or shorter than their normal sleep time. This information should be recorded.

An alternative cover story for the exercise could be that it is concerned with reaction times in general, since these are used as measures of performance for a wide variety of tasks in cognitive psychology. It is only necessary to provide a plausible rationale to the participants and any relevant story would be acceptable. It is left to the investigator's discretion which path to follow.

After the cover story has been given, the participant acting as the person to be experimented upon should be asked to leave the experimental setting for a brief period of time whilst the other member of the pair receives instructions on how to conduct the RT trials. The investigator should inform the participant that they will be acting as an experimenter and measuring the other participant's RT. In this exercise, RT will be obtained by the experimenter dropping a vertically held 30 cm ruler which the participant has to grasp as soon as possible. The method for conducting each trial should then be demonstrated to the experimenter.

In essence, the experimenter holds the ruler vertically at its top and at arm's length. The participant then lightly grasps the ruler at its base between finger and thumb to reduce the time for motor movements. A diagram illustrating the initial positions taken by the experimenter and the participant is illustrated in *Figure 1*.

Prior to each trial, the experimenter provides the participant with a 'Ready' signal to indicate that the trial is about to begin. After this signal the experimenter releases the ruler. As soon as the participant sees the ruler move, he or she should grasp it firmly between forefinger and thumb as quickly as possible. (The sequence of events for each trial is shown in *Figure 2*.)

The interval between the 'Ready' signal and the dropping of the

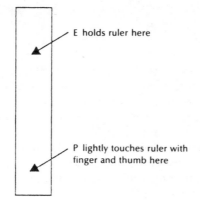

Figure 1. Positions taken up by subject and experimenter at the start of each trial.

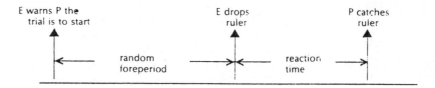

Figure 2. The sequence of events on each trial.

ruler is called the foreperiod. Experimenters should be told that the length of this foreperiod is to be randomly varied in order to prevent the participant from anticipating or guessing when the ruler will be dropped. The random period for each trial is taken from the data recording sheet in *Appendix 1*. The numbers appearing in the foreperiod column give the interval between the 'Ready' signal and the ruler being dropped. Experimenters should be told to count silently to the number presented for each trial at a rate of about three digits every two seconds. The copy of *Appendix 1* should be located so that when the experiment is underway, the participant whose RT is being measured cannot see it. The participant's RT on each trial is to be recorded by the experimenter, since the investigator will not be present during the RT trials. The distance the ruler drops is the measure of RT. Normally, the ruler will drop about 10 cm before it is caught. Any catches of less than 4 cm should be discarded since these can be regarded as anticipatory responses.

When the experimenter is familiar with the requirements of the task, potential bias is then introduced by the investigator. Half of the experimenters (Group 1) should be informed that 'longer foreperiods are associated with longer reaction times'. The other half (Group 2) should be informed that 'longer foreperiods are associated with shorter reaction times'. Experimenters may request clarification of this information, so in the case of Group 1 experimenters, it can be suggested that 'longer foreperiods are associated with longer reaction times because fatigue sets in' and that 'with shorter foreperiods fatigue does not set in and hence reaction time is quicker for short than for long foreperiods'. In the case of Group 2 experimenters, it can be suggested that 'because the "Ready" signal must be cleared from the central processing systems before the second signal (the falling ruler) can be dealt with, the longer the foreperiod the more likely the clearance is to have occurred and hence the easier the second signal is to deal with'. Group 2 experimenters could also be told that 'with a short foreperiod the first signal is not cleared before the second is presented and hence reaction time is longer'. Note that this explanation is simply suggesting that the refractory period effects exert an influence on RT.

After this information has been given to the experimenter, the participant should be re-introduced into the experimental setting and the exercise begun. A total of 40 RT trials should be conducted to provide a representative mean value of RT. This will enable a reasonable frequency distribution of RT values to be drawn. The experimenter should be told that he or she must record the distance the ruler has dropped using the appropriate column in the data recording sheet whilst ensuring that the participant does not see the results. The investigator should then leave the experimental setting and request that the pair bring the completed data recording sheet to him or her when all 40 trials have been performed.

Once all the trials have been conducted the experimenters and participants should be debriefed as to the real purpose of the study. After this, the questionnaire presented in *Appendix 2* should be administered to the experimenters and their responses recorded.

Results

First, the participant's mean RT values for the short and the long foreperiod trials should be computed. Short foreperiod trials can be defined as those which had a count of between one and five inclusive, whilst long foreperiod trials are those which had a count of between six and ten inclusive. The column headed 'Foreperiod' on the data recording sheet in *Appendix 1* has 20 values of between one and five inclusive and 20 between six and ten inclusive. Care should be taken when computing the mean values. The information for all participants should be tabulated as shown in *Table 1*.

The specific hypothesis was that there would be a bias effect in the direction suggested to the participants. Thus, Group 1 should produce shorter average reaction times after short foreperiod trials than after long foreperiod trials. It was predicted that there would be an opposite effect for those in Group 2. These predicted outcomes are illustrated in *Figure 3*. A similar figure showing the results obtained in this exercise should be drawn for comparison.

Analysis of the data involves testing the difference between the mean reaction times in the short and long foreperiods for the participants in Group 1. A significant difference in the predicted direction is positive evidence of an EBE. A significant difference between short and long foreperiods for the participants in Group 2 is also predicted, but in this case the short foreperiod trials should lead to longer

Table 1. Suggested format for tabulation of data

	Participant no.	Mean reaction time for short foreperiods	Mean reaction time for long foreperiods	Hours sleep the previous night	Difference between normal sleep and previous night's sleep
GROUP 1	1 2 3 etc.				
GROUP 2	21 22 23 etc.				

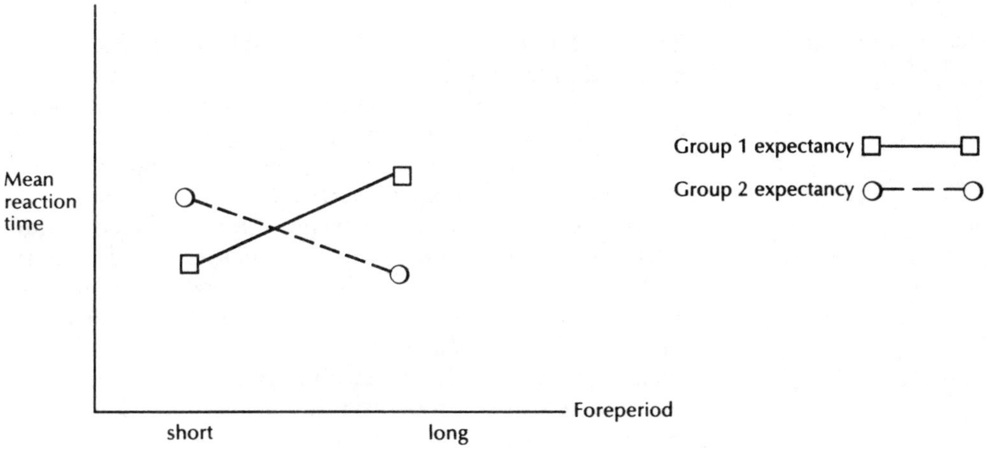

Figure 3. Predicted outcomes of the experimenter effect.

reaction times than the long foreperiod trials.

Since the RT data are distances, either a non-parametric test (such as the Wilcoxon) or a parametric test (such as the related 't') is appropriate for comparing the mean reaction time values obtained. Note that it is possible for the analysis of the data to produce a significant effect with a non-parametric test but not with a parametric test. This is because it is not the size of the reaction time differences which is important, but whether the difference is in the predicted direction. In this instance a numerically very small difference may be just as important psychologically as a very large difference. An even simpler approach is to count the number of participants whose results are in the direction of the imparted bias. If there was no bias, an equal number of results would be expected in each direction. This can be assessed using a binomial test.

Once it has been established that an EBE has been found, it remains to determine whether such effects are due to intentional factors. The evidence here comes from an individual analysis of the answers experimenters gave to the questionnaire (*Appendix 2*). It is not easy to obtain a straightforward assessment of this, but responses to some of the questions could be particularly revealing. Intentional bias would be indicated by those experimenters who admitted giving feedback to participants relating to their expected responses (saying, for example, 'Good!') and who had told the participant the experimental hypothesis (*Questions 1* and *3*). Data fabrication would be indicated by those experimenters who admitted misrecording some or all of their data (*Question 4*).

A record should be kept of all those experimenters who exhibited either of these types of bias. The number of participants showing a bias on reaction times in the predicted direction should then be identified. It ought to be possible to determine whether any bias is intentional by calculating what percentage of those showing reaction time bias in the predicted direction was paired with experimenters who admitted bias on the questionnaire.

Discussion

The most important task is to establish whether or not any bias occurred in the exercise. From a theoretical point of view it does not really matter whether the results show a definite bias or not, since the implications are equally important either way.

If no detectable bias has been observed, then this bodes well for science (and psychology in particular), since the implication is that it is relatively easy for experimenters to be objective. However, the scientific literature indicating that bias effects do occur cannot be neglected (Barber and Silver's (1968) views notwithstanding). There needs to be some discussion of possible reasons for non-observation of bias. Is it really due to experimenters being objective? How far is such objectivity likely to extend beyond the present exercise? Would the same results be produced in situations where there are rewards for experimenters getting the required results?

Apart from the rewards available in commercial and industrial environments, even the scientific world provides powerful incentives. Faber (1974) has pointed out that we are 'naïve to believe that dishonesty in research is unique and aberrant'. In some cases, rewards such as prestige, ego enhancement and large salaries, can prove too tempting to researchers. The fraudulent behaviour of William Summerlin (reported in Barber, 1976) is a case in point, and worthy of some consideration.

If a bias has been observed, it is important to distinguish whether or not it is intentional. Some suggestions as to how this can be accomplished have been made in the Results section, but there may be others. If it turns out that any bias observed is largely intentional, then this would argue against Rosenthal (1963; 1966/1976; 1967). It would also be good for experimentation in general, since once routes for intentionality have been identified they can be reduced or eliminated. (Kahneman *et al.* 1982).

Alternatively, if any observed bias appears to be largely unintentional, then Rosenthal's account of EBEs is supported. Even if it eventually turns out that seemingly unintentional biases are actually intentional, it will still be important to obtain some idea about whether other EBEs can be classified in the same way. This is an important issue because the body of evidence for EBEs is substantially empirical and consequently its refutation must be beyond the scope of any individual piece of research.

There are several variations which could be introduced into the procedure to increase or decrease the probability of obtaining EBEs. For example, would experimenters be more likely to be rigorous in their data gathering if they were told that the findings would be published? A further point to consider in this context is the way in which expectancies conveyed to the experimenters might change any potential bias. In the present exercise bias was transmitted directly, but what types of more subtle hints could be used?

One of the most important factors likely to influence the manifestation of an EBE is the nature of the task employed. In the present exercise experimenters carried out the simple mechanical operation of reading a data value on a ruler. With such a task EBEs are unlikely to intrude unless there is a deliberate fabrication of the data-recording, although there is liable to be a certain amount of ambiguity about where the ruler is caught. In many areas of psychology, however, tasks are used which contain a much greater subjective component and the criteria for making judgements are more ambiguous. What sorts of task would be included here and in what direction might the experimenter, consciously or unconsciously, bias the results? It might even be worth considering how the personality of the experimenter might interact with other aspects of the situation to produce an EBE and also whether there may be any positive aspects to EBEs.

Although it should be clear that experimenters do have the potential to influence the data they gather, it is also worth examining some of the problems involved in claiming that particular data demonstrate the presence of an EBE. In most studies in this area, and in the present exercise, experimenters act on behalf of a main investigator. Does this constitute an adequate simulation of 'real' experimenters doing 'real' research? A further problematical aspect in relation to the present exercise is the use of a questionnaire to assess what has happened during the data-gathering process. Can participants choose what information they wish to release? If irregularities were admitted, how could it be decided whether subsequent admissions were truthful?

Bibliography

General Background References

CALFEE, R.C. (1985) *Experimental Methods in Psychology*. New York: Holt, Rinehart and Winston.
COOLICAN, H. (1990) *Research Methods and Statistics in Psychology*. London: Hodder and Stoughton.
MATHESON, D.W., BRUCE, R.L. and BEAUCHAMP, K.L. (1978) *Experimental Psychology: Research, Design and Analysis*. New York: Holt, Rinehart and Winston.

Specific Background References

BARBER, T.X. (1976) *Pitfalls in Human Research – Ten Pivotal Points*. Oxford: Pergamon.

HYMAN, H.H. (1954) *Interviewing in Social Research*. Chicago: University of Chicago Press.

KAHNEMAN, D., SLOVIC, P. and TVERSKY, A. (1982) *Judgement under uncertainty: Heuristics and biases*. Cambridge: Cambridge University Press.

O'LEARY, K.D. and KENT, R. (1973) Behaviour Modification for Social Action: Research tactics and problems. In L.A. Hamerlynch, L.C. Handy and E.J. Mash (Eds) *Behaviour Change: Methodology, Concepts and Practice*. Champaign, Illinois: Research Press.

ROSENTHAL, R. (1966/1976) *Experimenter Effects in Behavioural Research*. (Enlarged edition) New York: Halsted Press.

Journal Articles

AZRIN, N.H., HOLZ, W., ULRICH, R. and GOLDIAMOND, I. (1961) The control of the content of conversation through reinforcement. *Journal of the Experimental Analysis of Behaviour*, 4, 25–30.

BARBER, T.X. and SILVER, M.J. (1968) Fact, fiction and the Experimenter Bias Effect. *Psychological Bulletin*, 70, Monograph Supplement.

COMPTON, J.W. (1970) Experimenter Bias: Reaction time and types of expectancy information. *Perceptual and Motor Skills*, 31, 159–168.

FABER, B.L. (1974) The Sloan-Kettering affair. *Science*, 185, 734.

JACOB, T. (1971) Experimenter Bias Effect as a function of demand characteristics and experimenter investment. *Psychological Reports*, 28, 1003–1010.

ROSENTHAL, R. (1963) On the Social Psychology of the Psychological Experiment: The experimenter's hypothesis as an unintended determinant of experimental results. *American Psychologist*, 51, 268–283.

ROSENTHAL, R. (1967) Covert communication in the psychological experiment. *Psychological Bulletin*, 67, 356–367.

ROSENTHAL, R. and FODE, K.L. (1963) Psychology of the scientist: Three experiments in experimental bias. *Psychological Reports*, 12, 491–511.

Appendix 1

Trial Number	Foreperiod (secs)	Reaction Time
1	6	
2	1	
3	5	
4	9	
5	4	
6	9	
7	7	
8	2	
9	10	
10	5	
11	8	
12	2	
13	3	
14	7	
15	8	
16	9	
17	10	
18	5	
19	6	
20	9	
21	3	
22	1	
23	7	
24	2	
25	1	
26	8	
27	4	
28	3	
29	9	
30	4	
31	6	
32	7	
33	4	
34	8	
35	6	
36	2	
37	10	
38	3	
39	5	
40	3	

Appendix 2

This questionnaire should be given to experimenters after they have completed the exercise and been informed about the true purpose of the study. Experimenters should answer 'Yes' or 'No' to the questions.

Question 1: During the experiment did you knowingly provide the participant with feedback of results, that is, did you knowingly provide any verbal or non-verbal information relating to your participant's responses and the expected outcome of the experiment?

Question 2: By the nature of the experiment you may have found it necessary to round-up to the nearest point. Did you, however, knowingly round-up in a systematic way so as to confirm the expected outcome of the experiment?

Question 3: Did you, at any time during the experiment, either implicitly or explicitly, tell the participant what the expected outcome of the experiment was?

Question 4: Did you, at any time during the experiment, and for whatever reason, misrecord any of the participant's reaction times?

Question 5: Do you think that when experimental work is carried out simply to introduce you to techniques and so on, that there is any ethical reason for you to faithfully record the results?

Question 6: If you were asked to be a participant in some research that you knew was important and likely to be published, do you think you would behave differently with respect to the conducting of the investigation?

PRACTICAL 2

Data gathering for parapsychological research: an investigation of water and metal divining

Andrew Rostron
University of Hull

Abstract

Many people claim that they are capable of divination – that is, detecting the presence of either water or metal when it cannot be observed by conventional sensory means. This practical exercise attempts to assess the claim for divination ability on an objective basis. In particular, it looks at evidence to see whether only a relatively small number of skilled diviners exists or if the ability is present in all of us to a greater or lesser extent. The exercise can also be used to examine the suggestion that apparently objective data-gatherers can be deceived by participants into believing that a given individual possesses some sort of parapsychological ability.

Several interesting discussion points are likely to emerge from this exercise. Amongst other things, it poses questions concerning the use of the psychological laboratory as a suitable location for parapsychological research, and asks whether divination abilities can best be explained without reference to 'extrasensory perception'. In addition, the practical exercise raises issues concerning the deception of investigators by those claiming to have some sort of extrasensory ability.

Materials
and Equipment

The exercise is best carried out by several investigative teams as this will allow a large amount of data to be collected in a relatively short period of time. The data can then be pooled for subsequent analysis. It is possible for a single team to generate its own data for analysis, though of course this will be more time consuming. Whichever approach is adopted, the data from at least 20 participants should be collected before any analysis is attempted.

Each investigative team should be composed of three members. The first will act as the experimenter and will be responsible for the overall course of events. The second and third members will act as 'target hider' and 'data recorder' respectively. Teams working in groups of three could alternate their roles during the course of the investigation. This strategy reduces experimenter bias and would allow members to see the investigation from different points of view which would be helpful when writing a formal report.

It is possible for a single individual to assume all three roles, but if this approach is taken he or she will need to spend some time devising a procedure which will allow the exercise to be conducted smoothly.

Several pieces of apparatus are needed to assess people's water divining abilities. Investigators should obtain ten suitable water containers such as old yoghurt cartons which should be identical to eliminate any visual clues. Ten sheets of fairly thick paper or card are

21

also necessary in order to conceal the containers. It is important that the paper or card used is sufficiently thick and large enough to completely hide the top of each container. Sheets of newspaper might be particularly suitable since the fold in a double spread provides a good potential hiding place for a small object. If investigators elect to investigate metal divining, a single piece of metal about 200 mm long, 20mm wide and 2/3 mm thick should be used.

Participants will also require a detection device or 'divining rod'. This can easily be prepared from two pieces of stiff wire about the same gauge as that used in metal coat hangers, and bent to form an L-shape. Alternatively, a wooden twig trimmed to form a Y-shape could be used as the detection device.

A minimum of 20 participants should be used, and each participant can be tested in five to ten minutes. Investigative teams working as part of a class should be able to collect and analyse sufficient data within three hours. Single teams generating and analysing their own data should allow extra time for testing participants.

Introduction and Hypotheses

The notion that the mind only receives information through the recognized senses has been questioned throughout recorded history (Inglis, 1977). There are numerous tales of people having intuitions and premonitions which later turned out to be true, and yet there is no apparent logical explanation of how such information could have been conveyed by conventional means (Rhine, 1925; Rhine and Platt, 1958; Hansel, 1966). The investigation of such phenomena is the subject matter of parapsychology.

Clearly it is beyond the bounds of a basic practical exercise to investigate scientifically this type of experience, but claiming to have the ability to detect metal or water by extrasensory means (divining or dowsing) is a skill which falls into the same area. Such a claim can be examined in a straightforward way and the purpose of this practical exercise is to look at ways of establishing whether there is any objective evidence for this type of ability. It also considers whether the techniques devised are liable to provide a reasonable opportunity for any hypothetical ability to be manifested.

For the purposes of this exercise, it is not whether the observed evidence is positive or negative that is of most interest. Rather, it is the techniques and methodology that are used to gather the evidence that are of greatest significance. It may be asked, for example, whether participants are allowed a fair opportunity to demonstrate any innate abilities and whether conditions are adequate to allow for any learning which might take place.

Metal or water detection is a suitable task for looking at possible parapsychological effects, as it has clear aims, can readily be set out in controlled laboratory conditions, and can provide objective measures of performance relatively easily. Furthermore, divining is a skill which has some commercial value since large and respectable business organizations have been known to employ dowsers to attempt to trace the location of unmarked pipes and ducts. Evidence for successful divining has been reported by Rhine (1950) and Barrett and Besterman (1926). As far as other real life applications of apparent

22

parapsychological abilities are concerned, it is worth mentioning that the police sometimes consult mediums in their searches for missing persons, although the real benefits of these approaches have not been well-documented (Inglis, 1984).

Another factor which needs to be taken into consideration in the area of parapsychological research is the role which may be played by the professional magician or by those deliberately aiming to deceive. The magician makes his or her living by making the seemingly impossible take place, and such skills could well be put to use in a water divining context. Marks and Cammann (1980) describe some interesting evidence here. They cite the example of Uri Geller, the so-called 'super-psychic', whose apparent powers stimulated articles in both the *New Scientist* (Hanlon, 1974) and *Nature* (Targ and Puthoff, 1974). It turned out that all Geller's powers could be duplicated by 'The Amazing Randi', a highly talented professional stage magician, and Marks and Cammann describe the techniques that Geller may have used to obtain his effects. To give some idea of how easy it is to create the illusion of successful divining, one aim of the present experiment is to set up a situation where two individuals attempt to cheat by conveying information successfully. The investigative team then have to see whether this cheating is detectable.

In practice, water divining is usually carried out in the open, but for experimental purposes better control is needed. In this practical exercise, the presence of a target, water or metal, has to be detected with participants using a suitable detection device. To ensure the best possible chance of success, a number of detection attempts are allowed, and feedback about where the target was hidden is given after each attempt. This methodological approach also allows an estimate of chance performance to be given; that is, some estimate can be made of the level of performance which would be attained if responses were made purely at random.

If there is any evidence of an ability to detect either water or metal, this should result in a number of scores above chance. Successful performance may be evident in different ways. For example, there may be just one or two talented individuals who show evidence of divining skill, or there may be some minimal ability which is evident in most people. One further behaviour which could be examined is inverse divining ability. This can be defined as a talent for consistently avoiding targets.

There is likely to be a wide range of attitudes to the exercise among participants. The majority will probably have a strongly sceptical attitude to the possibility of attaining positive results, but there is also likely to be a small but significant minority inclined to believe that something positive may be obtained. The exercise might be useful to both groups since it is primarily concerned with illustrating the advantages of relying on systematic evidence in reaching conclusions about claims made in this area of psychology. The exercise will also illustrate some of the problems involved in gathering evidence relevant to the issues at stake. In connection with this it is worth noting that in a survey of readers of the *New Scientist* journal (presumably people interested in science), Evans (1973) found that 88%

of respondents considered the study of extrasensory perception to be 'a legitimate scientific undertaking'.

Hypotheses

It is now possible to summarize the hypotheses that are the subject of this exercise. If there is any evidence for the notion of a divining ability, this should be evident in the following ways. First, if there are a very few individuals who have some divining ability, then this will result in a high rate of detection being maintained by them. This will be above a level expected by chance, even when they are re-tested. Second, if everyone has the ability to divine to some extent, the general detection scores will be above those predicted if purely chance factors were operating. Finally, it may be predicted that pairs of individuals, who attempt to deceive others that a divining ability is present, will be successful in this deception.

Procedure

The task that participants will undertake is one of water or metal detection. The procedural details presented here concern the water detection task. However, the basic procedure for both is identical even if the materials required are slightly different. Remember that investigators should work in teams of three, with one member acting as the experimenter and taking responsibility for the overall course of events. The second and third team members should act as 'target hider' and 'data recorder' respectively.

The procedure is as follows. First, in the absence of the participant, ten sheets of fairly thick card or paper should be laid out in a row either on the floor or on a table. This provides an overall target area which is effectively divided into ten sections. The pieces of card or paper should be numbered from one to ten.

Next, one of the ten water containers should be placed under each of the ten pieces of card or paper. One, and only one, of the containers should be filled with water. The water filled container is the target, and care should be taken that there are no visual clues as to its location. Should any difficulty be encountered in obtaining identical containers, the problem can be solved by the use of an eleventh container holding the target water which can then be placed at random in one of the ten targets. A diagrammatic representation of the target areas is given in Figure 1.

The choice of the location of the water-filled container should be made at random. A good way of deciding the position for the first and subsequent trials is to use a set of random number tables with 0 as the tenth position. Alternatively, the digits one to ten could be written on separate pieces of paper and placed into a box. Prior to each trial the box should be shaken and one of the numbers selected.

When the apparatus has been set up, the participant can be introduced into the experimental setting. Each participant will undertake ten detection trials. Participants should be informed that their task is to pass over the possible target locations with the aid of one of the detection devices, and make a decision about where the target is hidden. It should be emphasized to the participant that a decision

24

TARGET POSITION

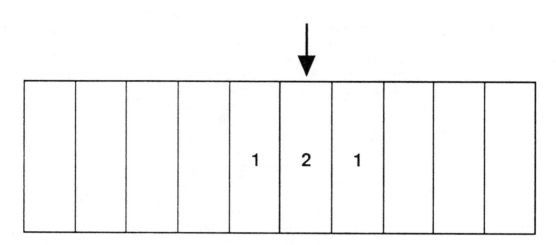

Figure 1. Schematic diagram of the experimental layout. (2 points awarded for hitting the the target and 1 point if the target is just missed.)

must be made even if the answer is based on guesswork. The assumption is that individuals need not necessarily be aware of any information from the targets. One, and only one, selection can be made.

Some participants may not be sure how the detection devices should be used. To a certain extent this is a matter of individual preference. However, the L-shaped stiff wire rods are traditionally held one in each hand rather like pistols, with the arms about 30 cm apart. The rods are lowered to within 50 cm or so of the individual potential target locations to detect any signals. In the case of the Y-shaped twig, the arms of the twig are grasped and the remaining section of the Y pointed to each target area in turn from about 50 cm or so away. The experimenter should be prepared to give participants a convincing demonstration of how the detectors might be used, and advise them what reactions they may experience.

Participants should be encouraged to do the best they can, even if they are not consciously aware of any signals from the target, and advised to test each possible location without spending too much time over it. Investigators should decide on a suitable time period in which a decision should be made. At the end of every trial participants should be given feedback about their performance (after all it may be a learning process that is being observed!)

Performance is scored as two for a direct hit and one for a 'near miss'. A 'near miss' is defined as nominating the zone adjacent to the target. After each trial the target should be repositioned as described. Clearly, it is vital that participants should not be aware of the new location either directly or indirectly. To ensure this, the participant should be asked to leave the experimental setting whilst the repositioning takes place, and investigators should stand out of sight of the participants during all trials.

Each participant's responses can be recorded using the table presented in the Appendix. This can be adapted according to the number of participants.

After all ten trials have been completed, the participant's score should be calculated. The minimum score is 0 and the maximum 20. When all participants have completed their trials the two highest scorers should perform another set of ten trials. The purpose of this is to establish whether their performance was due to chance factors or to some general detection ability.

It is left to the preference of individual investigative teams whether they wish to organize some way in which one of them and one of the participants cheat during the task. If it is decided to use this option, then the other members of the investigative team should be alerted to the fact that this will take place, but not informed of the identities of the deceivers. Potential deceivers should be able to improvise a means of deceiving the others fairly easily. However, generating maximum scores would not be a wise tactic since this is likely to arouse the suspicions of the other investigators.

Results

First, it is necessary to determine the level of performance which would be expected by chance; that is, if participants were behaving in a purely random fashion. The probability of a participant achieving a score on a single trial is 0.3, since there are three locations out of the ten which can result in a score. If a score is attained on a trial, the average value of any score will be 2 + 1 + 1 divided by 3, or 1.33 (remember that 2, 1, and 1 are the only scores that could be obtained on a single trial). The expected score on any given trial will be the probability of achieving a score (0.3) multiplied by the average value of that score (1.33). Therefore, in this case, the expected score is 0.4.

At first sight it might seem curious that any expected score on a trial is less than any score that can actually be obtained, but this results from the fact that it is quite likely that a score of 0 will be obtained on any random trial. What is being calculated here is the average expected score on any trial. If ten trials are performed, the average overall expected score will be the expected score on an individual trial multiplied by 10. In this case, then, the average overall expected score is 4. As a result, the expected distribution of scores of a large number of participants performing at chance levels will cluster around a mean of 4 as shown in Figure 2.

This expected value is not quite precise since, in a set of ten trials, each location in the overall target area will, on average, be occupied only once. If the target is in an 'end zone' a score can only be obtained in two locations rather than three. On a large number of trials this is likely to happen twice in any ten trials. The average value of any score in this case is 1 + 2 divided by 2 or 1.5, since 2 and 1 are the only scores that can be obtained. The expected score is, therefore, the probability of achieving a score (0.2) multiplied by the score that is likely to be obtained (1.5). This produces a value of 0.3. Given this,

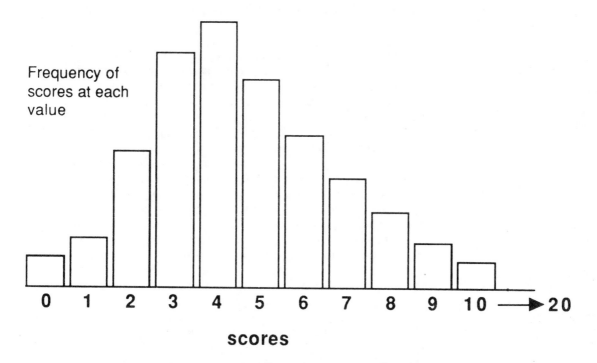

Frequency of
scores at each
value

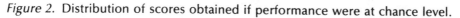

0   1   2   3   4   5   6   7   8   9   10 ——► 20

scores

Figure 2. Distribution of scores obtained if performance were at chance level.

the overall expected score will actually be slightly less than 4. In fact it is 3.8. This value arises from adding the average of the eight cases where the target is not in an 'end zone' (3.2), to the two cases where it is (0.6).

Each participant will have a total score ranging from 0 to 20, with the exception of the two highest scoring participants who will have an additional score resulting from their second attempt at the task. The data generated by the participants should be tabulated and the mean score calculated. The distribution of scores attained by participants could be presented as shown in Figure 2.

The data from the two highest scorers are the easiest to deal with. If their performances are due to successful detection by some means or other, then their levels of performance should be maintained on the second trial. However, if their first scores were due to chance factors, then their second scores should fall nearer the expected value.

As far as the evidence for a small but more general detection ability is concerned, there are a number of ways in which the data can be looked at. If there is any evidence of a general detection ability, the mean scores for the participants should all be above the expected value of 3.8. The scores obtained by the participants can be broken down further and the number of individuals scoring above the expected value compared with those scoring below it. (Scores at the expected value are ignored.) The difference between the size of these two groups can be assessed using a binomial test.

Suppose, for example, that out of a total of 11 scores, two are below the expected value and nine are above it. A table of exact probabilities for the binomial test indicates that the probability of actually obtaining nine or more scores out of 11 in the predicted direction is only 0.033, if chance factors alone are operating and there is therefore an equal likelihood of any score being in the predicted or the non-predicted direction. (Note that this is equivalent to the probability of getting nine or more heads in a series of 11 tosses of an unbiased coin.)

Since this is better than the 0.05 level of significance, it would look as if a general detection ability has been observed. However, this significance value is only appropriate if a specific prediction of success has been made. Unfortunately, in this instance, such a prediction is not really possible and a two-tailed test of significance must apply. This gives a probability level of 0.066 which is just above the 0.05 level of significance. The probability level must be doubled for a two-tailed test since, as is the case with tossing a coin, an effect can result from either a large number of heads or a large number of tails being obtained in a sequence of tosses. The data could also be analysed by using the Wilcoxon test where each obtained score is compared against the expected score of 3.8.

Another useful way of assessing the data is to examine the frequency distribution of the scores obtained. If there is any evidence of a small detection ability amongst all participants, the distribution will peak at a score larger than 4. Another indication that there may be several participants with some detection ability is if the frequency distribution does not fall away smoothly at values above the expected value. With relatively small data sets, as are likely in this practical exercise, there are bound to be some irregularities in the frequency distribution.

This situation can, however, be improved by cumulating the data over a range of scores. The following ranges could be used: less than 1, 1–2.9, 3–4.9, 5–6.9, 7–8.9, 9–10.9, over 11. Conversely it should be remembered that if the scores are cumulated over too large a range, this is likely to mask any small detection effects, as high frequencies at particular values will be smoothed out if the data are averaged over a wider range of scores.

Discussion

The data generated by the exercise will fall into one of three broad categories. First, there may be no evidence whatsoever for any detection ability. Second, there may be some evidence indicating that one or more individuals can perform at a level above that which would be expected if chance factors alone were operating. Finally, the evidence may be equivocal in that it neither supports nor rejects the notion that hidden objects can be located successfully without the use of the recognized senses. All of these possibilities will need to be considered.

At first sight, it looks as if the first outcome is the easiest to deal with. In a sense it is, since no (uncomfortable) evidence has to be explained away. However, jumping from a lack of evidence to the conclusion that the experiment refutes all detection claims is a rather large one and goes beyond any available evidence. The question that must be addressed is the extent to which the present data provide an argument against the existence of dowsing.

One issue to consider is whether the conditions were appropriate for any detection skills to be evident. Relevant factors to discuss are the size of the targets, the adequacy of the detection devices, the quality of the feedback that was given, the length of time allowed on each trial, and so on. In the case of the water divining task, it might well be the case that some alleged diviners are only sensitive to moving water, such as that in a stream or a pipe. Another set of problems involve motivation – were participants suitably motivated and did they remain so throughout the procedure? It would be worth considering the improvements that could be made to the procedure in order to maintain motivation levels. For example, would some small incentive for successful detections be likely to help?

A more fundamental point to consider is whether a small-scale laboratory simulation is a suitable location for any ability to be manifested. Could it possibly be the case that skilled detectors are hindered by the very act of being observed? What techniques might be adopted if this objection is raised by some participants? The issues outlined here do not constitute an exhaustive list and investigators should consider whether there are others which might merit discussion. Useful research to consider in this context is that reported in McMahan (1947), Rhine (1950) and Targ and Puthoff (1974).

As far as the second outcome is concerned, positive evidence is no real reason in itself to suggest that some explanation involving extrasensory perception should be invoked. The task, in this instance, is to review what factors might be producing the data. Might it be the case that some participants have simply adopted a good guessing strategy? Alternatively, could poor experimentation be responsible? Investigators might, for example, have given subtle and unintended non-verbal cues to the successful participant. It is up to individuals to suggest their own reasons for positive results and they must be satisfied that none of these can account for the data in hand before resorting to more speculative reasons. Useful discussions of some of the issues involved can be found in Soal and Bateman (1954), Krippner (1978), and Nash (1978).

It is at this point that those instructed to cheat should be considered. As the skills of professional magicians indicate, it is often possible for people to be deceived into believing that something extraordinary has occurred. This evidence should also be considered before the existence of a detection ability based on extrasensory perception is asserted. Such an assertion implies that all other routes of information transmission have been successfully ruled out in the exercise conducted, and this would demand an extremely confident and competent investigator! The possibility that some participants may possess an inverse divining ability could also be discussed.

In the case of the evidence being equivocal and neither strong enough to support some detection ability nor to state with confidence that there is no sign of correct detections, the issues associated with both of the first two outcomes remain and should be elaborated upon.

Particular attention should be paid to the ways in which the experimental design might be made more sensitive without giving participants opportunities to make correct detections via conventional means.

One final issue to consider is the extent to which experimental methodology can provide answers to the major questions raised in this practical exercise. In other words, can suitable situations be developed to successfully evaluate claims of extrasensory perception? Essentially the suggestions put forward will reflect the writer's attitude towards this type of phenomena but some elaboration of the advantages and limitations of the experimental approach is well worth presenting.

Bibliography

General background references

BARRETT, W.F. and BESTERMAN, T. (1926) *The Divining Rod*. London: Methuen.

HANSEL, C.E.M. (1966) *ESP: A Scientific Evaluation*. London: McGibbon and Key.

INGLIS, B. (1977) *Natural and Supernatural: A history of the paranormal from earliest times to 1914*. London: Hodder and Stoughton.

INGLIS, B. (1984) *Science and Parascience: A history of the paranormal, 1914–1939*. London: Hodder and Stoughton.

RHINE, J.B. (1925) *ESP*. London: Faber and Faber.

RHINE, J.B. and PLATT, J.G. (1958) *Parapsychology*. Oxford: Blackwell.

Specific background references

KRIPPNER, S. (1978) (Ed.) *Advances in parapsychological research 2: Extrasensory perception*. London: Plenum Press.

MARKS, D. and KAMMANN, R. (1980) *The Psychology of the Psychic*. New York: Prometheus Books.

NASH, C.B. (1978) *Science of PSI, ESP, and PK*. Springfield, Illinois: Charles C. Thomas.

SOAL, S.G. and BATEMAN, F. (1954) *Modern Experiments in Telepathy*. London: Faber and Faber.

Journal Articles

EVANS, C. (1973) Parapsychology – what the questionnaire revealed. *New Scientist*, *57*, 209.

HANLON, J. (1974) Uri Geller and Science. *New Scientist*, *64*, 170–185.

MCMAHAN, E.A. (1947) A review of the evidence for dowsing. *Journal of Parapsychology*, *11*, 175–190.

RHINE, J.B. (1950) Some exploratory tests in dowsing. *Journal of Parapsychology*, *14*, 278–286.

TARG, R. and PUTHOFF, H. (1974) Information transfer under conditions of sensory shielding. *Nature*, *251*, 602–607.

Appendix: DATA RECORDING TABLE

Participant	Trial										Mean Score
	1	2	3	4	5	6	7	8	9	10	
1											
2											
3											
4											
5											
6											
7											
8											
9											
10											
11											
12											
13											
14											
15											
16											
17											
18											
19											
20											
21											
22											
23											
24											
25											
26											
27											
28											
29											
30											

PRACTICAL 3 **Hand preference and hand skill**

Marian Annett
University of Leicester

Abstract

This exercise examines the distribution of patterns of hand prefer-ence, the distribution of differences between the hands in skill, and the relationship between these two distributions. A naturally-arising group of participants (such as a class group), not selected for handed-ness, each perform a number of simple tasks to demonstrate habitual hand use to an observer/partner. Each participant also performs a test of hand skill, using each hand alternately for a number of trials.

Previous research has shown that 30–40% of people prefer to use the left hand for at least one of the actions observed. A large number of patterns of preference emerge. For the purpose of this practical exercise, preferences can be classified as consistent left hand prefer-ence, mixed left, mixed right or consistent right. It has been found that the distribution of people in these classes is usually J-shaped. The hand skill task typically shows a continuous and roughly normal distribution of differences in skill between the hands. A scattergram of right–left hand differences in each of the four hand preference classes will show considerable overlap but an association between preference and skill should be evident on inspection.

Materials
and Equipment

The number of participants can vary with the size of the natural group, but at least thirty should be involved. It may be possible to combine data from more than one class. Students should work in pairs or in threes, acting as participant and investigator in turn.

The materials for the hand preference assessment are a question-naire (*Appendix 1*) and the objects mentioned for each item contained in it (for example matches, scissors, needle and thread, playing cards). It is desirable to have as many real or toy objects available as possible, but mime can be used where necessary. (For instance, it is not in-tended that participants should actually brush their teeth with the toothbrush, nor is it necessary to physically strike the matches.) It is recommended, however, that participants deal some real playing cards, unscrew a jar lid, and thread a needle because the method used is often a surprise for the participant.

The test of hand skill suggested here is placing dots between target circles as this needs no special equipment other than a stopwatch, pencil and paper. Circles with diameters of 0.5 inches should be drawn 8 inches apart on A/4 sheets. If two pairs of circles are printed per sheet, one for each hand, and if each participant has a practice trial followed by five test trials, six sheets will be needed for each participant. The investigator will need a sheet of printed instructions with space for recording the times for each trial (see *Appendix 2*).

The basic testing can be done easily in one class period (45–55 mins) and scoring, checking and pooling class data will take a second

32

period; that is, the whole practical can be completed in a two-hour period or spread over two sessions.

Introduction and Hypotheses

Most people use the right hand for writing (dextrals) but some prefer the left hand (sinistrals). Many people use one hand for writing and the other hand for other skilled actions (mixed handers). Very few people are equally able to use either hand for writing (ambidexters). Notice that the term 'ambidextrous' is used here to refer to inconsistent preference between different trials of the *same* action. The term 'mixed hander' is used to refer to inconsistent preference between *different* actions (although one hand is usually strongly preferred for any particular action).

Psychologists and others such as neurologists, teachers and biologists, are interested in this aspect of human individual differences because of its possible association with asymmetry of the cerebral hemispheres (see an introductory textbook such as Atkinson *et al.* (1990)). Speech production and the understanding of speech depend on parts of the left hemisphere in most people (including, in particular, Broca's and Wernicke's areas). Because the motor neurones cross as they leave the brain and enter the spinal cord, the left side of the brain controls the right hand. Thus, for most people, the left side of the brain has a major role in speech and in the use of the preferred hand. The question of whether this connection is causal or accidental has no generally accepted answer at present.

There are exceptions to this majority pattern. Some people's speech production is controlled by the right hemisphere, and some people do not prefer the right hand. The exceptions for brain and hand do not necessarily go together. The question of what rules, if any, govern these asymmetries is an important puzzle and currently forms the subject of much research (Annett, 1991). Solutions to puzzles depend on facts and the theories which can be based on them. In this practical exercise some important facts about handedness are demonstrated.

Handedness and other asymmetries such as eye and foot preferences have been investigated in many studies. (Asymmetries of perception have also been studied by techniques such as dichotic listening and the brief presentation of stimuli in the left or right visual fields, but these are outside the scope of this practical exercise.) In the area of hand preference, research has been carried out to try and establish whether there are differences between types of groups: animal versus human, male versus female, child versus adult, mentally impaired versus not impaired, learning disabled versus not disabled. It has also been asked whether some races, or certain professional groups such as artists, mathematicians, surgeons or sportspeople differ for handedness. Much of the evidence is conflicting because large and representative samples are needed. The groups must also be examined in exactly the same way, and the assessor should be blind to group status if possible. However, it would be very rare for this condition to be met.

Our closest primate relatives (apes and monkeys) are typically reported to be 50/50 right- and left-handed, but this evidence has been challenged. Gender comparisons in humans typically find females fractionally more often right-handed than males but, as in most areas of research, large samples are needed for statistical significance. Young children may be uncertain which hand to use at first, but there is no convincing evidence that hand-preferences change with age once they have been established. Questions about changes with age are complicated by the social changes that have occurred, liberalizing attitudes towards the use of the left hand for writing in school. Today there are fewer left-handers among elderly people than there are among young people. The question about twins contained in the questionnaire (*Appendix 1*) was included because of the suggestion that twins are more often left-handed than the single-born. The evidence was previously not good enough to decide on this question, since large samples of twins and non-twins assessed in exactly the same way have not been available until recently. It now seems that twins are more often left-handed than non-twins. Tennis professionals and cricketers, but not soccer goalkeepers, are more often left-handed (Wood and Aggleton, 1989).

The main point to notice in all of these comparisons is that any excess of left-handers is likely to be small; of the order of a few percent. Such differences could easily arise through different methods of assessment or changes in the criteria for classification. To be convincing, very careful methodology is required, as are clear rules for classification, preferably specified in advance. Bishop (1990) has shown that it is not difficult to find differences between groups for handedness after the event (*post hoc*) by shifting criteria. One of the main purposes of this practical is to show that the apparently simple question, 'Are you right-handed or left-handed?' does not have a simple answer. One would have to say, 'Well, it depends on what you mean. . .'.

Hypotheses

The specific hypotheses for this practical exercise are:

1. There are considerable individual differences in hand preference. About 25–35% of people are mixed handers and 3–4% consistent left-handers. When numbers of people showing various degrees of hand preference are plotted, the distribution will take the form of a J (if consistent left-handers are at the left and consistent right-handers at the right of the plot).

2. Differences in skill between the hands are normally distributed in a bell-shaped (normal) curve. For certain tasks, including peg moving (Annett, 1970; 1985) and the dotting task recommended here, the distribution is likely to be unimodal, with considerable overlap between right-handers and left-handers.

3. Although the distributions mentioned look very different in overall shape, levels of hand preference will be related in an orderly fashion to levels of difference between the hands in skill.

These three findings from previous work have important theoretical implications for the analysis of handedness and its relationship with cerebral dominance for speech. These wider issues are not directly relevant to this practical, but investigators may find them of interest.

Procedure

The tasks can be done in any order, as materials become available. Students should work in pairs or threes, acting as participant and investigator in turn. It should be ensured that the name of the participant is on the questionnaire and on the hand skill form where the participant's data are recorded.

Hand preference. The participant should perform each of the actions listed on the hand preference questionnaire (as in *Appendix 1*), miming or pretending when appropriate. The participant should not answer the questionnaire items without the investigator observing the performance. 'Either' (E) responses should only be recorded when the participant is truly indifferent to the hand preferred.

The participant should be classified as one of the following four groups, depending on the combination of R and L responses (E alone not counting as evidence of mixed handedness).

1. Consistent Right – all answers R or R + E.

2. Right Mixed – R for writing but L for any other tasks.

3. Left Mixed – L for writing but R for any other tasks.

4. Consistent Left – all answers L or L + E.

The number of participants in each category in the group should be counted.

Hand Skill. A copy of the instructions/record form and six sheets of paper will be needed for the dotting task. Investigators should practise using a stopwatch to time intervals to an accuracy of at least one tenth of a second. The instructions should be read carefully, and it should be ensured that the procedure for dotting and timing is clear to both participant and investigator. (A demonstration by the class tutor might help to standardize the procedure.)

The participant should try to avoid errors, but should not stop to correct them. If more than three dots fall outside either circle, it would be desirable to restart the trial with a new form (or different coloured pen on the same form). The investigator should practise starting the stopwatch on 'Go' and counting as the participant returns to the first circle, stopping the watch on 'ten'. The time should be recorded in the correct column for each hand. The participant may start with the preferred hand but it should be ensured that the hands alternate.

After the times for the trials for each hand have been added up, investigators should then calculate the average time for each hand. The difference between left- and right-handed performances should then be calculated. For most people the left hand takes longer so the difference is positive. Some right-handers and most left-handers will have a negative difference.

Results

Three descriptive analyses will demonstrate the main points arising from this practical exercise.

1. The distribution of hand preference: A bar chart

Participants have been classified for hand preference in four categories and the numbers counted in each category. The frequency of each type can be plotted in a bar chart. This could be done using the raw numbers on the vertical (y) axis if numbers are small, or the percentage of each type in the total group could be worked out and then plotted on the y-axis. The x-axis will have the four hand preference classes. (See *Figure 1* for a bar chart of the preference distribution on the sample data in *Appendix 3*.)

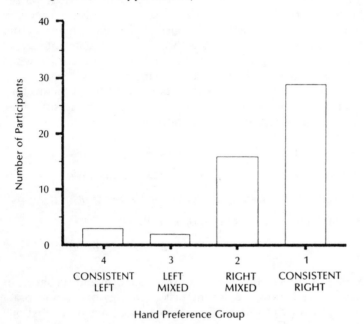

Figure 1. Bar chart showing the distribution of hand preference.

2. The distribution of L–R hand skill: A frequency curve

The L–R difference will be in units of tenths of a second, ranging from perhaps −2.0 to +2.0 (or more). The times should be grouped in intervals that seem appropriate for the data (0.5 second intervals should give about eight groups), and then plotted on the x-axis of a graph. Particular care should be taken where the scores change from − to + around zero. On the y-axis, N or percent should be plotted. It should be shown how many of the sample fall in each L–R interval. A straight line drawn between the points will give a frequency polygon. (See the example in *Figure 2*, using the sample data in *Appendix 3*.)

3. The relation between hand preference and hand skill: A scattergram

The same intervals of L–R time should be marked along the x-axis of another graph, as well spaced out as possible. 1–4 (well spaced) should then be marked on the y-axis to represent the hand preference classes. A tally should be made for each participant showing the preference class and L–R interval. Examination of the resulting scat-

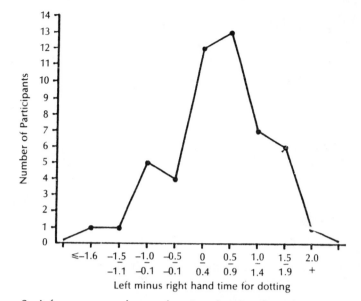

Figure 2. A frequency polygon showing the distribution of differences between the hands in skill.

tergram will indicate whether hand preference and hand skill are independent or related. The starting point for all good statistical analysis should be a plot of the distributions and a good look ('eyeball test') at the data. It is possible to practise this here, without going on to further statistics at this stage. (*Figure 3* gives a scattergram of the data in *Appendix 3*.)

Discussion

Consideration should be given to the findings in each of the three main sections of results, in the light of the initial hypotheses. It is often a good start to summarize in one sentence (not more than two) what was found. This may or may not resemble what was expected and investigators should state which or how far it was unexpected. Investigators should comment on any particular features of their data, keeping close to the actual results. Were there any special factors which might have influenced findings, such as distracting events, shortage of time, low numbers of participants, temperamental stopwatches, or uncomfortable working conditions? Investigators should try to be as analytical as they can with regard to their own data. It is real data and that usually means that it falls short of what might be thought ideal. Students should not be afraid to say what they think the data's shortcomings might be. If the experiment were repeated, how could it be improved? What further analyses might have been useful, given time and opportunity? The most important consideration in a good discussion is to keep what was actually done, and what was actually observed, in focus, and avoid escaping into the nether world of 'might have beens' too soon.

With regard to wider theoretical issues, was the data in any way surprising? Did it expand the students' ideas of human individual differences? What reply should be given to someone who asks 'How many people are left handed'?

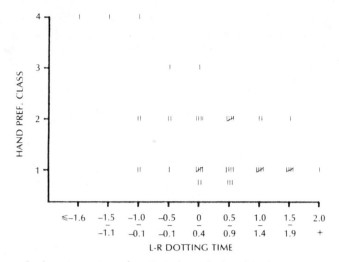

Figure 3. A scattergram showing the relationship between hand preference and hand skill.

Suggestions for further work

There may be enough time to collect more data, such as for eye preference or foot preference. *Eye preference* can be assessed by any one of several simple methods. The focus of interest is on which eye the participant prefers when only one can be used; this is not necessarily the same as the best eye in the sense of visual acuity.

1. The participant should be asked to look through a tube at a distant object. (The tube could be a paper towel or toilet roll holder or a roll of paper.) The investigators should say 'Look through this tube at the clock/lamppost/etc.' They should *not* say 'Show me which eye you use to look. . .' because a spontaneous action is wanted, not one which the participant stops to think about.

2. The investigator could ask the participant to point to an object with an outstretched finger and then, holding the finger steady, close each eye in turn (or cover with a small card). Which eye is lined up with the object?

3. Using a piece of cardboard with a single hole cut in it, the participant should be asked to hold the card out in front of them with both hands, and look at a distant object. They should keep the object in view and bring the card up to their nose. Which eye does it come to?

4. The participant could be handed a kaleidoscope and asked to look into it, and the investigator should note which eye it is raised to.

If two or more of these tasks are used, investigators can ask how many people are consistent or inconsistent for eye preference, and then this can be compared with the consistency and inconsistency of hand preference.

For *foot preference*, the participant should be asked to kick a large

38

soft ball, or to trace a square on the floor with the point of their shoe. How does foot preference go with hand preference? Are the proportions of left eye preference and left foot preference similar? It is generally found that many people are left eyed (about one in three right-handers) while only one in ten or less is left footed.

Another variable which could be investigated easily is familial sinistrality, that is, family left-handedness. A family tree could be drawn up, with boxes labelled 'Father', 'Mother', 'Brothers', 'Sisters', (and 'Sons' and 'Daughters' for mature students), and participants then asked to indicate handedness for each relative. (It should also be recorded whether this is unknown, or if the relation is step or adopted.) All the full relatives are known as first degree relatives, as they share half their genes (on average for siblings) with the respondent. More distant relatives can be included but most people are vague about handedness, even in the immediate family so the reliability of the information would be doubtful. It is usual to classify for the presence or absence of a close left-handed relative. Familial sinistrality present is denoted as FS+, and familial sinistrality absent as FS−. However, the use of these labels varies, so the definition should be read carefully in publications. In this exercise it could be asked whether the FS± variable has any effect on the variable previously assessed. It should be noted that the FS± classification does not usually have much effect.

The statistical analyses can be extended as required in line with the students' stage of learning. For example, the differences between the hands for dotting time could be used for a repeated measures t test in a group of students. The scattergram could be used as the basis of a correlation, if numbers were assigned to the hand skill groups, as well as to the hand preference classes.

Bibliography

General background references

ATKINSON, R.L., ATKINSON, R.C., SMITH, E.E., BEM, D.J., and HILGARD, E.R. (1990) *Introduction to Psychology.* 10th edn. Harcourt. Brace, Jovanovich. Chapter 2, pp. 46–56.

Specific background references

ANNETT, M. (1980) Handedness in M. Jeeves (Ed.) *Psychology Survey No. 3.* London: George Allen and Unwin.

ANNETT, M. (1985) *Left, Right, Hand and Brain: The Right Shift Theory.* London: Lawrence Erlbaum Associates.

SPRINGER, S.P. & DEUTSCH, G. (1985) *Left Brain, Right Brain.* 2nd ed. San Francisco: W.H. Freeman. Chapters 1 and 5.

Journal articles

ANNETT, M. (1970) A classification of hand preference by association analysis. *British Journal of Psychology, 61,* 641–652.

ANNETT, M. (1991) Annotation: Laterality and cerebral dominance. *Journal of Child Psychology and Psychiatry, 32,* 219–232.

BISHOP, D.V.M. (1990) How to increase your chances of obtaining a significant association between handedness and disorder. *Journal of Clinical and Experimental Neuropsychology, 12,* 812–816.

WOOD, C.J. and AGGLETON, J.P. (1989) Handedness in 'fastball' sports: Do left-handers have an innate advantage? *British Journal of Psychology, 80,* 227–240.

Acknowledgements. I am indebted to many psychology students at Aberdeen, Hull, Leicester, and the Open Universities and Coventry Polytechnic, from whose laboratory classes I have collected data. John Ashworth drew the figures.

APPENDIX 1. HAND PREFERENCE QUESTIONNAIRE

Name:_____   Age:_____   Sex:_____

Were you one of twins or triplets at birth, or were you single-born?..

Please indicate which hand you habitually use for each of the following activities by writing R (for right), L (for Left), E (for either).

Which hand do you use:

1. To write a letter legibly? ....

2. To throw a ball to hit a target? ....

3. To hold a racket in tennis, squash or badminton? ....

4. To hold a match whilst striking it? ....

5. To cut with scissors? ....

6. To guide a thread through the eye of a needle (or guide needle on to thread)? ....

7. At the top of a broom while sweeping? ....

8. At the top of a shovel when moving sand? ....

9. To deal playing cards? ....

10. To hammer a nail into wood?..

11. To hold a toothbrush while cleaning your teeth? ....

12. To unscrew the lid of a jar?..

If you use the RIGHT HAND FOR ALL OF THESE ACTIONS, are there any one-handed actions for which you use the LEFT HAND? Please record them here.

....
....
....

If you use the LEFT HAND FOR ALL OF THESE ACTIONS, are there any one-handed actions for which you use the RIGHT HAND? Please record them here.

....
....
....

(From Annett, 1970, Questionnaire 2)

Appendix 2. HAND SKILL: DOTTING
BETWEEN TARGETS

NAME:_____   SEX:_____

Apparatus: Sheets of A4 paper printed with half inch diameter circles,
8 inches apart, centre to centre. Stop watch.
I = Investigator   P = Participant

Task and Procedure: P should *stand* at a table on which is placed a
sheet of paper with circles. The arrow should point toward P. P holds
a pencil or ballpoint, with the point placed in the further circle. On a
signal from I, P moves to the nearer circle and makes a dot, and then
back again, to and fro until ten movements have been made in each
direction. I must count the moves aloud, starting with 1 as P returns
to the far circle, and counting each return up to 10. P moves as fast
as possible, but all the dots must be *inside* the circle.

I starts the stopwatch on a 'Go' signal and stops on the 10th return to
the far circle. Record the time to the nearest 1/10 second e.g. 6.5 or
8.4.

P should start with the preferred hand, then repeat the task with a
new pair of circles with the other hand. Do 5 trials with each hand in
turn. Record the times in the spaces below. Make sure the right hand
times are in the right hand column and similarly for the left hand,
and that the hands alternate between trials.

Instructions to P: 'Place the point of your pencil here (indicating the
further circle) and when I give the signal "go" move as quickly as you
can to the other circle and place a dot anywhere inside it; then move
straight back to the first circle and keep tapping to and fro as fast as
you can till you have 10 dots in each circle. I shall count out loud
when you return to the first circle and stop when we reach 10. Go as
fast as you can making sure all your hits are inside the circle. Ready?
Go!'.

Participant's times   Left hand   Right hand
                          _____   _____
                          _____   _____
                          _____   _____
                          _____   _____
                          _____   _____

SHEETS FOR DOTTING

Left **Right**

Appendix 3. SAMPLE DATA: PSYCHOLOGY STUDENTS

(Students should complete the Hand preference class and L−R column.)

No.	Sex 1 = M 2 = F	Age in yrs	Hand pref. Questionnaire items 1 = R 2 = E 3 = L												Hand pref. class	Dotting time in seconds		
			1	2	3	4	5	6	7	8	9	10	11	12		Right	Left	L–R
01	2	18	1	1	1	1	1	2	2	1	1	1	1	1	1	10.2	09.8	0.4
02	2	18	1	1	1	1	1	2	2	1	1	1	1	3	2	08.6	08.0	0.6
03	2	20	1	2	1	1	1	1	1	1	1	1	1	2	1	10.3	09.7	0.6
04	2	18	1	1	1	1	1	1	3	1	1	1	1	1		09.4	08.8	
05	2	21	1	1	1	1	1	1	1	1	1	1	1	1		08.1	07.8	
06	1	19	1	1	1	1	1	1	3	3	1	1	1	1		09.4	10.1	
07	2	19	1	1	1	1	1	1	2	2	1	1	1	1		10.2	09.5	
08	2	20	1	1	1	1	1	1	1	1	1	1	1	1		12.1	10.5	
09	2	19	1	1	1	1	1	1	1	1	1	1	1	2		11.3	09.9	
10	2	19	1	2	1	1	1	1	1	1	1	1	1	2		13.0	11.5	
11	1	19	1	1	1	1	1	2	1	1	1	1	1	1		08.9	09.5	
12	2	18	1	1	1	1	1	3	1	1	1	1	1	3		09.7	09.0	
13	2	21	1	1	1	1	1	1	1	1	1	1	1	1		08.7	08.7	
14	2	19	1	1	1	1	1	1	1	1	1	1	1	1		13.0	11.1	
15	1	18	3	3	2	2	3	3	2	2	2	3	2	2		10.0	11.4	
16	2	19	1	1	1	1	1	2	1	1	1	1	1	1		12.6	11.1	
17	2	18	1	1	1	1	1	1	3	2	1	1	1	1		11.5	09.8	
18	1	22	1	1	1	1	1	2	1	3	3	1	3	3		10.7	09.7	
19	1	18	3	3	3	3	3	3	3	3	3	3	3	3		08.6	09.4	
20	1	18	1	1	1	1	1	1	1	1	1	1	1	3		09.0	08.7	
21	1	19	1	3	3	2	1	1	1	1	3	1	1	3		05.9	05.7	
22	1	19	1	1	1	1	1	1	1	1	1	1	1	3		09.5	09.1	
23	1	19	1	1	1	1	1	1	1	1	1	1	1	1		09.7	09.9	
24	1	20	3	3	3	3	1	3	3	3	3	3	3	2		09.9	09.9	
25	1	24	1	2	2	1	1	1	2	1	1	1	1	2		10.3	09.3	
26	1	19	1	1	1	1	1	1	1	1	3	1	1	3		11.5	11.6	
27	1	19	1	1	1	1	1	1	1	1	1	1	1	2		10.7	10.2	
28	1	19	1	2	1	1	1	2	2	1	2	1	1	2		06.4	07.0	
29	1	22	1	1	1	1	1	1	1	1	1	1	1	1		07.8	06.5	
30	1	18	1	1	1	1	1	1	1	1	1	1	1	1		12.1	11.2	
31	1	19	1	1	1	1	1	1	1	1	1	1	1	1		10.8	09.8	
32	1	20	1	1	1	1	1	1	1	1	2	1	1	2		08.1	08.1	
33	1	18	1	1	1	1	1	1	1	1	1	1	1	1		10.6	10.3	
34	1	19	3	2	3	3	1	1	1	1	3	2	2	3		10.0	10.5	
35	1	18	1	1	1	1	1	2	1	1	1	1	1	2		10.8	09.1	
36	1	22	1	1	1	1	1	1	3	3	1	1	1	1		09.7	09.5	
37	2	19	1	1	1	1	1	1	1	1	1	1	1	1		10.4	09.9	
38	2	19	1	1	1	1	1	1	1	1	1	1	1	1		08.4	07.5	
39	2	19	1	1	1	1	1	1	3	3	1	1	1	1		10.1	09.2	
40	2	18	1	1	1	1	1	3	1	1	3	1	1	1		08.1	08.3	
41	1	18	1	1	1	1	1	1	2	1	3	1	1	3		11.0	10.0	
42	2	18	1	2	2	2	1	2	2	1	1	2	2	2		08.4	08.4	
43	2	19	1	1	1	1	1	1	1	1	1	1	1	1		10.3	10.1	
44	2	20	1	1	1	1	1	1	1	1	3	1	1	3		10.7	10.2	
45	1	19	3	3	3	3	3	3	3	3	3	3	3	3		10.1	11.9	
46	2	19	1	1	1	1	1	1	1	1	1	1	1	2		09.8	09.3	
47	2	24	1	2	2	3	1	3	1	2	2	1	1	3		11.2	12.1	
48	2	20	1	1	1	1	1	1	1	1	1	1	1	1		12.4	11.1	
49	2	20	1	1	1	1	1	1	1	1	1	1	1	2		11.2	10.5	
50	1	20	1	1	1	1	1	1	1	1	1	1	1	1		12.4	10.3	

PRACTICAL 4   **Estimating I.Q.**

Louise Higgins
Chester College

Abstract

The term 'self-concept' refers to our ideas of who we are and what we are capable of doing and achieving. One aspect of self-concept is the notion of how our intelligence compares with others'. Research has shown that when people are asked to estimate their own I.Q. and that of their mother and father, there are consistent differences in the estimates (Hogan, 1978; Higgins, 1987). Men give higher estimates of their own I.Q.s than women do, while both sexes estimate their father's I.Q. as higher, but their mother's I.Q. as lower, than their own. The purpose of this practical exercise is to find out whether these conclusions are still true. The discussion of results considers why such sex differences are found and suggests some possible reasons for them.

Materials
and Equipment

This is a very straightforward exercise to carry out, simply requiring pen and paper to record the participants' sex and answers to the three questions which appear in the Procedure section. A minimum of 30 participants, (with equal numbers of males and females) should be included in this exercise. Investigators may work individually, or in groups, and should be able to collect and analyse the data produced within one two-hour session.

Introduction
and Hypotheses

In order to understand the purpose of this practical exercise, it is necessary to be familiar with three important topics in Psychology. These are *intelligence*, *self-concept* and *sex-role stereotyping*. Brief backgrounds to these areas follow.

Intelligence. There is a great deal of argument amongst psychologists over just what is meant by intelligence. There are many different expressions of intelligence, but in general terms, intelligent behaviour involves understanding the relationships between things and being able to apply this understanding in new but related circumstances.

Certain aspects of intelligence can be measured by psychometric tests (intelligence tests). These concentrate on verbal, numerical and visual-spatial abilities, often the factors linked to success in academic training. We know that as children grow and develop, their mental abilities grow too, but at varying rates. Therefore, we can describe children in terms not only of their real (chronological) ages but also in terms of their mental ages, that is, their level of mental functioning compared with that of other children of the same age. Mental age is worked out by comparing individual scores on a test with the average scores produced by large numbers of children of the same age on the same test. An individual intelligence quotient (I.Q.) is derived by taking the ratio of mental age to chronological age and multiplying it by 100 in order to remove decimals. For example, an eleven-year-old girl who has a perfectly average mental ability for her age, will have an IQ of

$$\frac{\text{Mental Age}}{\text{Chronological Age}} \times 100 \quad \text{i.e.} \ \frac{11}{11} \times 100 = 100$$

Thus, by definition, an I.Q. of 100 means 'average'. A figure of less than 100 means below-average intelligence, and a figure of more than 100 means above-average intelligence, as measured by an intelligence test. When the intelligence test is for adults, the 'mental age' concept is not really applicable (there is no difference between being 'mentally 24' as opposed to 'mentally 25'). Therefore, psychologists structure such tests by a process of standardization, often providing a 'normal distribution' of scores with a mean score of 100 and a standard deviation of 16 (see Figure 1), so that most people's I.Q. scores fall between 84 and 116. To find out more about the nature and construction of intelligence tests see Anastasi (1988).

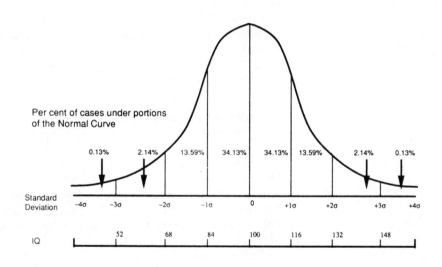

Figure 1. A normal distribution curve of I.Q.s.

It should be noted that during this standardization procedure, sex differences are deliberately minimized so that the average score for both males and females is 100. Nevertheless, it is argued that there are some real sex differences in intelligence: for example, more males than females tend to fall at the extreme ends of the I.Q. scale, and females are often found to excel in verbal abilities while males often excel in mathematical abilities. For a more detailed assessment of sex differences and intelligence, look at Singleton (1986). Remember, however, that this practical is not actually concerned with measured intelligence, but simply with people's perceptions of their own intellectual ability.

Self-concept. Burns (1979 p. i) describes self-concept as:

> a composite image of what we think we are, what we think we can achieve, what we think others think of us and what we would like to be.

The self-concept was one of the first aspects of mental life to be studied by early psychologists. William James (1890) believed that our idea of self had three elements – the material, the social and the spiritual. Cooley (1902) wrote about the 'looking-glass self', stressing the way in which we form opinions about ourselves as a result of feedback from other people. A more recent explanation of self is that offered by Bem (1967). According to him, we gain knowledge of ourselves by observing our own behaviour and making inferences from it. Thus, if 'I give money to lots of charities', then 'I must be a generous person'.

Self-concept involves an evaluative element known as self-esteem or self-worth. It is generally a part of healthy adjustment to have a positive sense of one's own self-worth, although this does not imply self-conceit. We acquire this self-esteem largely as a result of the way in which parents and others treat us in childhood. In infancy we absorb their impressions of us as we come to differentiate ourselves from the world around us, and as we grow older, their comments and reactions are incorporated to form our self-identities.

Sex-role stereotypes.   Finally, the effect of sex-role on our developing self-concept has to be considered. Everyone is immediately classified by sex (a biological distinction) at birth, and begins to be treated differently according to gender (that is, as masculine or feminine) from then on. Much research shows that parents treat male and female babies very differently and indeed expect them to react differently (see Dworetzky (1990)). Gradually we learn that certain behaviours and ideas are appropriate for our gender-role, and these ideas become part of our self-concept.

Another factor to be considered is the effect of stereotyped ideas. These are widely held expectations that certain categories of people will behave in particular ways. Sex stereotypes, therefore, are expectations that men and women will exhibit certain consistently different patterns of behaviour and personality. Such ideas may vary greatly from one culture to another, but the expectations are strongest regarding tasks which are labelled as most appropriate for one sex, for example, that women exhibit caring behaviour towards small children.

How then do sex-role stereotypes come to influence our idea of our own intelligence level? In general, the female role is not expected to involve a demonstration of mastery, competence or intelligence (except perhaps in domestic matters). Torrance (1963) showed that even when girls had performed as well as boys on a science test, both sexes still thought that the boys had done better. Connell *et al.* (1975) reported that when children rated themselves on scales indicating mental abilities, physical abilities and school performance, the boys rated themselves consistently more favourably than the girls. Even by middle-childhood, therefore, girls had a less positive view of their abilities than boys. Thus, when Hogan (1978) asked people in the United States to estimate their own I.Q. in comparison with the national average I.Q. of 100, it was not surprising that he found significant sex differences. He noted that:

> compared with male self-perceptions, the females invariably underestimated their I.Q. scores,. . .the females typically attributed higher I.Q.s to others than they claimed for themselves. . .and . . .male and female [participants] projected higher I.Q.s on to their fathers than their mothers and invariably perceived their fathers having higher I.Q.s than they perceived themselves having (p. 138).

Higgins (1987) obtained similar results in England, and also noted that both males and females placed their mothers lower on the I.Q. scale than themselves.

Hypotheses

On the basis of Hogan's (1978) and Higgins' (1987) findings, the following one-tailed hypotheses may be proposed:

1. Male participants will give higher estimates of their own I.Qs than female participants.

2. Participants will estimate higher I.Qs for their fathers than for their mothers.

3. Participants will estimate higher I.Qs for their fathers than for themselves.

4. Participants will estimate lower I.Qs for their mothers than for themselves.

For each of the hypotheses, the null hypothesis predicts that there will be no significant differences in estimates of I.Q. scores, and that any differences obtained will be due to chance factors.

Procedure

In this exercise, investigators may work individually or as a group. A single investigator would need to gather data from about 30 participants, ensuring that there are equal numbers of males and females. A group of investigators could each collect some scores and then pool their results for analysis.

The participants should be completely naïve with respect to the nature of the exercise. Psychology students may already be too well informed about this area of research, and so should not be used as participants. Additionally, people who claim to know their real measured I.Q. (or that of their parents) should be excluded from the exercise. Participants should be questioned individually and preferably in private. They should be informed that the investigators are conducting a psychological investigation and asked if they would be willing to answer three short question. Investigators should use the following questions which have been used in previous research.

1. *By comparison with the national average I.Q. score of 100 (one hundred), what do you estimate your I.Q. would be, should you take one of the standard, objective tests?*

2. *By comparison with the national average I.Q. score of 100 (one hundred), what do you estimate your mother's I.Q. would be, should she take one of the standard, objective tests?*

3. *By comparison with the national average I.Q. score of 100 (one hundred), what do you estimate your father's I.Q. would be, should he take one of the standard, objective tests?*

The answers provided by each participant should be noted down as well as his or her sex. There is no need for names or other identification. When the participant has given his or her answers, he or she should be debriefed as to the purpose of the questions, and the expected sex differences explained. Some participants may be interested in the concept of intelligence, so investigators should be prepared to explain just what psychologists believe intelligence to be and how it can be measured. Participants may have their own explanations for the predicted sex differences, and these may be worth noting down for use in a written report.

Results

Once all the data has been collected, the four one-tailed alternative hypotheses may be tested. The first hypothesis suggested that male participants would give higher estimates of their own I.Q. scores than female participants would. The relevant data to analyse are the participants' responses to the first question which they were asked. Mean estimated I.Q. scores and standard deviations should be calculated for male and female participants, in order to look for a difference between the means of the two groups. The appropriate statistical test to use is the independent 't' test, which is a parametric test whose use requires that the data satisfy certain criteria. If the data do not meet the requirements for the independent 't' test, then the non-parametric equivalent (the Mann–Whitney U-test) should be used. When referring to probability tables to check for significance, it should be remembered that the hypothesis was one-tailed, that is, the direction of the differences which would occur was predicted beforehand.

The second hypothesis predicted that participants would estimate higher I.Q.s for their fathers than they would for their mothers. The mean estimated I.Q.s and standard deviations for fathers and mothers should be calculated. This time, since each participant has provided two scores, the related 't' test is the appropriate method to use to test for significant differences. However, once again, if the necessary criteria are not met for using a parametric test, then a suitable

48

non-parametric test, such as the sign test or the Wilcoxon test, should be employed.

The third hypothesis suggested that participants would estimate their father's I.Q. to be higher than their own. As with the second hypothesis, each participant provided two scores. As before, depending on the data, a related 't' test, a sign test or Wilcoxon test should be used.

The fourth and final hypothesis predicted that participants would estimate that their mother's I.Q was lower than their own. Again, each participant provided two scores, and the correct test to use for this one-tailed hypothesis is the related 't' test or a suitable non-parametric alternative.

Discussion

If the results agree with Hogan's, some explanations will need to be offered, perhaps in terms of socialization, child rearing practices and sexual stereotypes. It should be remembered that there is no evidence for consistent sex differences in real I.Q. scores because of the way in which intelligence tests are devised. This practical exercise is not about actual I.Q. scores, but rather about self-perception of intelligence.

Hogan's work was published in 1978. Since then, a whole generation of our society has been reared in an age of alleged sexual equality. Would younger participants show the same sex differences as older participants? These investigations might be continued by taking groups of children of different ages as participants and looking for differences between them. What predictions might be made, given the findings of this exercise? Could the lower self-estimations of I.Q. by females be the result of greater modesty? Bird (1984) showed that females' estimates of their performance on a memory task were actually lower when given in private than in public. This would suggest that it was not public modesty which shaped their judgements, but negative self-perceptions. Could this variation of procedure be implemented with the questions given in this exercise? There is very little psychological literature on modesty, but immodesty is generally perceived negatively, especially in females (Heatherington *et al.* 1989). When self-esteem levels are measured, they are widely found to be higher in males than in females (see Pathare and Kanekar's (1990) study on an Indian student population). If awarding oneself a high I.Q. score is seen as one aspect of having high self-esteem, what other questions involving self-description might male and female participants be asked in the expectation of finding significant sex differences?

The socially conditioned underrating of self found in females may have important real-life consequences. Hogan (1978, p. 137) noted that '*thinking* one has either more or less intelligence than another person may matter every bit as much as how the individual may actually score on a so-called I.Q. test'. For instance, in 1972, Dickstein and Kephart reported that females who were told that they were expected to do well on an intelligence test actually improved their level of performance. How could this effect be checked for in the present exercise?

A subtle variable which might influence some of these sex-role difference findings is the sex of the investigator. Do female participants become even more modest in their estimates in the presence of male investigators? Again, how could an investigation be designed to study the effect of the investigator's sex on the participant's responses? Is it possible to check whether the sex of the person asking the questions made any differences or not in the present study?

A survey of the literature on sex-roles will reveal the important influence of Sandra Bem's writings in the 1970s. Many people would agree with her that there are not simply two categories of maleness and femaleness, but that there are instead varying degrees of sex-typing, and we all have some of the characteristics of the opposite sex. This idea would enable us to elaborate the sex-differences in I.Q. findings. For example, Kelly and Smail (1986) showed that children who were strongly sex-typed showed less interest than those who were not in learning about those areas of science traditionally seen as the province of the opposite sex. Similarly, Selkow (1985) found that perceived gender role, in terms of maleness and femaleness, was more relevant to demonstrated sex differences in mathematical ability than was biological sex. We could hypothesize, therefore, that very feminine females might give the lowest self-estimated I.Q.s of all. How could this be investigated? It might be necessary to use one of the published sex-role inventories about which Kaplan and Sedney (1980) provide useful information. Wilkinson (1986) includes a critical evaluation of Bem's contribution to the sex-role debate. Will the commonly held sex-role stereotypes ever change? Would more assertiveness training for females make a difference?

The other findings need to be explained as well. Why are mothers seen as less intelligent than fathers? Is it because they often do the less intellectually demanding chores at home, such as washing and dusting, or is it perhaps that men deliberately choose to marry women who seem less intelligent than themselves, and therefore mothers are accurately perceived by their children as being less intelligent than fathers?

If the results of this study do not agree with previous research, it will be necessary to try to explain why this is the case, and investigators should decide whether the differences arose because of their sample or because of their methods. The questions given in the Procedure section are worded in exactly the same way as in previous studies. Would altering the wording of the questions or giving participants more information about I.Q. tests beforehand change the results? How privately was the questioning done? How did the investigators react verbally and non-verbally to the answers given?

The 'experimenter effect' is a well-known source of error in psychology experiments. When investigators are aware of the hypothesis, there is a tendency for their findings to turn out in the predicted direction. (See the practical on 'Experimenter Bias Effects' in this section.) Perhaps it would be better for the investigators to be 'blind' as to the purpose of this study in order to eliminate these possible subtle influences. How could this be arranged?

Whatever the results of this practical exercise, it is highly likely to produce interesting and lively debate.

Bibliography

General background references

ANASTASI, A. (1988) *Psychological Testing*, 6th edn. London: Collier Mac-millan.

DWORETZKY, J.P. (1990) *Introduction to Child Development*, 4th edn. St. Paul: West Publishing Company.

KAPLAN, A.G. and SEDNEY, M.A. (1980) *Psychology and Sex Roles: an Androgynous Perspective*. Boston: Little, Brown and Company.

SINGLETON, C.H. (1986) Sex roles in cognition. In D. Hargreaves and A. Colley (Eds) *The Psychology of Sex Roles*. London: Harper Row.

WILKINSON, S. (1986) *Feminist Social Psychology: Developing Theory and Practice*. Milton Keynes: Open University Press.

Specific Background References

BURNS, R.B. (1979) *The Self Concept*. Harlow, Essex: Longman.

CONNELL, W.F., STROOBANT, R.E., SINCLAIR, K.E., CONNELL, R.W. and ROGERS, K.W. (1975) *Twelve to Twenty*. Sydney: Hicks Smith.

COOLEY, C.H. (1902) *Human Nature and the Social Order*. New York: Schocken Books.

HIGGINS, L.T. (1987) The Unknowing of Intelligence. *The Guardian* 10 February.

JAMES, W. (1890) *The Principles of Psychology*, Volumes 1 and 2. New York: Holt.

Journal References

BEM, D.J. (1967) Self Perception: An alternative interpretation of cognitive dissonance phenomena. *Psychological Review*, 74, 183–200.

BEM, S. (1974) The measurement of psychological androgyny. *Journal of Consulting and Clinical Psychology*, 42, 155–162.

BIRD, J.E. (1984) Gender differences in expectations of children when anticipated feedback and anonymity are varied. *Genetic Psychology Monographs*, 110, 307–325.

DICKSTEIN, L. and KEPHART, J. (1972) Effect of explicit examiner expectancy upon W.A.I.S. performance. *Psychological Reports*, 30, 207–212.

HEATHERINGTON, L., CROWN, J., WAGNER, H. and RIGBY, S. (1989) Towards an understanding of the social consequences of 'feminine immodesty' about personal achievements. *Sex Roles*, 20, 371–380.

HOGAN, H.W. (1978) I.Q. Self-estimates of males and females. *Journal of Social Psychology*, 106, 137–138.

KELLY, A. and SMAIL, B. (1986) Sex stereotypes and attitudes to science among 11-year-old children. *British Journal of Educational Psychology*, 56, 158–168.

PATHARE, S.S. and KANEKAR, S. (1990) Self-esteem, intelligence and academic achievement of Indian College students in relation to sex roles. *Irish Journal of Psychology*, 11, 31–40.

SELKOW, P. (1985) Male/Female differences in mathematical ability: a function of biological sex or perceived gender role? *Psychological Reports*, 57, 551–7.

TORRANCE, E.P (1963) Changing reactions of pre-adolescent girls to tasks requiring creative scientific thinking. *Journal of Genetic Psychology*, 102, 217–223.

PRACTICAL 5

Evaluating a technique to aid the learning of people's names

Vicki Bruce
University of Nottingham

Abstract

This practical exercise investigates techniques for improving people's memories and, in so doing, introduces and illustrates the use of *repeated measures* (sometimes referred to as *within subjects*) and *independent* (sometimes referred to as *between subjects*) designs. If conducted within a class setting, the exercise can begin with a preliminary demonstration of the use of the 'One is a bun' mnemonic (see *Appendix 1*) for remembering the serial positions of words. The main experiment involves designing and executing an evaluation of the use of a similar technique to learn the names of people (after Morris *et al.*, 1978). Discussion points which may arise include the theoretical basis of any benefit obtained using such mnemonic techniques and more complex experimental designs which could be used in future work.

Materials
and Equipment

Two groups of 10–20 participants are required, with participants being randomly allocated to each group. Lists of nouns are needed for the preliminary demonstration (see *Appendix 2* for suggestions). Fifteen names and faces are needed for the main experiment. Surnames may be obtained by sampling from the phone book (excluding very long or complicated ones). Faces may be obtained from newspapers or magazines (photocopy quality is acceptable), or may be provided by the students' own faces. Faces may be presented using slides or an overhead projector to a whole group of participants or may be shown as photographed (or photocopied) sheets to participants tested individually. A stopwatch or wrist-watch with a second hand is needed to time presentation of the stimulus material.

If the experiments are conducted within a class, with the initial demonstration described followed by the main experiment and analysis, the exercise will take about two hours. The data collection itself only takes a tiny proportion of the class time, and the activities could easily be divided between two shorter class sessions.

Introduction
and Hypotheses

The Sunday newspapers often contain advertisements for schemes to help improve one's memory. Do such systems work? And if so, how? Many of the 'commercial' packages for improving memory involve training people to use one or more mnemonic devices for improving recall. Mnemonic tricks have been used throughout history to help people learn things they would otherwise find difficult. Most such systems involve making meaningful links between things that would otherwise be meaningless lists to remember (e.g. Richard Of York Gained Battles In Vain for the colours of the spectrum), or often use

52

rhyme ('Thirty days hath September. . .' for the number of days in a month) or imagery. The Greek orators used to learn their speeches by mentally placing each topic at a different place along a familiar route. When delivering the speech, they mentally 'walked' the route, retrieving the topics in order as they encountered each imagined landmark.

If techniques such as those used by the Greek orators sound bizarre, try participating in a simple demonstration. This can be run as an introductory 'experiment' at the beginning of a class, though it is less suitable for an individual studying alone. This demonstration shows how the use of a 'pegword' mnemonic ('One is a Bun') helps people to remember a list of words and the serial position in which each word occurs. Students are read out a list of ten words preceded by their numbers (for example, Number 1, tiger), and then tested on their ability to reply to questions of the sort, 'What was Number 3?' Then they are taught the rhyme 'One is a bun, two is a shoe, etc.' (full rhyme appears in *Appendix 1*). When trying to remember a second list of words, they are told to associate each word to be remembered with the corresponding 'pegword'. They may be given one or more examples from the old list to help them think about this: for example, if Number 1 is tiger, they might imagine a tiger eating a bun. Later, when asked, 'What is Number 1?' they will remember 'bun', see the tiger, and recall the word correctly. Usually students are sceptical that such an elaborate procedure will work, but typically it produces gains of about three or four words correctly recalled compared with the first list.

However, the limitations of the conclusions which can be drawn from this demonstration must be discussed. Would students have improved anyway on their second attempt? Was the second list of words easier than the first? The class can be invited to consider what type of design would be needed for a rigorous test of the efficacy of this technique. This class discussion can be used to introduce a comparison of the advantages and disadvantages of repeated measures versus independent subjects designs. The main experiment which follows makes use of an independent subjects design.

Remembering that 'Number 1 is tiger' is not something that would be found generally useful in everyday life. The 'Improve Your Memory' books promise benefits that will carry through to improve your work and social life. What about a mnemonic system for remembering the names of people that we meet? Names can be extraordinarily difficult to remember – we frequently have temporary blocks for the names of people we may know quite well (Young *et al.*, 1985), and names are harder to learn than other information about a person – for example, what they do for a living. Indeed, it is harder to remember that someone is called 'Mr Baker' than that he is a 'baker', even though the same words are used (McWeeny *et al.*, 1987). Cohen (1990) has suggested that names are hard to remember because they are not integrated into the semantic system (that part of long-term memory which stores the meanings of words). Some accounts of person identification propose that names are held in a different store from that in which other knowledge about people is held (e.g. Bruce and Young, 1986).

Lorayne (1958) describes a technique which can be used to improve people's memories for the names of people that they meet. There are two stages. First a 'meaningless' name is turned into a more concrete version (e.g. Bruce = Bruise), and then a link is made between this word and some prominent feature of the person's face. For example, to learn the name 'Bruce', you might imagine a person with a bruise over one eye. When you see the face again, you imagine the 'name' covering part of the face, and retrieve it appropriately. Morris *et al.* (1978) evaluated this technique and showed, in an experiment using photographs of named faces, that it did indeed improve people's abilities to retrieve names. The aim of this practical exercise is to replicate Morris *et al.*'s study, though using a somewhat simpler design. If the practical involves learning the (real or made-up) names of volunteers, rather than photographed people, then the additional aim is to examine whether the technique works when applied to a real-life situation.

Hypotheses

The experimental hypothesis is that a group of participants taught to use Lorayne's technique will remember a different number of names from a group not taught the technique. The null hypothesis is that there will be no difference between the groups.

Procedure

To keep the statistical analysis simple, an independent subjects design should be used. Participants are randomly allocated to two equal groups. A minimum of ten participants, but preferably 20, will be needed per group for the design to have enough 'power' to reveal significant effects of the mnemonic, given the within-groups varia-bility that is obtained in memory tests such as this. The experimental group is taught the mnemonic technique; the control group is not. All participants then receive the same set of faces and names to learn. Thus the independent variable is whether or not the mnemonic tech-nique is taught, and the dependent variable is the number of names correctly remembered.

The procedure itself may involve either testing individuals or a group test; whichever is used will depend on the teaching context. Students working in small groups may go out separately and recruit their own participants for this design, testing each individually. If an individual student is able to recruit as many as 20 participants in total, then each student may act as an independent experimenter, collecting and analysing data for a complete experiment. However, it is more likely that students will collect data from just a few partici-pants and the data will be pooled in class. Whichever method is adopted, if students are to act as experimenters outside class, they must be told how to recruit volunteers, how to debrief them, and how to reassure them if they are worried about their performance of the tasks. Students must be taught about the random allocation of parti-cipants to conditions, and be made aware of the necessity of ensuring that experimental procedures are kept constant in all respects except for the manipulation of the independent variable.

If the exercise is being carried out in the class and the class comprises at least 20 students, then the experiment may be conducted within the class session, with students allocated to the two conditions and acting as participants. In this case, the participants may be tested simultaneously as a group. However, for the experiment to be at all plausible, some way must be found to keep the control group unaware of the mnemonic technique until after the experiment has been conducted, so that they are not tempted to employ it. In order to end up with equal-sized groups, students can get into pairs and toss a coin within each pair to determine which member enters each group. The control group should be sent away while the mnemonic technique is explained to the experimental group.

Participants in the experimental condition should have the mnemonic procedure explained to them, and be invited to practise its use with a set of faces and names not used in the experiment proper. Then all participants should be invited to try to remember the names of 15 people (this is a long enough list to avoid any risk of ceiling effects). These may be presented as 'faces' using an overhead projector or slides (photocopy quality pictures are fine for a practical of this sort). If the class is very large, a set of students may volunteer to be given 'new' names or, if it is very early in the course before students have got to know each other, their own names may be used. Please note, however, the possible sensitivities involved if, through random allocation of 'new' names to people, someone ends up with a rather unfortunate label that may stick throughout their student career (e.g. an overweight student ends up being given the new name 'Mr/Ms Wait', for example).

The faces, or people, with the names allocated to them randomly (with exceptions as discussed above), should be presented to the experimental participants in a random order. Each face or person is 'introduced' for a fixed period of time ('This is Mr Green', etc). It is recommended that participants are exposed to each face for at least ten seconds so that the mnemonic group have time to try to link the name with the face. The names can either be read out by the experimenter (in which case, of course, the spelling of the name is irrelevant), or they may be printed on to cards or on to the slides so that participants can see as well as hear them. After all the faces/names have been presented, the participants should be asked to count aloud backwards by threes from a three-digit number for approximately 30 seconds to prevent rehearsal of the most recent items.

The faces, or people, are then presented again, in a different order, without their names. As each is shown, the participants must try to write down the name. A record of the test order used will be needed in order to check whether the answer is right or wrong. A decision must be made about what counts as a 'right' answer (e.g. what if the spelling is wrong?). Scores are then collected in.

Results

However the experiment has been conducted, the data will comprise scores (out of 15) for two independent groups. Data may be summarized by computing the mean score and a measure of spread for example, the standard deviation, for each group. Histograms showing the scores obtained in each group may be plotted and compared and the class asked to comment on these. A Mann-Whitney U-test may be used to compare the scores obtained by the two groups. The test should be two-tailed, since it is not impossible for the mnemonic to depress performance relative to control if its use prevented more effective natural strategies (again this is a point for discussion with the class). If parametric tests are preferred, then an independent samples t-test can be used, provided that the necessary assumptions for employing the test have been met.

Discussion

If a significant difference in the predicted direction is obtained, then discussion can focus on the possible reasons for the improvement produced by the mnemonic. Do both stages of the mnemonic strategy contribute to the improvement? Perhaps it is merely the instruction to make names more concrete which makes them more memorable? Why are imagery instructions used so frequently in mnemonic systems? Are images useful because they are particularly vivid (but then what of people who have poor powers of mental imagery?); or, is it that imagery instructions encourage the formation of novel or bizarre associations? Consideration could be given to the kinds of follow-up study which would be needed to explore in more detail the mechanisms by which the mnemonic helps memory. While emphasizing the practical and theoretical implications of their result, students should also consider the limitations of the design used. Ideally, the design would follow that used by Morris *et al.*, involving two independent groups of participants and giving both groups the same pretest, before teaching only one group the mnemonic technique. There is nothing to prevent the use of this design in class, though it does require more faces, more names, more time and (ideally) more complex statistical methods. Limitations of the procedure could also be discussed. For example, how do we make sure that participants try to link the name with the face rather than the clothing worn by the people to be remembered? A useful technique must survive changes in clothing – perhaps clothing should be concealed during the experiment?

In my experience, significant effects are obtained in most but not all attempts at this practical. If no significant difference was found between the two groups, consider possible reasons for the failure to replicate Morris *et al.'s* result. Did the experimental group have enough practice at applying the method? Was the time allowed for each 'introduction' to the faces/names sufficient to allow application of the method? Were members of the control group 'cheating' by devising similar strategies themselves, given the earlier discussion of imagery techniques? However, even if no significant differences were found, the class should be encouraged to think about the reasons why mnemonic systems of this kind can work.

Further exercises may be developed. For example, the class could be invited to make use of what they have learned about mnemonic techniques to suggest further potentially beneficial strategies for remembering difficult things, such as the dates of people's birthdays, and could design an experiment to test this.

Bibliography

General background references

Any general introductory text (such as ATKINSON, R.L., ATKINSON, R.C., SMITH, E.E., BEM, D.J. and HILGARD, E.R. (1990) *Introduction to Psychology*. 10th edn. New York: Harcourt, Brace Jovanovich) will have a section on memory, and most will include some reference to mnemonic strategies, placed in the context of a discussion of organization in memory.

Specific background references

BADDELEY, A.D. (1990) *Human Memory*. London: Lawrence Erlbaum Associates. Chapter 8.

LORAYNE, H. (1958) *How to Develop a Super-power Memory*. Preston: Thomas.

See also Morris *et al.*, in Journal articles section.

Journal articles

BRUCE, V. and YOUNG, A.W. (1986) Understanding face recognition. *British Journal of Psychology*, 77, 305–327.

COHEN, G. (1990) Why is it difficult to put names to faces? *British Journal of Psychology*, 81, 287–298.

MCWEENY, K.H., YOUNG, A.W., HAY, D.C. and ELLIS, A.W. (1987) Putting names to faces. *British Journal of Psychology*, 78, 143–149.

MORRIS, P.E., JONES, S. and HAMPSON, P. (1978) An imagery mnemonic for the learning of people's names. *British Journal of Psychology*, 69, 335–336. (This very short paper is well worth photocopying and distributing to the class (allowed by BPS journals for educational purposes) since it provides a specific reference on which the practical is based.)

YOUNG, A.W., HAY, D.C. and ELLIS, A.W. (1985) The faces that launched a thousand slips: Everyday difficulties and errors in recognizing people. *British Journal of Psychology*, 76, 495–523.

Acknowledgement: To the best of my (unaided) memory, the 'One is a bun' demonstration and the lists of words used were adapted from a practical class suggestion given to me by Alan Baddeley when I was about to embark on my first teaching post.

Appendix 1. ONE is a BUN

Mnemonic for remembering serial position of words

ONE is a BUN
TWO is a SHOE
THREE is a TREE
FOUR is a DOOR
FIVE is a HIVE
SIX is STICKS
SEVEN is HEAVEN
EIGHT is a GATE
NINE is a LINE
TEN is a HEN

Appendix 2

List A
1. LEGGINGS
2. MACKEREL
3. CANYON
4. DAFFODIL
5. PIGMY
6. MALLET
7. BORROWER
8. MINERAL
9. INCUBATOR
10. ASPARAGUS

List B
1. AWARD
2. GINGER
3. WRINKLE
4. BOTTLE
5. SPICE
6. STEEL
7. DISPENSARY
8. CHOCOLATE
9. FERTILIZER
10. PARTRIDGE

PREFACE TO THE OBSERVATIONAL METHOD

Paul Humphreys
Worcester College of Higher Education

Until relatively recently observation was viewed very much as the poor relation of psychological research methodologies. Early psychological investigation was based upon *positivist* principles which reject all things metaphysical, and advocate the use of 'scientific' methods, such as the experiment. By and large the followers of Watson's Behaviourism thoroughly embraced these principles, with the result that psychology was substantially dominated until the last two or three decades by a behaviouristic/positivistic/experimental orientation. One of the earliest and most significant turning points came with an address given by D.O. Hebb to the American Psychological Association. In this address, Hebb, generally regarded as a mainstream (or conventional) positivist psychologist, contended that psychology had 'lost its mind'. The thrust of his argument was that the discipline of psychology had become dominated by an adherence to methodological doctrines, especially Watsonian Behaviourism, effectively debarring the study of much of its original subject matter, mental life. Mainstream psychology today is characterized by a much richer diversity of methodologies than has probably ever before been the case. This is the result of many factors, some specific to psychology, others more attributable to attitudinal and ideological/political changes in American and Western European cultures. It is worth briefly considering three factors which have contributed to the de-emphasizing of the laboratory and the experimental method in psychology.

The question of the *ecological validity* of psychological research was raised in the *Preface to the Experimental Method*. Ecological validity is the extent to which psychological research and data accurately measure and reflect phenomena or events which are either of the real world or can be justifiably extrapolated to it. To put this another way, studies of participants trying to recall nonsense syllables in a laboratory may actually tell us nothing more than how well people can recall nonsense syllables in a laboratory. Note that Bruce's practical in the *Experimental Method* section, *Evaluating a Technique to Aid the Learning of People's Names*, is designed for a 'real-world' setting: the classroom. Furthermore, the activity concerned is a highly pertinent one in this context, and useful to candidates preparing for psychology examinations. It could be argued that observations of 'slices' of real-world behaviour have greater ecological validity than contrived experimental manipulations. However, it should be pointed out that by no means all observational studies are non-interventionist or carried out in non-laboratory settings.

A second factor worth particular attention is the question of ethics. You will, no doubt, have noticed that the contributors to this book use the term 'participants' rather than the more traditional term 'subjects'. This is in keeping with recent (1990) guidelines issued by the British Psychological Society, and it is indicative of the way in which practising psychologists are being encouraged to be more aware of their moral responsibilities to the people or animals involved in their studies. It also extends to a movement towards an increased awareness of the relationship between psychology and the culture of which it is a part. For example, psychologists are being encouraged to consider fully the uses and implications of their research. Might it conceivably be used, for example, to fuel racism or denigrate women? Many of the psychological studies of bygone years which are now deemed to be ethically contentious (such as Harlow's (1959) classic studies of maternal deprivation in rhesus monkeys) have used the experimental method. Many writers claim that observation studies reduce the likelihood of such participant 'exploitation'. However, the issue is far from simple. One of the other main arguments advanced against the practice of psychological research in general concerns the issue of *deception*, in particular, the *deliberate* and *intended* withholding of important information, or the provision of incorrect information to participants. Milgram's (1963) studies of obedience will come readily to mind as clear examples of such deception. The fact is that many studies would not work if participants knew the true purpose of the study. Psychologists today are urged to weigh up such dilemmas very carefully indeed before undertaking such research. Furthermore, it could be argued that deception is just as likely to occur in non-experimental and non-laboratory studies, such as participant observation. One final point for ethical consideration may also be raised here; that of invasion or loss of privacy for participants. Again, it might be argued convincingly that this is just as likely to happen in observational studies as in those using an experimental methodology. Indeed many participants in observational studies never actually knew that they were participants. This emphasizes the importance of obtaining informed consent from participants, and fully debriefing them immediately after a study has been completed. However, exactly what constitutes invasion of privacy is a contentious issue. For Westland (1978), observation of behaviour that takes place within the public domain cannot possibly be construed as an invasion of privacy; only when behaviour occurs in private would any attempt to observe it be construed as an invasion of privacy. Lang's practical, *Observational Studies of Pedestrian Behaviour*, is a good example of social psychological investigation in the public domain, as it concerns the observation, recording and analysis of behaviours which are available for all in visual range to see. Notwithstanding Westland's contention, it is clearly desirable to obtain informed consent from participants where this will not compromise the logic of the investigation and, if at all possible, to debrief participants immediately after a study has been completed.

The third general issue to be raised here concerns another recent trend associated with the modern reduced emphasis on the experimental method. This concerns the increasing amount of strictly qualitative research to be found in mainstream psychology. The term qualitative is used here to mean 'non-numerical' (that is, verbal descriptions), and thus contrasts with quantitative or numerical research. It should be made clear that the distinction between the two styles of research is rarely clear-cut: the vast majority of quantitative research also generates much description, and vast number of qualitative studies generate numerical data. It is rather a matter of relative emphasis. Think, for example, of the clearly different ways in which Piaget, with his usage of the clinical interview, and Eysenck, with his usage of psychometric testing, have studied human intelligence. The former is an example of qualitative orientation, and the latter, quantitative.

Many teachers will be aware that, in recent years, several writers have argued that psychology has been too much dominated by a desire for quantification. For example, Reason and Rowan (1981) claim that

> there is too much measurement going on. Some things which are numerically precise are not true; and some things which are not numerical are true. Orthodox research produces results which are statistically significant but humanly insignificant; in human inquiry it is better to be deeply interesting than accurately boring.

Several observational techniques lend themselves rather better to qualitative research than does the experimental method. (Correlational analysis is, of course, by definition, quantitative.) Examples of largely qualitative observation methods are:

(i) the case study, which itself raises the contentious issue of the relative values of nomothetic research, (where a plurality of participants is involved) and idiographic research (which is, generally, the in-depth study of a single individual or event)

(ii) clinical observation (as used by Piaget and Freud)

(iii) the diary method; this involves daily recording of the behaviour of a specific person.

Most of the practicals in this book, however, such as the content analysis of television advertisements (see page 69) and attribution for success and failure made by English soccer managers and players (see page 78) do lead to numerical analysis.

Before we turn our attention to particular types and classifications of observational methods, three points need to be made. First, as Coolican (1990) points out,

> there is ambiguity in the use of the term 'observational' in research literature. It can refer to the use of observation as a technique for gathering data about behaviour in a study which might in general be referred to as an experimental design. On the other hand, 'observational' might refer to the overall design of a study, in contrast to a controlled experiment.

It is this latter definition I will adopt here.

Second, by observation I do not just mean casually watching something. Issues such as definition of units of behaviour or observation, structure, procedure, interpretation and recording are crucial. As Miller (1964) has pointed out, our ancient ancestors learned relatively little about the world through centuries of merely casual observation.

Finally, a note to students: carrying out an observational, as opposed to experimental, study, is *not* a licence for sloppy reporting and writing-up. Very rarely will an unstructured, essay-type presentation be appropriate. There are clear conventions for the writing-up of observational studies, even those which are purely qualitative. (See *Appendix 2* to the *Manual* for notes on report writing.)

Different types of observation

In the *Preface to the Experimental Method*, I pointed out that the experimental method is actually a collection of methodological practices and procedures united by principles such as abstraction, and IV/DV differentiation. Similarly, there are many different types of observational studies, and just as we identified some criteria by which experimental methodologies could be distinguished and classified, so it is possible to produce a number of criteria to help us differentiate observational methods. The following list is not intended to be definitive, but may be useful.

Some criteria for differentiating observational studies

Naturalistic versus controlled observations. Earlier I differentiated naturalistic experiments from other forms of experimentation. Remember that in naturalistic experiments the experimenter takes advantage of naturally occurring or fortuitous IV manipulation. In the naturalistic observation the investigator observes naturally occurring behaviour, whereas in a controlled observation study the researcher makes some attempt to structure or influence the type of behaviour or response to be observed. Note that, as with the distinction between naturalistic and field experiments, the emphasis is not on the setting but on the natural occurrence of the event.

Let us briefly consider examples from the field of child psychology to illustrate the distinction in practice. Ainsworth *et al.* (1971) studied what has been called the 'strange situation' in babies. She was interested in the development of attachments and sociability in very young children and, as part of this, she arranged the following situation in order to observe the behaviour of babies. The baby would first be observed playing with its caregiver (usually the mother), who would then leave the room. The baby would usually display distress (one of the characteristics of the existence of an attachment bond) and when this occurred, another adult, not known to the baby, would come into the room and pick the baby up and offer comfort. Ainsworth and her colleagues compared this behaviour with that displayed by the baby when the caregiver re-entered the room and picked the baby up. Note that it is the researcher who is 'fixing' the scenario; it is not naturally occurring behaviour which is being observed. Readers may be interested to check this study against the ethical guidelines discussed by Wadeley in *Appendix 1* to this *Manual*. There has been a growing emphasis in recent years on the ethics of experimentation and observation, in particular when involving animals or children. It is probably fair to say that several studies which were carried out in the past would not be deemed justifiable today.

In contrast to Ainsworth's study, Sylva *et al.* (1980) observed the naturally occurring behaviour of pre-school children in playgroups, making no attempt whatsoever to influence what they were observing. In fact, Sylva and her colleagues went to considerable lengths to blend into the playgroup setting so that the behaviour they observed would not be influenced by their presence. This potential contamination factor – where the presence of the observer distorts the behaviour displayed – is called *subject reactivity* (or observer effects) and is something which observational researchers must always be mindful of.

Setting. As with the experimental method, we can make distinctions between observational studies according to their setting. Again, the differentiation is usually (but not necessarily) between so-called natural environments and contrived or artificial ones (such as the laboratory). For instance, many of Ainsworth's studies were carried out in a laboratory setting, whereas Sylva's occurred in an environment which was natural to the children.

Let us consider a rather different type of example to illustrate specifically an observation in a natural setting, and look to the world of animal behaviour. The discipline of ethology, which concentrates on the behaviour of animals in their natural habitats, was pioneered in the 1930s by Lorenz. The results of ethologists' observations, which aim to give as complete pictures of a particular form of animal behaviour as possible, are called *ethograms*.

Structure of data categorization, recording and analysis. Observations can differ massively according to how behaviour is classified, recorded and analysed. Let us consider some examples. The point was made earlier that we learn little from merely watching – we need to be rather more purposeful and structured. One of the most important decisions an observational researcher has to make is what counts as a 'unit'. He or she may concentrate on units of behaviour, producing a list of behaviours which count as aggressive which can then be used to study, for example, gender differences with respect to aggressive behaviour. (See Cardwell's practical on *Gender Differences in the Aggressive Behaviour of Schoolchildren* in this section.) Bales (1950) produced a behavioural classification system called *Interactional Process Analysis* (IPA). He classified the behaviours (including verbal behaviours) demonstrated by people working in groups according to two overriding criteria: whether the behaviour was task- or emotion-orientated (for example, 'I think we could best deal with this problem by. . .'versus 'I don't think getting angry with each other is going to help'), and whether the behaviour was positive or negative. As can be seen from the examples given, the two criteria usually interact, and so Bales was able to produce a 12-types classification which was divided into four overall categories: emotional-positive, task-positive, task-negative and emotional-negative.

Bales went to great lengths to ensure that different observers could be trained to use his IPA in a uniform and consistent way, thus ensuring there is both *intra-* and *inter-rater reliability*. By intra-rater reliability we mean that there is consistency of observation within the same observer on different occasions (for example, if he or she watched a different piece of behaviour on video tape on different occasions, there should be close agreement between the outcomes of the two observations). Inter-rater reliability refers to agreement and consistency between different observers watching the same behaviour. Again, these issues must be of great and continuing concern to all observational researchers, and the related issue of validity (that is, whether our observations are 'meaningful') must be considered. The task of the observational researcher has been made much easier by technological developments in equipment for recording events. In the days of early observers such as Darwin and Freud, reliance was usually placed upon pen, paper and memory to record events that had taken place. Since then, the emergence of audio tape recorders, film and video has not only facilitated total (as opposed to selective) recording of events, but also given researchers the means to endlessly re-run and review recordings of behaviours. These facilities greatly enhance our ability to standardize the information available to observers, thus increasing reliability.

At the beginning of this section we considered the issue of categorizing behaviours by defining units of behaviour. However, an alternative approach is to categorize or define behaviour by 'time units' or other pre-determined criteria. The following examples are given by Wadeley (1991, unpublished).

Specimen description is a method pioneered by Barker and Wright (1951) who made a record of an American boy's day. The observer makes as full an account as possible of behaviour in a chosen segment of the individual's life, by recording what is happening, the context in which it is happening, and the other people involved. This is a very time-consuming method and frequently there are problems concerning the reliability of the observation, and observer effects.

Event sampling involves focusing on a specific type of behaviour and recording the number of times it occurs, the context in which it occurs and events surrounding it. One famous study of infant crying reported by Bell and Ainsworth (1972) employed this technique. The researchers were able to show how a quick and sensitive response by the mother to the infant's cries in the first months was linked to less infant crying at one year of age and a greater variety of vocalizations. Event sampling is particularly time-saving where the type of behaviour to be recorded occurs infrequently and it is especially good for preserving the context in which the event occurs.

Time sampling is perhaps more suitable where the behaviour of interest occurs relatively frequently. The researcher observes for 30 seconds and records for 60 seconds. The presence or absence of the behaviour during each observation interval can be recorded to give an idea of how frequently it occurs. By varying the time intervals for observations, the researcher can give full attention to a number of children during one session and gain an overall impression of how a group of them operates in terms of, say, aggressive or helpful behaviour.

64

The *Target Child Method*, a system using time as criterion, was used by Sylva *et al.* (1980). It involved focusing attention for a specified period of time on one particular child and at specified and pre-determined times (for example, every 30 seconds) noting what the child was doing. This technique is particularly useful for reducing distraction, as it ensures that behaviour is recorded evenly and according to the given criteria.

Another widely used observational technique which is primarily characterized by data categorization and analysis is *content analysis.* According to Crano and Brewer (1973):

> Content analysis broadly describes a heterogenous domain of techniques which are focused upon the [more or less] systematic, objective and quantitative description of a communication or series of communications.

Note the description of the procedural techniques ('systematic, objective and quantitative') and what it is applied to ('communication'). It was originally pioneered by researchers such as Berelson (1952) as a means of analysing media messages of the Second World War. In this section, the practical exercise by Wadeley analyses the content of evening television advertisements for gender stereotypes. One of the important differences between content analysis and other forms of observation is its focus – communication. McIlveen's practical exercise studies the explanations given by football managers and players as to why their teams won or lost a particular game.

One recent important development in observational analysis is *discourse analysis* (for example, Parker and Shotter, 1990) which examines, in qualitative rather than quantitative terms, how social situations and interactions are engineered and manipulated by participants through the intricacies of the specific language used.

Qualitative versus quantitative methods. Some observational techniques are used to gather numbers whereas others (such as the diary method) generate discursive descriptions. If you look back at the last examples given in the previous section (p. 61) you will see that content analysis is a quantitative analytical task whereas discourse analysis is purely qualitative.

Holistic versus 'divisional' techniques. A characteristic which psychology drew from positivism is that analysis should be of 'bits' of behaviour, such as a person's personality, intelligence, motivation. This is consistent with the experimental principle of abstraction. However, there has been a recent trend in psychology, derived from the writings of such humanistic psychologists as Rogers and Maslow, to emphasize the wholeness of the human being. Only by doing this, they argue, does the study of human behaviour and experience make any sense. Holistic studies, therefore, take the 'whole person' into consideration emphasizing not only what people do, say and feel, but also the all-important psychological and social contexts in which these behaviours and cognitions occur. The vast majority of observational techniques are very clearly divisional; indeed the very purpose of many observational techniques, such as event sampling, is to do just this. There are, however, some observational techniques such as the specimen description and the diary method which are holistic.

Nomothetic versus idiographic techniques. The distinction here concerns the *number* of participants included in the observation. Nomothetic studies use large groups of participants, who themselves usually represent an even larger group, such as a sample drawn from a population, whereas the idiographic technique uses a very small number (often one) of individuals. Earlier I contrasted the approaches of Piaget and Eysenck as they studied human intelligence. Another difference between the two psychologists concerns the nomothetic/idiographic dimension: Eysenck's intelligence and personality tests have been used on thousands of people, whereas Piaget preferred to use the 'clinical interview', a free-flowing, unstructured, reactive technique almost always carried out on a one-to-one basis between psychologist and participant.

One extreme form of the idiographic method is the *case study*, the in-depth, usually longitudinal study of a very small number of individuals. The patients Freud worked with can be considered to constitute a series of case studies. Another example of the case study is the *diary method*, mentioned before. It involves the daily recording of descriptions and observations of the behaviour of a specific person. Piaget, for instance, kept detailed diaries chronicling the developmental processes he observed in his own children. One of the strongest advocates of the case study was Allport (1947) who argued that the most preferred form of psychology was the 'science of biography'.

The strengths of the idiographic method (including the case study) are obvious: they give us, for example, a richness of detail and depth which is difficult to obtain with nomothetic methods. They may also provide us with insight into the uniqueness of human experience. The main difficulty of this method concerns its generalizability, that is, the extent to which we can generalize the results of a study carried out on a handful of participants to a larger group of people. Such concerns did not prevent Freud from developing a whole branch of psychology from his case studies of a relatively small number of patients, including only one child. Many other psychologists have expressed rather more concern!

Other criticisms made about case studies (such as those carried out by Freud) are that they deal with unreliable retrospective data, such as the memories of early childhood events and emotions, and they are particularly open to observer bias in interpretation. However, many case studies deal with current events, and advocates of this method argue that observer interpretation is always potentially problematic, and no more problematic in this technique than in any other form of observation.

Participant versus non-participant observation. Almost all of the examples of observation which we have looked at have involved looking in from the 'outside'. However, one way to obtain real insight into, for example, the working of a group, is to study it from the inside. Thus, some observers actually participate in what they are observing. The observer may try to blend unobtrusively into the group, and act as another member (such as Festinger *et al.* did in their (1956) study of an 'end-of-the-world' group). Or, perhaps because of practical difficulties in establishing credible 'cover', the observer may seek to enter the group in a special capacity. A good example of this strategy can be seen in Whyte's classic (1943) study of 'street corner society', in which he studied an Italian gang in Chicago. Since Whyte could not convincingly pass as a 'typical' member, his cover was that he was writing a book on the area. This raises the very sensitive ethical and practical problem of *disclosure*. It could be argued that many of the advantages of using the method of participant observation (such as real-world validity, insider experience and insight) would be lost if the group were aware of the real intentions of the researcher. However, one must seriously challenge the ethical issues involved in such deception. We may note in passing that the discipline of anthropology makes very extensive use of participant observation.

Direct versus indirect observation. The observational techniques I have described so far all involve direct or 'eyes-on' observation, but sometimes we may wish to make use of indirectly observed data (data not generated by the observer him/herself). This may be because of the sensitivity of the area being observed, for example in HIV and AIDS diagnosis communication, or because the phenomena are inaccessible (for example, they may be historical). In such cases researchers may make use of data gathered from other sources, such as medical records or archival data.

Summary

Historically, observation has been regarded by several writers and researchers as the 'poor relation' of the psychology methodologies. At the beginning of this *Preface* I gave a number of reasons for the greater acceptability and 'respect' acquired by observational methodologies during the last two or three decades. These reasons include the claim for greater ecological validity, a concern for ethical considerations in many manipulative and interventionist experimental studies, and an increasing acceptance in mainstream psychology of non-quantitative research. However, it was emphasized that humankind has gained little from centuries of casual, unsystematic observation. Most of the observational techniques and studies described in this *Preface* are as systematic and well designed as any experiment. The point was also made, and should be reiterated, that observational research is not an excuse for sloppy or unstructured reporting. In fact, students may find writing-up an observational study more demanding than writing-up an experiment.

The remainder of the *Preface* classified observational techniques and studies by the following eight criteria:

(a) naturalistic versus controlled observation;
(b) setting;
(c) structure of data categorization, recording and analysis;
(d) qualitative versus quantitative methods;
(e) holistic versus 'divisional' techniques;

(f) nomothetic versus idiographic techniques;

(g) participant versus non-participant observation;

(h) direct versus indirect observation.

Within this framework, many examples of different observational techniques were described. Several of these, including content analysis, are included as exercises in this *Manual*.

References

AINSWORTH, M., BELL, S.M. and STAYTON, D. (1971) Individual differences in strange situation behaviour of one-year olds. In H.R. Schaffer (Ed.) *The Origins of Human Social Relations*. London: Academic Press.

ALLPORT, G.W. (1947) *The Use of Personal Documents in Psychological Science*. London: Holt Rinehart and Winston.

BALES, F.R. (1950) *Interactional Process Analysis: a method for the study of small groups*. Cambridge, Mass.: Addison-Wesley.

BARKER, R.G. and WRIGHT, H.F. (1951) *One Boy's Day*. New York: Harper and Row.

BELL, S.M. and AINSWORTH, M.D.S. (1972) Infant crying and maternal responsiveness. *Child Development, 43*, 1171–90.

BERELSON, B. (1952) *Content Analysis in Communication Research*. New York: Free Press.

BRITISH PSYCHOLOGICAL SOCIETY (1990) *Ethical Principles for Conducting Research with Human Participants*. Leicester: The British Psychological Society.

COOLICAN, H. (1990) *Research Methods and Statistics in Psychology*. London: Hodder and Stoughton.

CRANO, W.D. and BREWER, M.B. (1973) *Principles of Research in Social Psychology*. New York: McGraw Hill.

FESTINGER, L., RIEKEN, H.W. and SCHACHTER, S. (1956) *When Prophecy Fails*. Minneapolis: University of Minnesota Press.

HARLOW, H.F. (1959) Love in Infant Monkeys. *Scientific American, 200*, 68–74.

MILGRAM, S. (1963) Behavioural study of obedience. *Journal of Abnormal and Social Psychology, 67*, 371–8.

MILLER, G.A. (1964) *Psychology: The science of mental life*. Harmondsworth: Penguin.

ORNE, M.T. (1962) On the social psychology of the psychological experiment: with particular reference to demand characteristics and their implications. *American Psychologist, 17*, 776–83.

PARKER, I. and SHOTTER, J. (Eds) (1990) *Deconstructing Social Psychology*. London: Routledge.

REASON, P. and ROWAN, J. (Eds) (1981) *Human Enquiry: A sourcebook in new paradigm research*. Chichester: Wiley.

ROSENHAN, D.L. (1973) On being sane in insane places. *Science, 179*, 250–8.

SYLVA, K., ROY, C. and PAINTER, M. (1980) *Childwatching at Playgroup and Nursery School*. London: Grant McIntyre.

WESTLAND, G. (1978) *Current Crises of Psychology*. London: Heinemann.

WHYTE, W.F. (1943) *Street corner society: The social structure of an Italian slum*. Chicago: The University of Chicago Press.

WILLIAMS, J.E., BENNETT, S.M. and BEST, D.L. (1975) Awareness and expression of sex stereotypes in young children. *Developmental Psychology, 11*, 635–42.

PRACTICAL 6

Sex role stereotyping in British television advertisements

Alison Wadeley
Filton College, Bristol

Abstract

There is a wealth of psychological theory and research evidence to suggest that one of the chief ways in which humans of all ages learn is by observing others. The mass media – television, radio, video, newspapers, magazines, books – are rich sources of models of behaviour. Well-known areas of concern include the possible influences of the portrayal of aggression and of sex-stereotyped behaviour by the media.

The general aim of this practical is to investigate the portrayal of men and women through the mass medium of television. In particular, the exercise aims to build on recent research which suggests that sex-role stereotyping is evident in British TV advertisements. Content analysis of advertisements will be carried out in order to see whether they depict men and women differently, and if so, in what ways.

The procedure most closely resembles that used in a similar study by Harris and Stobart (1986) although some modifications have been made. The data collected will enable comparisons to be made with Harris and Stobart's findings and those of other researchers. On the assumption that some evidence of sex-role stereotyping will be found, the discussion of the results could focus on the nature of the stereotype, whether it bears any resemblance to reality and whether people's attitudes and behaviour really are influenced by what they see on television.

Materials
and Equipment

This exercise can be carried out by a single investigator or a group of investigators. Whichever approach is used, investigators will need access to commercial television showing approximately 60 suitable advertisements between agreed times and dates. If investigators choose to work in a group, they may collect data independently and then pool it; alternatively, it may be possible to video a suitable number of advertisements and arrive at a judgement about the content of each one together. The second method would lead to greater inter-observer reliability (that is, agreement between observers) but has the disadvantage of being extremely time-consuming. A group of, say, 12 investigators could quite easily collect sufficient data during normal viewing time over one week. Each investigator will need a copy of the Notes for Completing Tables (see *Appendix 1*) and a copy of the Data Tables and Advertisement Checklist (see *Appendix 2*).

Introduction
and Hypotheses

Any investigation into the effects of the media on attitudes and behaviour must begin with observational research into the actual content of those media. If people really can be influenced by media messages, what do those messages consist of and is their content a true reflection of real life? Television advertisements are just one area of interest. To be effective, adverts must have wide appeal and contain images to which the viewer can relate. In a sense, a commercial presents us with a condensed, stereotypical view of current life-styles and cultural values; there is so much more to it than just the message to buy. Advertisements may not be accurate reflections of everyday life but they do selectively reinforce certain aspects of it and, in particular, the roles of men and women.

In 1975, McArthur and Resko presented evidence for sex-role stereotyping in American TV commercials. This was followed by a similar British study by Manstead and McCulloch (1981) who analysed 309 advertisements broadcast by Granada TV between 6 p.m. and 11.30 p.m. over seven days in July 1979. When advertisements containing only children, animals or fantasy characters were discarded, 170 suitable examples remained. Adult central figures were identified in each advert and classified on a number of criteria. The researchers found that males and females were portrayed in markedly different ways. Women were significantly more likely than men to be shown as product users, to be cast in a dependent role, to produce no arguments in favour of a product, and to be shown at home.

In 1986, Harris and Stobart extended and refined Manstead and McCulloch's study, this time comparing daytime with evening advertisements and also voice-overs with visual presentations in relation to the gender of the central character. With the exception of the location of the central figure, they supported Manstead and McCulloch's findings and were also able to conclude that sex-stereotyping was stronger in evening than in daytime advertisements and that voice-overs were overwhelmingly male (189 males, 26 females). The authors of these studies agreed that the stereotyped image of males and females bears no relation to the social reality of family or working life. They also speculated about the effect on the viewer of the models provided by such images.

The study suggested here is based mainly on Harris and Stobart's research and its aim is to update and partially replicate their findings on visually presented central characters. It involves content analysis of as many TV advertisements as possible in order to investigate a number of hypotheses. Harris and Stobart analysed eight aspects of visually presented central figures but it is suggested that, in this practical, investigators examine just four. These are: credibility basis, role, argument, and product type. (These terms are explained in *Appendix 1*, Notes for Completing Tables.) For a more elaborate study, investigators may like to create new hypotheses and draw up new tables for the other four categories – location of the central character, type of reward provided by the product for the central character, gender of the background figures, and humour. Another possibility would be to categorize the age of the central character, their attractiveness or physique.

Hypotheses

Alternate hypothesis: There is an association between the gender of the central figure in a TV advertisement and each of the variables examined. For each of the alternative hypotheses, the null hypothesis predicts that there is no association between the gender of the central figure in a TV advertisement and each of the variables examined. Any association will be due to chance.

Procedure

Familiarization with the data collection procedure is vital as it will be necessary to work fast and there will be little thinking time. A pilot study (a trial period of data collection) should be carried out and before the main study commences, there should be some discussion to iron out any practical difficulties and increase reliability of categorization. At the very least, investigators should practise classifying some well-known advertisements before the exercise begins.

Investigators should then decide on the time period (for example, 6 p.m. to 11.59 p.m.) and the television channel(s) to be used. Advertisements which show a readily identifiable, speaking or non-speaking, adult, central figure should be chosen. If, in any single advert there are two central figures of the same gender, only one should be selected. If they are of opposite genders one should be chosen at random. It is permissible for different advertisements for the same product to be included.

Advertisements which show children or animals with no adult present, which use fantasy settings or cartoon figures and which have no easily identifiable central figure, should not be included. Classification of voice-overs is not part of this exercise so they should be ignored, although the rest of the advertisement can be used. Investigators may find that many advertisements are unsuitable for this exercise but they should not be put off by this as there will still be plenty of usable examples.

Chosen adverts should be assigned a letter and this letter entered once only in every table, (see example in *Appendix 1*). The use of letters is important at this stage so that investigators know which to discard if it is later discovered that others have classified the same advertisements. (Once the 26 letters have been used, investigators should start again with a new list, using A1, B1, and so on.) A quick note of the product should be made against the appropriate letter on your checklist. This is important so that investigators can avoid using the same advertisement twice. At least 60 different advertisements should be classified, although investigators should attempt to gather more if possible. One way of achieving this is to divide the task between members of the investigative team.

Results

If the collected data are to be combined, all duplicated advertisements should be discarded and the data then pooled by casting the frequencies of observations into the appropriate cells in each table. Some categories will have been used infrequently or not at all and, in these cases, investigators will need to decide whether to discard the category or collapse the table by combining categories. Investigators should ensure that each table contains the same total number of males and the same total number of females. If this is not the case, it means data are missing. To avoid this, it is essential that investigators are diligent in ensuring that each advertisement is entered into every table once only, as described in the procedure.

The data contained in the contingency tables should be presented in an appropriate form to enable visual inspection of the results. One way of achieving this is to take each table in turn and calculate the percentage of males in each category and then the percentage of females. The use of percentages takes into consideration the very likely event that more central figures of one gender than the other will have been observed and allows for easier comparison. Using these data, bar charts can then be drawn to give an initial impression of any patterns (see *Figure 1*).

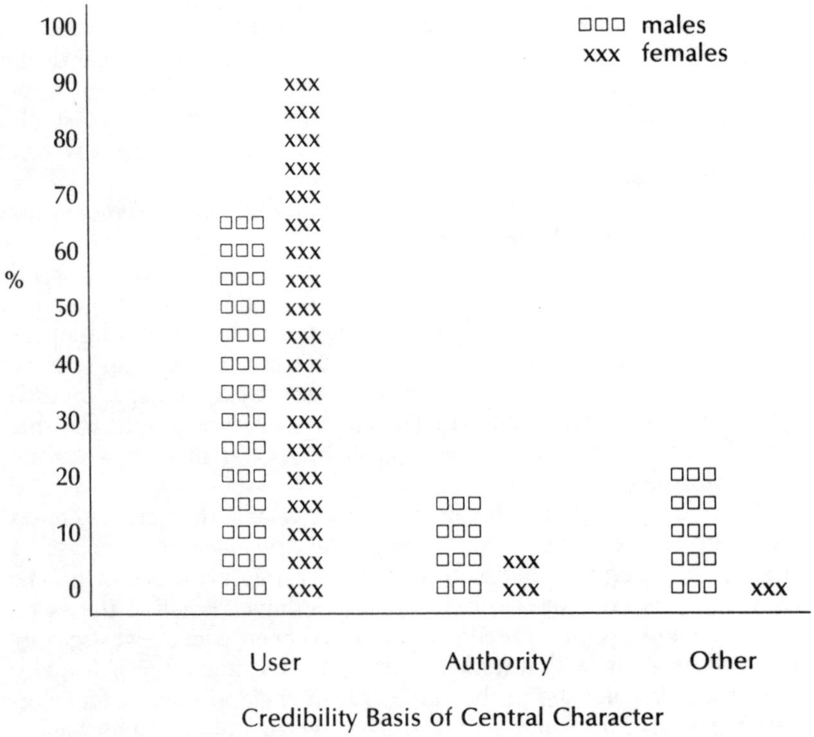

Figure 1. Example of bar chart for visual presentation of data.

If sufficient data have been collected, the raw data tables should lend themselves to chi-square analysis. With such analysis, it is important to ensure that observations are independent (that is, a letter must not appear more than once in each table). A significance level of 5% (i.e. $p \leqslant 0.05$) should be adopted. Significant results indicate that there is an association between the gender of the central character and the aspect of content being analysed. Examination of the percentages will indicate which categories are responsible for the effect. Great care should be taken not to over-interpret the results. Chi-square is a fairly crude statistical measure which in this case, allows us to see if there is a significant difference between the observed frequencies and those one might expect to see if chance alone determined them. Chi-square does not permit the results to be interpreted in terms of gender causing differences in frequency, nor in terms of there being any specific pattern of relationship. All that could be said is that gender and the variable of interest are in some way associated and do not operate independently of each other.

Discussion

The discussion of results should begin with an examination of the aims and hypotheses in the light of the statistical analyses carried out. The first point to address is whether the null hypotheses can be rejected. This is a good place to discuss the tables and bar charts so that ideas can be formed about significant associations between the variables in question. Non-significant results should not be overlooked: they are equally important and informative. How can the results obtained be explained and what is the nature of the stereotype (if any) that has been observed?

It is important to make comparisons with previous research and there is plenty to choose from. The paper by Manstead and McCulloch (1981) is a good source of data and it is also summarized in Gross (1990). The ideal comparison is, of course, with the percentages and other findings described in Harris and Stobart's (1986) article. Is there any evidence that the stereotype is changing or is there some other explanation for the findings?

The procedures used and the data collected in this exercise should be critically examined, bearing in mind that whenever this is done, it is important that constructive points should also be offered. How reliable were the scoring systems and how could their reliability be improved? The method of data collection and analysis are rather crude. Could they be refined? There is a possibility that male and female observers might interpret the same advertisement in different ways. How could this be checked and what could be done about it?

The method of content analysis used could be seen as reductionist, that is, specific aspects of the advertisements have been lifted out of their context so that the overall sense of the message may be lost. Non-verbal messages, for example, can contradict verbal ones and humour can change the nature of the communication, as can voice-overs. For instance, men may well be seen doing more domestic tasks or child-care but the hidden message may be that they are only helping out and/or making a mess of it, while for women such work is routine. Something else that could be looked for is the beneficiary of the man's domestic work. Is it the man himself or his friends or family? There may also be complex interaction effects, such as the gender of the central character and the type of product advertised — do women advertise men's shavers? Do men advertise tampons? These factors should all be considered.

If significant associations between the variables have been found, it could be asked whether this really matters. Remember, the exercise has provided some good descriptive data, but that is all. Durkin (1985c) says that the evidence linking television and behaviour is mixed; some researchers show that the content of television fare affects the behaviour of the viewer, while others find no effect. Perhaps research now needs to focus on individual differences in receptiveness and ask what the viewer brings to the situation. After all, the viewer is not a passive recipient of information but an active processor of it. What individual differences would be worth examining in this respect?

An issue worth considering is the extent to which advertisements reflect reality; but this is difficult to assess. If investigators have access to survey data on the division of labour between men and women in the home, or the number of men and women employed in full- or part-time work outside the home, they can compare their own findings with this data. It is commonly felt that women in full-time work still do most of the housework compared to their male partners. Work on counter-stereotyping, summarized by Durkin (1985d) is salient here. Again the evidence is mixed. Is there really a trend for greater equality and, if not, should television be leading the way in breaking the stereotype?

If students wish to extend this exercise, there is plenty of additional content analysis of advertisements which could be carried out. The content may change with the seasons, the time of day or the medium concerned. Furnham and Schofield (1986) investigated sex-role stereotyping on commercial radio. Magazine, newspaper and hoarding advertisements are other possible sources of information. Voice-overs in television advertisements are predominantly male but does the content of the message differ according to the gender of the speaker? Finally, in which direction could research move in order to balance the concentration on content?

Bibliography

General background references

GROSS, R.D. (1987) *Psychology, the Science of Mind and Behaviour*. London: Edward Arnold. Chapter 22.

HARTNETT, O., BODEN, G. and FULLER, M. (1979) *Sex-role Stereotyping*. London: Tavistock Publications Ltd.

HETHERINGTON, E.M. and PARKE, R.D. (1987) *Child Psychology, a Contemporary Viewpoint*. New York: McGraw Hill. Chapter 15.

Specific background references

DURKIN, K. (1985a) *Television, Sex Roles and Children*. Milton Keynes: Open University.

DURKIN, K. (1986) Sex roles and the mass media. In D.J. Hargreaves and A.M. Colley (Eds) *The Psychology of Sex Roles*. London: Harper and Row.

GROSS, R.D. (1990) *Key Studies in Psychology*. London: Hodder and Stoughton. Chapter 8.

HETHERINGTON, E.M. and PARKE, R.D. (1987) *Child Psychology, a Contemporary Viewpoint*. New York: McGraw Hill. pp. 179–182.

SMITH, P.K. and COWIE, H. (1988) *Understanding Children's Development*. Oxford: Blackwell. Chapter 4.

Journal Articles

DURKIN, K. (1985b) Television and sex-role acquisition 1: Content. *British Journal of Social Psychology*, 24, 101–113.

DURKIN, K. (1985c) Television and sex-role acquisition 2: Effects. *British Journal of Social Psychology*, 24, 192–210.

DURKIN K. (1985d) Television and sex-role acquisition 3: Counter-stereotyping. *British Journal of Social Psychology*, 24, 211–222.

FURNHAM, A. and SCHOFIELD, S. (1986) Sex-role stereotyping in British radio advertisements. *British Journal of Social Psychology*, 25, 165–171.

HARRIS, P.R. and STOBART, J. (1986) Sex-role stereotyping in television adver-tisements. *British Journal of Social Psychology*, 25, 155–164.

MANSTEAD, A. and McCULLOCH, C. (1981) Sex-role stereotyping in British tele-vision advertisements. *British Journal of Social Psychology*, 20, 171–180.

McARTHUR, L. and RESKO, B. (1975) The portrayal of men and women in American television commercials. *Social Psychology*, 97, 209–220.

Appendix 1. NOTES FOR COMPLETING TABLES

Add to these notes as appropriate after trying out the procedure.

You may like to add new classification tables of your own. Harris and Stobart used location of central character, type of reward provided by the product for the central character, gender of background figures, and humour.

Table 1. Credibility basis of central character

User	– primarily a user of the product.
Authority	– primarily a source of verbal information about the product.
Other	– neither a user nor a source of information.

Table 2. Role of central character

Dependent	– e.g. spouse, parent, home-maker, boyfriend/girlfriend, lover, sex-object, grown-up son/daughter/relative.
Autonomous	– e.g. career person, worker, professional, interviewer, narrator, celebrity.
Other	– a character who appears to be neither dependent nor autonomous.

Table 3. Argument spoken by central character (in favour of product)

Factual	– scientific or objective argument.
Opinion	– subjective, non-factual argument.
None	– argument implied in person's behaviour or words, but not directly verbalized.

Table 4. Product type used by central character

Food/drink	– any edible product or non-alcoholic drink.
Alcoholic drink	– beer, spirits, wine, cocktails.
Body	– products concerning health, hygiene, cleansing or clothing.
Household	– any product relating to home or housework.
Other	– e.g. financial services, cars, petfood, petrol.

Appendix 2. DATA TABLES AND ADVERTISEMENT CHECKLIST

Table 1. Credibility basis of central character

	Male	Female
User		A
Authority		
Other		

Table 2. Role of central character

	Male	Female
Dependent		
Autonomous		A
Other		

Table 3. Argument spoken by central character

	Male	Female
Factual		
Opinion		
None		A

Table 4. Product type used by central character

	Male	Female
Food/drink		A
Alcohol drink		
Body		
Household		
Other		

Advertisement Checklist

Advert	*Product*
A	Gold Blend
B	
C	
D	
E	
F	
G	
H	
I	
J	
K	
L	
M	
N	
O	
P	
Q	
R	
S	
T	
U	
V	
W	
X	
Y	
Z	
A1	
B1	
C1	
etc.	

PRACTICAL 7

An investigation of attributional bias in a real world setting

Rob McIlveen
Springwood High School, King's Lynn

Abstract

Attribution theory is a general theoretical perspective in social psychology concerned with social perception; that is, the processes by which people explain their own and others' behaviour. The purpose of this two-step practical exercise is to investigate one of the sources of bias in the attribution process, namely the 'self-serving' or 'hedonic bias' first described by Miller and Ross (1975). The self-serving bias refers to people's tendency to take credit for successful behaviour or outcomes but to deny responsibility for unsuccessful ones. Unlike much attribution research, which has little relevance to real world settings, these exercises examine actual remarks (attributions) made by English soccer team managers and players following matches in which their team had been successful or unsuccessful.

The existence of the self-serving bias amongst athletes was first reported by Lau and Russell (1980) who looked at attributions for success and failure made by coaches and players from American baseball and football teams. The exercises have two aims. The first attempts to determine whether there is any evidence for the existence of the self-serving bias amongst English soccer team managers and players, while the second investigates one of the proposed explanations for the existence of the self-serving bias. Discussion points arising from the data generated by the exercises focus on competing explanations for the self-serving bias and on avenues of research which could be investigated further.

Materials and Equipment

The first exercise can be conducted by a single investigator who codes statements made by English soccer team managers and players for their attributional content. However, there is no reason why a small group of investigators should not work together in coding the statements. This might give rise to some lively discussion about how the statements should best be coded. The second exercise requires the investigator(s) to perform an additional coding task in order to test one of the proposed explanations for the self-serving bias.

The apparatus needed for the exercises consists of the statements and information presented in the *Appendix*. It is recommended that copies of the Appendix be made available to each investigator. The coding tasks and analysis of the resultant data should take no longer than two hours. Investigators can, if they wish, collect their own attributions rather than use those given in the Appendix. Any newspapers providing a reasonable coverage of sport would be suitable. Investigators who decide to create their own attributional data base should, however, confine their searches to lengthy articles, as shorter articles are usually confined to descriptions of a particular match and rarely contain explanations offered by coaches or players for the outcome of the match.

Introduction and Hypotheses

Understanding the processes by which we explain our own and other people's behaviour has long been a topic of research in social psychology. A number of theories of causal attribution have been proposed (e.g. Heider, 1958; Jones and Davis, 1965; Kelley, 1967), accounts of which can be found in most introductory textbooks (e.g. Hewstone *et al.*, 1988).

One of the most influential theories of causal attribution is the covariation theory offered by Harold Kelley. Like many other attribution theorists, Kelley (1967) argues that attributions about the causes of behaviour are typically made in terms of internal or dispositional causes (that is, some aspect of the individual), external or situational causes (that is, some aspect of the social or physical world), or a combination of the two. In brief, Kelley proposes that causal attribution is a highly rational process through which people arrive at explanations for behaviour by examining three types of information.

The first type of information is called 'consensus'. This refers to the extent to which other people share the same reaction to the same stimulus as the person whose behaviour is being explained. Kelley terms the second type of information 'consistency'. This refers to the extent to which the person in question reacts in the same way to the same stimulus on other occasions. The last type of information is termed 'distinctiveness' and refers to the extent to which the person in question reacts in the same way to other stimuli. Whether an attribution is made to internal factors, external factors or a combination of the two depends on what the three types of information reveal.

Kelley's theory is a normative model of the attribution process which indicates how people *should* make causal attributions. However, one problem with his theory is that the attribution process is liable to a number of systematic biases: that is, systematic distortions of an otherwise correct procedure (Fiske and Taylor, 1984). These biases include the 'fundamental attribution error' (Jones and Harris, 1967), the 'actor-observer effect' (Jones and Nisbett, 1972) and the 'self-serving' or 'hedonic bias' (Miller and Ross, 1975). Since it is this last bias which forms the basis of the exercises presented here, it will be the only one considered in detail. However, excellent accounts of the other two biases can be found in Pennington (1989).

The self-serving bias is concerned with attributions made for success and failure, and refers to people's tendency to attribute success to internal (or dispositional) factors and failure to external (or situational) factors. For example, suppose that a student has just passed a psychology examination and is asked to explain this successful event. All sorts of explanations could be forthcoming but, in such instances, people tend to explain their behaviour in terms of internal factors such as having a 'high IQ' or 'all the hard work I put in'. Far less frequently do people attribute success in examinations to external factors such as 'a simple paper' or 'soft marking'.

Suppose, however, that a student has just failed a psychology examination and is asked to explain this unsuccessful event. Again, any sort of explanation could be forthcoming, but the most common explanations would relate to external factors such as 'poor teaching' or 'a very difficult examination paper'. Much less frequently is failure in examinations attributed to internal factors such as 'not being clever enough' or 'failing to revise sufficient material'.

The existence of the self-serving bias has been demonstrated in a number of studies (for example, Van der Pligt and Eiser, 1983) and several explanations for the bias have been suggested. Two broad positions can be identified. The first proposes that the bias can best be explained in motivational or 'need-serving' terms. One such motive is the need to enhance or protect one's self-esteem (Greenberg *et al.*, 1982): if a person explains success in terms of internal factors, his/her self-esteem is enhanced. An explanation for failure in terms of external factors protects one's self-esteem. Another similar possibility is that the self-serving bias may reflect a motivation to appear in a favourable light to other people (Weary and Arkin, 1981).

The second position proposes that the self-serving bias can best be explained in cognitive or 'information processing' terms. Miller and Ross (1975) and Feather and Simon (1971) argue that people typically intend and expect to succeed at a task, although there are, presumably, occasions on which they expect to fail. Consequently, intended and expected outcomes tend to be attributed to internal factors whilst unintended and unexpected outcomes tend to be attributed externally.

In addition to seeking evidence for the existence of the self-serving bias, Lau and Russell (1980) attempted to discriminate between motivational and cognitive explanations for the occurrence of the bias. Rather than basing their research in the psychological laboratory, these researchers decided to explore the generality of attribution research by looking at athletic competition – a real world setting.

Lau and Russell examined 33 major American football and baseball events reported in eight daily newspapers during the autumn of 1977. Each of the 107 resulting newspaper articles was then coded for attributional content, yielding a total of 594 attributions. In order to establish the existence of the self-serving bias, attributions made by players and coaches were first sorted according to whether the team had won the game (Success) or lost it (Failure). Then, attributions were coded as either Internal (if the attributor said something about his own team) or External (if the attributor said something about the other team or the circumstances under which the game took place). As predicted, the analysis produced strong evidence for the existence of the self-serving bias. Thus, victories tended to be attributed to internal factors whilst defeats tended to be attributed to external factors.

With respect to the motivational explanation for the self-serving bias, Lau and Russell reasoned that if attributions do serve self-presentational purposes, then the occurrence of the bias should increase with the ego-involvement of the attributor. Thus, the self-serving bias should be stronger amongst coaches and players than among sportswriters, since the former should be more concerned with the outcome of the game than the latter. Analysis of the data did indeed support this prediction.

With respect to the cognitive explanation for the occurrence of the bias, Lau and Russell suggested that 'expected outcomes' (whether successful or unsuccessful) should result in more internal than external attributions, whilst 'unexpected outcomes' (whether successful or unsuccessful) should result in more external than internal attributions. Thus, when a team was the pre-match favourite to win, and did so, their success was coded as 'expected'. When the favourites lost, their failure was coded as 'unexpected'. On those occasions when the 'underdogs' won, their success was coded as 'unexpected' whilst on those occasions when the underdogs lost, their failure was coded as 'expected'. Analysis of the data did not, however, lend any support to the predictions derived from the cognitive explanation of the self-serving bias.

Hypotheses

The purpose of the first exercise is to investigate whether or not the self-serving bias operates amongst English soccer team managers and players. If it does, then victories will tend to be attributed more frequently to internal than external factors, whilst defeats will tend to be attributed more frequently to external than internal factors. The null hypothesis predicts no significant association between Outcome and Locus of Causality. The second exercise takes the investigation further and attempts to find support for the cognitive explanation of the self-serving bias. On the basis of the cognitive explanation, it may be predicted that 'expected outcomes' will tend to be attributed more frequently to internal than external factors, whilst 'unexpected outcomes' will tend to be attributed more frequently to external than internal factors. The null hypothesis predicts no significant association between Outcome Expectancy and Locus of Causality.

Procedure

The raw data for this practical exercise have already been collected and can be found in the Appendix. The data consist of 34 attributions for success or failure made by managers or players of English soccer teams. The attributions were collected in the following way. First, reports in several national newspapers of soccer matches held between October 1986 and February 1987 were scrutinized for attributional content. Only those games which did not result in a draw were analysed. Each attribution was written on a card and a note was made of the attributor, his team, and the outcome of the game. Later (for the purposes of testing the cognitive explanation), predictions made by independent soccer results forecasters were collected. The predictions of six forecasters from six national newspapers were used for this purpose.

Exercise 1

In order to test for the existence of the self-serving bias, each of the 34 attributions should be coded according to two dimensions: OUTCOME (Success or Failure) and LOCUS OF CAUSALITY (Internal or External). An outcome should be coded as a Success if the attributor's team won the match, and a Failure if the attributor's team lost the match. Locus of Causality should be coded as Internal if the attribution refers to something good or bad about the attributor's team's ability or that of a team member. If the attribution refers to something good or bad about the opposition's ability either as a team or a specific individual and/or something about the circumstances, it should be coded as External. A justification of this coding system can be found in Lau and Russell (1980, p. 32).

Coding for outcome should be straightforward. However, coding for Locus of Causality might be more difficult. The following examples, adapted from Lau and Russell (1980), will serve as illustrations:

Example 1. Attribution made by losing Dodgers' manager: 'It took a great team to beat us, and the Yankees definitely are a great team.' This is an attribution to the Yankees' ability and since it was said by a Dodger whose team lost, it would be coded as Failure–External.

Example 2. Attribution made by winning Yankees' manager: 'Piniella (a Yankees player) has done it all.' This attribution refers to a Yankees player and since it was said by the Yankees' manager whose team won, it would be coded as Success–Internal.

Example 3. Attribution made by losing Dodgers' manager: 'You're supposed to keep the ball in on him (a Yankees player). Well, we didn't.' In this case the attribution is something 'we' (the Dodgers) did, something 'we' presumably could have done better but did not. The attribution would therefore be coded as Failure–Internal.

Example 4. Attribution made by winning Dodgers' manager: 'I don't think we hit the ball right. We were lucky.' Here, the attributor's team has won but the success is clearly an attribution to good fortune. Consequently it would be coded as Success–External.

The codings for the 34 attributions in the *Appendix* should be placed in a clearly labelled 2 (Outcome) × 2 (Locus of Causality) contingency table as shown in *Table 1*. It is possible that some of the attributions may not give rise to straightforward codings (especially if investigators are working together in small groups). Lau and Russell allowed their coders one minute to reconcile their differences. If reconciliation could not be achieved within this time, the attribution was discarded. It is recommended that this procedure is followed by investigators conducting this practical exercise.

Exercise 2

The second exercise involves an examination of the cognitive explanation for the self-serving bias. It will be recalled that according to this explanation, expected outcomes (whether successful or unsuccessful) should be attributed more frequently to internal than external factors, whereas unexpected outcomes (whether successful or unsuccessful) should be attributed more frequently to external than internal

Table 1. Suggested contingency table for *Exercise 1*

	LOCUS OF CAUSALITY	
	Internal Attribution	External Attribution
Outcome Success		
Failure		

factors. Therefore, in order to test this explanation, each of the 34 attributions must be coded according to LOCUS OF CAUSALITY (Internal or External) and OUTCOME EXPECTANCY (Expected or Unexpected).

Locus of Causality should be coded in the manner described in *Exercise 1*. Outcome Expectancy is more difficult to code. It could, for example, be determined by looking at the results of previous encounters between the teams in question or by considering their relative positions in the league. For the purposes of this exercise, however, Outcome Expectancy has been related to the forecasts made in national newspapers by independent soccer results forecasters. The *Appendix* also includes, for each of the 34 attributions, information concerning the forecasters' predictions for the game in question.

If four or more forecasters out of the six examined were in agreement that a team would win a particular match, then the outcome can be coded as Expected or Unexpected for the team's attributor. For example, if the majority of forecasters agreed that Liverpool would beat Grimsby and this outcome occurred, Liverpool's win (or Grimsby's defeat) would be coded as Expected. If, however, Grimsby had won, then their victory (or Liverpool's defeat) would be coded as Unexpected. In those cases where there is not a two-thirds majority of opinion amongst the forecasters, or if the majority prediction is for a drawn game, the attribution should be discarded.

The coding procedure described here is not as complex as that employed by Lau and Russell (1980), nor does it measure the 'subjective' expectancies of the attributor. As Lau and Russell (1980, pp. 32–33) point out, 'players and coaches would probably rarely admit to expecting to lose. . .but certainly [they] are not unaware of the roles of the favourite or underdog in any game.' However, the measure of Outcome Expectancy employed in this exercise is at least a rough indicator of subjective expectancies.

Table 2. Suggested contingency table for *Exercise 2*

	LOCUS OF CAUSALITY	
	Internal Attribution	External Attribution
Expected		
Unexpected		

Outcome Expectancy

The attributions should be placed in a clearly labelled 2 (Locus of Causality) × 2 (Outcome Expectancy) contingency table as shown in *Table 2*.

Results

Exercise 1

The data for this exercise have been collected at the nominal level of measurement: that is, categories have been established and the number of observations falling into each category recorded. Statistical evidence for the existence or otherwise of the self-serving bias can be assessed by means of a 2 × 2 chi-square test. This test calculates the value of chi-square with two independent variables (i.e. Outcome and Locus of Causality) each having two levels (i.e. Success/Failure and Internal/External).

The 2 × 2 chi-square test examines the null hypothesis that there is no significant association between two independent variables. A significant chi-square would indicate that there was a difference between successes and failures in the relative proportion of internal and external attributions. Interpretation of such a result can be made by inspection of the contingency table. If the self-serving bias does operate amongst English soccer team managers and players, there should be a greater proportion of internal than external attributions for success and a greater proportion of external than internal attributions for failure. The data from the contingency table could be presented in pictorial form, perhaps using a bar chart.

Exercise 2

The data for the second exercise have also been collected at the nominal level, and statistical evidence or otherwise for the cognitive explanation of the self-serving bias can similarly be assessed by means of a 2 × 2 chi-square test. In this case, the two independent variables each having two levels are Locus of Causality (Internal/External) and

Outcome Expectancy (Expected/Unexpected). A significant chi-square would indicate that there was a difference between expected and unexpected outcomes in the relative proportion of internal and external attributions. Once again, interpretation of such a result can be made by inspection of the contingency table. If the cognitive explanation is supported, then there should be a greater proportion of external than internal attributions for unexpected outcomes, and a greater proportion of internal than external attributions for expected outcomes.

Discussion

The initial discussion point of the first exercise must be the extent to which the self-serving bias was present amongst English soccer team managers and players and, therefore, the extent to which *Exercise 1* replicates the findings of Lau and Russell (1980). The degree of support for the cognitive explanation of the self-serving bias obtained in the second exercise should also form a central discussion point, especially given that Lau and Russell failed to find any support for this explanation in their study. In addition to these fundamental talking points there are a number of other issues which could be usefully incorporated into a discussion of the results of the two exercises, and these are outlined below.

Attribution research has been criticized for its tendency to have participants (typically college undergraduates) 'provide causal explanations for their own or some other person's behaviour in hypothetical or fairly trivial situations . . . [using] forced-choice, closed ended scales' (Lau and Russell, 1980, p. 29). As Lau and Russell (1980, p. 30) have noted, 'players and coaches have a much greater range of possible responses available to them' and therefore 'the scope of possible explanations is much greater in such free responses than is usually the case in the laboratory'. The attributions made by politicians for the success or failure of certain policies could form another area of research. Are there other people who often make statements in public about their behaviour and who therefore might employ the self-serving attributional bias?

According to Reis (1981), the tendency to make internal attributions for success occurs with greater frequency than the tendency to make external attributions for failure. Is this the case for the attributions that were analysed in the first exercise? Would people ever learn from their mistakes if they habitually explained away their failures by attributing them to external factors? What sorts of interpersonal friction might arise as a result of excessive use of the self-serving bias?

Lau and Russell (1980) argued that if the self-serving bias serves self-presentational purposes (a motivational explanation), then the bias should be greater for coaches and players than for sportswriters, since the former should be more ego-involved with the outcome of the game. As noted previously, Lau and Russell's data supported this viewpoint. The present exercises could not, however, look at this aspect of a motivational explanation because sufficient information was not available. What information would need to be gathered to conduct such a study and how would the study be conducted?

Lau and Russell have also suggested that evidence for or against a motivational explanation could be influenced by the setting in which the attribution is made. For example, players and coaches make their attributions publicly and are, therefore, constrained by plausibility and the informal norm that exists amongst athletes to be humble about their successes and to accept blame for their failures. These factors would tend to decrease any evidence of a self-serving bias for players and coaches. Equally, however, since players and coaches are much more involved in the outcome than is true of participants in most laboratory experiments, this could accentuate a self-serving bias (if the motivational interpretation is correct). Are these suggestions plausible? Are there any soccer players or managers whose attributions often seem *not* to be constrained by plausibility and who are not humble about their successes?

The attributions offered by the soccer managers and players were made in public. It could be argued that they serve more to justify performance than to reach an abstract causal understanding of events. For Lau and Russell this raises the question of whether public attributions differ from the private explanations made by managers and players. Private attributions are clearly not readily accessible for assessment, but Lau and Russell believe that the answer to this question is most certainly 'yes' in some circumstances and 'no' in others. Thus, where there are norms concerning behaviour (e.g. bravado or humility), public explanations may differ from private beliefs. A manager may, for example, publicly attribute a victory to superior skill, but privately explain the outcome in terms of luck. Equally, it could be argued that there are occasions when, to maintain consistency, an attributor brings his/her private attributions into line with his/her public statements. For example, a manager attributing a defeat to bad luck, even though it may generally be agreed that 'the better team won', may come to believe that the elements genuinely did conspire against the team.

A study conducted by Greenberg *et al.* (1982) is interesting in this respect. These researchers were able to show that the self-serving bias can appear under private as well as public conditions. This finding is consistent with the view that the self-serving bias stems from ego-defensive needs, and might suggest that private attributions are not that different from public attributions. How could the issue concerning public and private attributions be addressed experimentally in the context of attributions made in the sporting world?

In connection with the issue of whether the self-serving bias is best explained in cognitive or motivational terms, Ross and Fletcher (1985) have suggested that cognitive explanations actually contain motivational aspects and that motivational factors can have an effect on information processing. In the light of these points, some researchers suggest that it is virtually impossible to choose between the two types of explanation since both are likely to be correct. As Ross and Fletcher (1985, p. 105) have noted, 'people are both rational and rationalizers'. Are there any circumstances additional to those posited by Lau and Russell which might permit discrimination between the cognitive and motivational explanations?

The coding of free-response attributions from archival sources is not without its problems, since the issue of what is internal and what is external is not always evident. Monson and Snyder (1977) have suggested that most internal attributions can be rephrased as external statements and vice versa. Thus, 'they played better than we did' could just as easily be phrased 'we played worse than they did'. Although the two statements are semantically equivalent, the former would be coded as external and the latter as internal in Lau and Russell's coding system. However, despite the semantic equivalence of the two statements, Lau and Russell suggest that this does not necessarily imply that they are psychologically equivalent. Is the way in which the attributor chooses to make an attribution the best way of coding it, and if so, why?

Bibliography

General background references

FISKE, S.T. and TAYLOR, S.E. (1984) *Social Cognition.* New York: Random House.

HEWSTONE, M., STROEBE, W., CODOL, J.P. and STEPHENSON, G.M. (Eds) (1988) *Introduction to Social Psychology.* Oxford: Blackwell. Chapter 6. pp. 111–141.

PENNINGTON, D.C. (1989) *Essential Social Psychology.* London: Arnold.

ROSS, M. and FLETCHER, G.J.O. (1985) Attribution and social perception. In G. Lindzey and E. Aronson (Eds) *Handbook of Social Psychology, Vol. 2,* 3rd edn. New York: Random House.

Specific background references

HEIDER, F. (1958) *The Psychology of Interpersonal Relations.* New York: Wiley.

JONES, E.E. and DAVIS, K.E. (1965) From acts to dispositions: The attribution process in person perception. In L. Berkowitz (Ed.) *Advances in Experimental Social Psychology, Vol. 2.* New York: Academic Press.

JONES, E.E. and NISBETT, R.E. (1972) The actor and the observer: divergent perceptions of the causes of behaviour. In E.E. Jones, D.E. Kanouse, H.H. Kelley, R.E. Nisbett, S. Valins and B. Weiner (Eds) *Attribution: Perceiving the Causes of Behaviour.* Morristown, N.J.: General Learning Press.

KELLEY, H.H. (1967) Attribution theory in social psychology. In D. Levine (Ed.) *Nebraska Symposium on Motivation,* Vol. 15. Lincoln: University of Nebraska Press.

REIS, H.T. (1981) Self-presentation and distributive justice. In J.T. Tedeschi (Ed.) *Impression management theory and social psychological research.* New York: Academic Press.

WEARY, G. and ARKIN, R.M. (1981) Attributional self-presentation. In J.H. Harvey, W.J. Ickes and R.F. Kidd (Eds) *New Directions in Attributional Research,* Vol. 3. Hillsdale, N.J.: Erlbaum.

Journal articles

FEATHER, N.T. and SIMON, J.G. (1971) Attribution of responsibility and valence of success and failure in relation to initial confidence and task performance. *Journal of Personality and Social Psychology, 18,* 173–188.

GREENBERG, J., PSYZCZYNSKI, T. and SOLOMON, S. (1982) The self-serving attributional bias: Beyond self-presentation. *Journal of Experimental Social Psychology, 18,* 56–67.

JONES, E.E. and HARRIS, V.A. (1967) The attribution of attitudes. *Journal of Experimental Social Psychology, 3,* 1–24.

LAU, R.R. and RUSSELL, D. (1980) Attributions in the sports pages. *Journal of Personality and Social Psychology, 39,* 29–38.

MILLER, D.T. and ROSS, M. (1975) Self-serving biases in the attribution of causality: Fact or fiction? *Psychological Bulletin, 82,* 213–225.

MONSON, D.T. and SNYDER, M. (1977) Actors, observers and the attribution process: Toward a reconceptualization. *Journal of Experimental Social Psychology, 13,* 89–111.

VAN DER PLIGT, J. and EISER, J.R. (1983) Actors' and observers' attributions, self-serving bias and positivity bias. *European Journal of Social Psychology, 13,* 95–104.

Appendix

ATTRIBUTION NO. 1 – Tottenham manager after his team had been beaten in a league game:
'We were awful, a complete contrast to last week. . .we won't win anything if we go on playing like this.'
Five of the six forecasters predicted a Tottenham victory, and the sixth predicted a drawn game.

ATTRIBUTION NO. 2 – Crystal Palace manager after his team had won a league game:
'I have to admit that the goal was a little bit lucky, but who cares? At the end of the day winning is the only thing that matters.'
The six forecasters were unanimous in predicting that Crystal Palace would lose the game.

ATTRIBUTION NO. 3 – Manchester United player following victory in a cup-tie:
'When Bryan [Robson, a Manchester United player] is fit he's worth a goal start to us. His return to the side today really spurred us on.'
Three of the forecasters predicted a draw, two a Manchester United victory, and one a victory for the opposition.

ATTRIBUTION NO. 4 – Burnley manager after his team had lost a league game:
'When you hit the bar and the post you know it isn't going to be your day, and it wasn't ours today.'
Five forecasters predicted a Burnley victory, with the sixth predicting a drawn game.

ATTRIBUTION NO. 5 – West Ham player after his team had won a league game:
'We've got it together now and are playing like a team. We should do very well this season.'
Four forecasters predicted a West Ham victory. The other two predicted a drawn game.

ATTRIBUTION NO. 6 – Tottenham manager after his team had lost a league game:
'The penalty decision turned it. It was a diabolical decision. They weren't in it until that happened.'
Five forecasters predicted a Tottenham victory and one predicted a drawn game.

ATTRIBUTION NO. 7 – Stoke City player after this team had lost a league game:
'Davison [centre forward for the opposition] is a great player. We couldn't stop him. . .he was the difference between the two teams.'
Three forecasters predicted a Stoke City victory and three predicted an opposition victory.

ATTRIBUTION NO. 8 – Manchester United player after his side had won a cup-tie:
'I wasn't expecting it to be as easy as that. I don't think they played as well as they are capable of playing.'
Three forecasters predicted a drawn game, two a Manchester United victory and one a victory for the opposition.

ATTRIBUTION NO. 9 – Everton manager after his team had lost a league game:
'You create your own luck in this game. They did and we didn't. That's why we lost.'
All six forecasters predicted that Everton would win the game.

ATTRIBUTION NO. 10 – Arsenal manager after his team had won a league game:
'There was no stopping us today. On this form we'll be there or thereabout at the end of the season.'
Four forecasters predicted an Arsenal victory and two predicted a drawn game.

ATTRIBUTION NO. 11 – Chelsea player after his team had lost a league game:
'We're not playing well at the moment. . .there doesn't seem to be a solution to the problems we've been creating for ourselves.'
One forecaster predicted a Chelsea victory and one predicted a drawn game. The other four forecasters predicted a victory for the opposition.

ATTRIBUTION NO. 12 – Derby manager after his team had won a league game:
'You need what happened today to win games. . .they were walking through our defence at will but not scoring. In all honesty the best side didn't win.'
All six forecasters were unanimous in predicting a victory for Derby.

ATTRIBUTION NO. 13 – Arsenal player after his side had won a league game:
'Charlie [Nicholas, then an Arsenal player] was the difference today. It was a brilliant performance by a brilliant player.'
All six forecasters were unanimous in predicting an Arsenal victory.

ATTRIBUTION NO. 14 – Liverpool manager after his team had lost a league game:
'It's about time the league outlawed these [plastic] pitches. Football is supposed to be played on grass.'
Five forecasters predicted a Liverpool victory and one predicted a victory for the opposition.

ATTRIBUTION NO. 15 – Everton manager after his team had lost a league game:
'You know we can't comment on referees, but if I was on the league panel I'd take a careful look at this one. He cost us the match.'
Three forecasters predicted a drawn game, two an Everton victory and one a victory for the opposition.

ATTRIBUTION NO. 16 – Norwich manager after his team had won a league game:
'I won't be drawn into making a comment about the referee. I think that the decision he made [a penalty to Norwich] was a bit fortunate for us, and in the end was the difference between the teams.'
Three forecasters predicted a drawn game, one a Norwich victory and two a victory for the opposition.

ATTRIBUTION NO. 17 – Millwall manager after his team had lost a league game:
'I don't think the hold-up [for a pitch invasion] helped us any. In fact, our own fans probably cost us the match.'
Four forecasters predicted a Millwall victory and the other two predicted a drawn game.

ATTRIBUTION NO. 18 – Coventry manager after his team had won a league game:
'We don't have stars in this team. Everything we achieve comes from hard work. We're triers and we deserved it today.'
All six forecasters were unanimous in predicting that Coventry would lose the match.

ATTRIBUTION NO. 19 – Arsenal manager after his team had lost a cup-tie:
'Obviously they're at an advantage. From one side of the pitch it's almost impossible to see the other. It's like playing on the side of a mountain.'
Five forecasters predicted an Arsenal victory and one predicted a drawn game.

ATTRIBUTION NO. 20 – Nottingham Forest manager after his team had lost a league game:
'We haven't practised penalty-taking in training because professional footballers should be capable of beating any goalkeeper from a direct kick twelve yards out. Our players obviously aren't.'
All six forecasters were unanimous in predicting that Nottingham would win the game.

ATTRIBUTION NO. 21 – Leeds United manager after his team had lost a league game:
'Their winner was the direct result of the referee's actions.'
Four forecasters predicted that Leeds would lose. The other two predicted that Leeds would win the game.

ATTRIBUTION NO. 22 – York City manager after his team had won a cup-tie:
'I suppose the conditions didn't help them. . .they're probably used to playing on a pitch with grass on it! The pitch stifled their play which made it easier for us to compete.'
All six forecasters were unanimous in predicting that York City would lose the game.

ATTRIBUTION NO. 23 – Colchester manager after his team had won a league game:
'We've been threatening to do this [score five goals] all season. There was no stopping us today.'
Four forecasters predicted that Colchester would lose the game, one predicted a draw and one predicted that Colchester would win the game.

ATTRIBUTION NO. 24 – Manchester City player after his team had lost a league game:
'He [another Manchester City player] has a four-inch gash on his thigh. You can't expect to win when you're being kicked to death like we were.'
Only one forecaster predicted that Manchester City would win the game. Four predicted a victory for the opposition and one predicted a drawn game.

ATTRIBUTION NO. 25 – Bristol City manager after his team had won a cup-tie:
'The result doesn't surprise me. The gap between a good Third Division side like us and most First Division sides isn't as great as it used to be. Third Division players are very skilful.'
Three forecasters predicted a drawn game, two predicted that Bristol City would lose and one predicted they would win.

ATTRIBUTION NO. 26 – Aston Villa player after his team had won a league game:
'We haven't done it many times this season, but today we thoroughly outplayed them and got three vital points.'
Four forecasters predicted that Aston Villa would win the game and two predicted a draw.

ATTRIBUTION NO. 27 – Arsenal player after his team had lost a league game:
'Everyone expects injuries and we've had our fair share. . .but today we barely had eleven fit players out there.'
All six forecasters were unanimous in predicting an Arsenal victory.

ATTRIBUTION NO. 28 – Nottingham Forest manager after his team had lost a league game:
'After that performance, I need to take a look at the transfer market. If there are eleven decent players on offer I might just sign them all.'
Three forecasters predicted that Nottingham Forest would win the game and three predicted a draw.

ATTRIBUTION NO. 29 – Oldham manager after his team had won a league game:
'I don't think the fact that the pitch is plastic made any difference to the outcome. We'd have won if the game had been at their place.'
Four forecasters predicted that Oldham would win the game and two predicted a draw.

ATTRIBUTION NO. 30 – Grimsby Town manager after his team had lost a league game:
'I'm not superstitious or anything like that, but the fact that we've yet to win might have something to do with our goalkeeper's jersey. Green is considered an unlucky colour by some Grimsby folk.'
Four forecasters predicted a drawn game and two predicted that Grimsby would lose.

ATTRIBUTION NO. 31 – Liverpool manager after his team had won a league game:
'We're possibly the best team in Europe at the moment. I doubt if anyone could match us after that performance.'
All six forecasters predicted that Liverpool would win the game.

ATTRIBUTION NO. 32 – Chelsea manager after his team had lost a cup-tie:
'The ground was too heavy for my players. Lower division sides are used to playing on mudbaths like that, but we're not.'
Five forecasters predicted that Chelsea would win the game and one predicted a draw.

ATTRIBUTION NO. 33 – Brighton player after his team had won a league game:
'The pitch was very heavy after that downpour. None of us have ever played on anything like that, it makes the game a lottery.'
All six forecasters predicted that Brighton would win the game.

ATTRIBUTION NO. 34 – Watford player after his team had won a league game:
'*I know we're supposed to beat teams like that, but to be quite frank we'd have beaten anyone with that performance.*'
Four forecasters predicted that Watford would win the game, one predicted a draw and one predicted a victory for the opposition.

PRACTICAL 8

Observational studies of pedestrian behaviour

Gillian Lang
Wakefield District College

Abstract

The practical exercises presented here are concerned with the behaviour of pedestrians. This behaviour is something which has been of interest to social psychologists, particularly those concerned with understanding non-verbal communication, interaction and gesture. The first exercise is a partial replication of a study conducted by Collett and Marsh (1981) who found that the way in which adults avoid colliding with one another on a pedestrian crossing differs according to gender. Thus, men tend to orient themselves towards the person they are avoiding, whilst women tend to orient themselves away from the person they are avoiding.

The second exercise extends Collett and Marsh's research by investigating whether the same difference is shown among young children. The data generated by this exercise could contribute to an understanding of why the gender difference in adults reported by Collett and Marsh exists. An optional third exercise examines overtaking behaviour amongst adult pedestrians. Previous research has indicated that pedestrians tend to pass on the right; the third exercise aims to establish whether pedestrians overtake on the right on a relatively uncrowded pavement.

The main discussion points will consider some of the possible explanations for the gender orientation difference in adults, including the implications of the same variation being present or absent in young children. Additionally, the overtaking behaviour of adult pedestrians will be examined in relation to their collision avoidance behaviour. Finally, some advantages and disadvantages of the observational method within the context of pedestrian behaviour are suggested.

Materials and Equipment

All of the exercises are best carried out by pairs of investigators working together as observers and data recorders who can then collect and analyse their own data. However, if the exercise is being conducted as a class practical, there is no reason why the class should not divide itself into pairs and then pool the data for subsequent analysis.

For the first exercise, a minimum of 30 mixed pairs of male and female pedestrians should be observed by the investigators. The second exercise can be carried out in the same manner as the first, the only difference being that child instead of adult male and female pedestrians will be observed. For these exercises it is necessary for investigators to make their observations in a relatively crowded area, but not one which is so densely populated that observation of the relevant behaviour becomes difficult.

For the third exercise, investigators should again work in pairs. This time, however, one investigator will act as a slow-walking pedestrian whilst the other will observe and record whether other pedestrians overtake on the left or right side. Again, at least 30 observations per pair of investigators should be made, and there is no reason why observations recorded by a number of pairs should not be pooled for subsequent analysis. For this exercise, investigations should be carried out on a relatively uncrowded pavement.

The only equipment needed for each of the exercises is a clipboard, paper, and a pen. The observations to be recorded for each exercise are described in the Procedure section. Data collection for each exercise should take pairs of investigators no longer than an hour to complete providing, of course, that observations are made in a relatively crowded area. Analysis of the data obtained for each exercise should also take no longer than an hour.

Introduction and Hypotheses	If we watch people walking along a street it is noticeable that they very rarely bump into one another. Furthermore, they seem to avoid each other with very little difficulty. This raises the interesting question of how collision avoidance amongst pedestrians is achieved.

If we watch people walking along a street it is noticeable that they very rarely bump into one another. Furthermore, they seem to avoid each other with very little difficulty. This raises the interesting question of how collision avoidance amongst pedestrians is achieved. Several studies have been carried out to investigate the behaviour of pedestrians, and descriptions of these can be found in Hirsch (1970), Henderson and Lyons (1972), Morris (1967) and Stilitz (1970).

Such studies reveal that people tend to keep to the right of the pavement: thus some will be walking on the inside, away from the road, and others, walking in the opposite direction, on the outside and close to the road. Goffman (1972) has termed this behaviour 'lane formation', whilst Collett and Marsh (1981) have called it 'pedestrian streaming'. Where lane formation occurs, those pedestrians who wish to quicken their pace may either weave their way through their own lane or along the interface between opposing lanes. On a crowded pavement, pedestrians frequently take to the road when lane formation is absent.

Although it may not be immediately obvious, some means clearly exists whereby lane formation is maintained and collisions avoided. It has been suggested that two processes are involved, which may be conscious or unconscious. Wolff (1973) has described how pedestrians scan the faces of those coming towards them and terms this behaviour 'monitoring'. Goffman (1972) has called the other process 'externalization' or 'body gloss'. This refers to observable body movements conveying information concerning someone's likely behaviour to both those approaching and following. For example, where an area is very crowded, a characteristic avoidance movement involving a slight turning of the shoulders and a hardly noticeable side step has been observed. Wolff (1973) refers to this as 'step and slide'.

Collett and Marsh (1981) were particularly interested in the relationship between collision avoidance and the processes of monitoring and externalization. They found that the best place to study collision avoidance was a controlled pedestrian crossing, since when the lights change and pedestrians cross they are obliged to find a way past each other. The movements of pedestrians were recorded over several days by means of a portable video-recorder and zoom lens from a building overlooking the crossing. The video-taped data were then analysed.

Several aspects of behaviour were studied, including passes between individuals, the direction of passes (to the left or right), the orientation of people when passing, and the position of their arms. The gender and approximate age of the individuals were also noted. Of particular relevance to the first exercise presented here are the passes that were made between single individuals.

When two adults are moving together with what Collett and Marsh term an 'approach overlap', they will collide at some stage unless one or both alters direction. If this is not done early enough then one or both pedestrians has to take avoidance action. Collett and Marsh found that men and women differed with respect to the way in which they oriented themselves to the person they were passing. Men tended to turn towards the person they were passing (termed an 'open pass') while women tended to turn away (termed a 'closed pass'). This difference in collision avoidance behaviour between the sexes was found to be statistically highly significant. The difference is illustrated in *Figure 1*.

Further examination of the data showed that the type of pass was not simply a natural orientation according to which leg was forward at the time of passing. Even when a closed pass needed more effort than an open one, women were still significantly more likely to angle

Figure 1. Modal patterns of pass. © Simon Collins.

themselves in this way. Collett and Marsh's explanation for this finding is that women wish to protect their breasts. Their explanation is supported by the movement of the arms during a pass: more women than men drew one or both of their arms across their body when passing another person. Again, this difference was statistically highly significant.

Kendon and Ferber (1973) found similar behaviour in their analysis of greetings or salutations. Significantly more women were observed to draw an arm across their bodies immediately prior to a close salutation. However, Kendon and Ferber pointed out that this might simply be due to the transference of an article such as a purse or a newspaper from one hand to another in order to prepare for the greeting. Collett and Marsh therefore excluded from their analysis all those who were carrying something. However, the sex difference remained. Thus the findings regarding arm movements do seem to support Collett and Marsh's view that female behaviour is self-protective.

Other research which may have relevance to the idea of open and closed passes is that reported by Jenni and Jenni (1976) who investigated book-carrying behaviour in students. The researchers identified two ways in which books tended to be carried. In one, the books were held supported against the body, whilst in the other, the books were carried at the side of the body with the long edge more or less horizontal. Jenni and Jenni's results indicated that approximately 90% of female students used the first method and approximately the same number of male students the second. This strong gender difference is reminiscent of the differences in collision avoidance behaviour between adult male and female pedestrians, and it is possible that the difference in book-carrying behaviour is due to anatomical factors and, in women, represents a form of self-protection.

One further finding reported by Collett and Marsh is of interest. As mentioned earlier, Goffman (1972) and Wolff (1973) reported that pedestrian streams tend to form on the right. Collett and Marsh found that, when adult pedestrian density reached a certain level, four streams developed as though two pavements were placed side by side, and that there was a clear pattern of walking on the right. The researchers wanted to know whether pedestrians avoiding collision moved to the right when no lane formation occurred.

Of course, when two pedestrians are not directly opposite one another, the direction of pass is determined by the position of the people concerned relative to one another. Thus, if right shoulders are overlapping people will move to the left. However, when two people are approaching each other head-on, a choice between moving left or right can be made. Collett and Marsh found that, in such a case, almost twice as many pairs of pedestrians moved to the right as the left. This finding would seem to be well established: pedestrians tend to move towards, and walk on, the right.

Hypotheses

The aim of the first exercise presented here is to attempt to replicate Collett and Marsh's (1981) finding that adult men and women orient themselves differently when avoiding a collision. Replication is an important part of the scientific process, and an attempt to confirm Collett and Marsh's findings would further our knowledge about pedestrian behaviour. On the basis of their research, it may be hypothesized that there will be a significant difference in the collision avoidance behaviour of adult men and women such that women will tend to make more closed than open passes and men more open than closed passes when avoiding other pedestrians. The null hypothesis predicts no significant differences in the type of collision avoidance behaviour of men and women.

The second exercise is related to the first and aims to determine whether the gender difference in collision avoidance behaviour observed by Collett and Marsh in adults is also present in children. The data generated by this second exercise could contribute to our understanding of why the gender difference observed in adults occurs. There is no available evidence to suggest whether there will or will not be a difference in collision avoidance behaviour between boys and girls, so generating a specific formal hypothesis for the second exercise is difficult. However, if Collett and Marsh's suggestion is accepted – that closed passes made by adult women are to protect their breasts – then a logical null hypothesis for the second exercise is that no significant difference will be found in collision avoidance behaviour between young boys and girls. The experimental hypothesis predicts that there will be a difference between young boys and girls.

The optional third exercise aims to build on the work of previous investigators such as Goffman (1972) and Wolff (1973) and add to the existing knowledge concerning the behaviour of pedestrians. This research indicates that adults tend to move to the right when passing others, although the pattern is less clear in overtaking behaviour. In view of the general tendency to move to the right, the hypothesis for this exercise is that significantly more adults, of both sexes, will overtake another person by moving to the right rather than to the left, on a relatively uncrowded pavement. The null hypothesis predicts that overtaking to the right will not occur significantly more frequently than overtaking to the left.

Procedure

Exercise 1: Collision avoidance behaviour in adults

In this exercise, the collision avoidance behaviour of adult males and females will be compared. Investigators should work in pairs, one acting as the observer and the other as the data recorder. Prior to conducting the exercise, it will be necessary for observers to familiarize themselves with the difference between an open and closed pass. For the purposes of this exercise, an *open pass* will be operationally defined as an attempt to avoid a collision by turning the body *towards* the approaching person. A *closed pass* will be operationally defined as an attempt to avoid a collision by turning the body *away* from the approaching person.

Collision avoidance behaviour which does not fall into either of these categories should be classified as *neutral*. This behaviour should be recorded, even though it will not form part of the subsequent data analysis. It is suggested that observers conduct their own pilot study prior to the exercise proper to ensure that they are completely familiar

Table 1. A 2 × 3 contingency table

TYPE OF PASS	GENDER	
	Male	Female
Open		
Closed		
Neutral		

with the difference between an open, closed and neutral pass.

Using their clipboards, paper, and pens, data recorders should keep a tally of the behaviours observed. It is suggested that data recorders construct a 2 (Gender : Male or Female) × 3 (Type of Pass: Open, Closed or Neutral) contingency table in which to record the observations as shown in Table 1. Pairs of investigators may wish to take it in turns to observe and record. The investigator acting as observer should verbally inform the data recorder of the type of pass made and the gender of the individuals concerned, for example: 'female closed – male open'.

When the pair of investigators are satisfied that they can competently observe and record the relevant behaviour, they should select an appropriate area in which to carry out the exercise. Any area where there is likely to be a relatively concentrated number of people moving in opposite directions would be suitable. Such locations include a pedestrian crossing, a corridor in a public building, or the entrance to a building where the door is permanently open, such as a bank or a shop. If investigators intend to share their data, then the choice of location for carrying out observations is clearly an important factor. All investigators should use the same type of location in order to control for any effect this might have. Investigators should observe at least 30 pairs of pedestrians and should try to include male–male, female–female, and male–female interactions. Investigators should also satisfy themselves that a sufficient number of males and females have been observed.

Exercise 2 : Collision avoidance behaviour in children

This exercise should be carried out using the same procedure described for the first exercise, the only difference being the age of those observed. It may be difficult for investigators to find as many children to observe as adults, but there are places where relatively large numbers of children may be found, particularly after school and at the weekend. These include shopping centres, swimming pools, playgrounds or any areas which offer some form of amusement. Additionally, it might be possible to observe children in a school, provided that permission is first obtained from the head teacher. The children studied should be of school age but no older than eleven.

Exercise 3 : Overtaking behaviour amongst adult pedestrians

As with the other two exercises, this optional exercise is best carried

Table 2. A 2 × 2 contingency table

| | GENDER | |
TYPE OF PASS	Male	Female
Open		
Closed		

out by pairs of investigators. One investigator should act as the pedestrian to be overtaken whilst the other, remaining at a discrete distance behind, should act as data recorder. The investigator acting as the pedestrian should walk slowly enough to warrant being overtaken by another pedestrian. It is essential that the investigator keeps to the centre of the pavement or walkway so that it is equally easy for someone following to overtake on the right or left.

The data recorder should only record overtaking when he or she is satisfied beyond all reasonable doubt that no other factors influenced it. Such factors include obstructions or other approaching pedestrians. The only information that the data recorder needs to note down is whether the overtaking was done on the left or right of the investigator acting as the pedestrian. As with the previous exercises, pairs of investigators should conduct a practice exercise until they are satisfied that they can competently undertake the proper exercise. Investigators should also decide on a suitable number of observations to be made and/or the time frame for the observation period.

Results

The raw data for *Exercise 1* will have been recorded in a 2 × 3 contingency table. However, the neutral passes are not relevant to the hypothesis under test for this exercise, and consequently they may be discarded from the analysis of results. (Note, however, that the proportion of neutral passes to open and closed passes might be worthy of some discussion.) Removing the neutral passes leaves a 2(Gender: Male or Female) × 2 (Type of Pass:Open or Closed) contingency table (see *Table 2*).

Since the exercise has involved establishing categories and then recording the number of observations falling into each of them, the appropriate inferential statistical test to employ is the 2 × 2 chi-square test. This test will contrast the observed values of open and closed passes with the values which would be expected if there were no difference between adult males and females in their collision avoidance behaviour. A significant value of chi-square will indicate that adult males and females are different with respect to their collision avoidance behaviour whilst a non-significant value will indicate that they are not particularly different with respect to this behaviour.

Whether or not Collett and Marsh's (1981) findings have been replicated does not, of course, depend solely on a significant value of chi-square. Their findings will only have been replicated if more men than women employed open passes and more women than men employed closed passes. The relationship between sex and type of pass employed could be plotted in the form of a graph to illustrate the findings from the exercise. The raw data should be converted to percentages in order to make the comparisons meaningful. This will indicate where any significant effect comes from.

The data generated in the second exercise should be analysed and presented in the same way as in *Exercise 1*. Remember, though, that if Collett and Marsh's interpretation of the differences in collision avoidance behaviour in adults is correct, then no significant difference should be observed in the behaviour of boys and girls. Any significant difference would tend to cast doubt on the legitimacy of Collett and Marsh's interpretation.

As far as the third exercise is concerned, previous research has indicated that adults tend to move to the right when passing others. If the same is true of overtaking behaviour, then significantly more pedestrians overtaking on the right should be observed than would be expected if overtaking behaviour were purely a chance or random affair. A simple one way chi-square test for deviation from an a priori expected frequency distribution will indicate whether the findings reported by previous researchers can be confirmed. As with *Exercises 1* and *2*, the data generated in *Exercise 3* could also be presented in an appropriate pictorial form.

Discussion

The major discussion point arising from the first exercise is the extent to which a gender difference in adult collision avoidance behaviour has been observed and hence the extent to which the findings of Collett and Marsh (1981) have been replicated. If the same pattern of results reported by Collett and Marsh has been found, then explanations for this difference need to be considered. Collett and Marsh's 'breast protection' explanation is just one of a number of possibilities. What other plausible explanations might account for the gender difference? Are there any differences between male–male, female–female, and male–female avoidance behaviours and could these be used to formulate a possible explanation? The work of Knowles (1972) on gender differences in response to invasions of personal space could also be made relevant here.

The data generated in *Exercise 2* might also be helpful in explaining the gender difference reported by Collett and Marsh. If a similar gender difference was observed in children, this would have strong implications for Collett and Marsh's 'breast protection' explanation. Or would it? It could be that imitation can explain gender differences in the collision avoidance behaviour of children. The work of social learning theorists would be relevant here. According to these theorists, the similarity between a child and a role-model is an important factor in imitation. Thus, children tend to imitate the behaviour of a same-sex model. Alternatively, a Freudian explanation for children's tendencies to imitate the same-sex parent might be applicable. Are these explanations for a similar gender difference in the collision behaviour of children plausible? What other sorts of explanation might be more plausible?

It could be that the data generated in *Exercise 1* failed to replicate the findings reported by Collett and Marsh. Does this suggest that there is something suspect about their findings or are there any limitations in the way in which *Exercise 1* was carried out which might account for a failure in replication? Again, the data generated in *Exercise 2* could be useful for any proposed explanation. For example, would the absence of a gender difference in both *Exercises 1* and *2* tend to cast doubt on the whole notion of sex differences in pedestrian collision avoidance behaviour?

The absence of a gender difference in *Exercise 2* coupled with its presence in *Exercise 1* would not necessarily refute Collett and Marsh's 'breast protection explanation'. It would, however, raise the interesting question of the age at which breast protection behaviour develops. Are there any ways in which this question could be addressed empirically and how would the data generated in such a study be analysed?

Although the number of neutral passes made by pedestrians in *Exercises 1* and *2* was not included in the analysis of the data, their proportion in relation to open and closed passes might form an interesting discussion point. For example, what would the implications be for Collett and Marsh's work if the proportion of neutral passes far outweighed the proportion of open and/or closed passes? (An entertaining alternative view of the significance of pedestrian collision avoidance behaviour and social psychological approaches to it can be found in Ryave and Schenkein (1974).)

The major discussion point which will arise from the optional third exercise is whether the results have indicated that pedestrians tend to move to the right even when overtaking on a relatively uncrowded pavement. If overtaking does appear to be a predominantly 'right-sided' behaviour (or even, perhaps, a 'left-sided' behaviour) why might this be? Could, for example, such behaviour be related to the way in which English motorists overtake? If this were so, what patterns of pedestrian overtaking behaviour would be expected in countries such as America or France?

In connection with this, Kemp's (1973) research on encounters between ships might be worth investigating. Alternatively, it might be asked whether consistently overtaking on the right confers any advantage to the overtaker and what this advantage would be? An important variable likely to influence overtaking behaviour is whether the pavement is crowded or not. Why might this be? What other sorts of variable could be investigated with respect to overtaking behaviour, and how would the data be collected and analysed?

An alternative finding might be that pedestrians tend to overtake on the outside of the pavement, regardless of whether this involves passing on the left or right. Possible reasons for this could be considered, such as politeness or an unwillingness to edge another pedestrian towards the outer edge of the pavement.

Finally, the use of the observational method within the context of studying pedestrian behaviour could be discussed. The observational method has both advantages and disadvantages (reviewed by Hutt and Hutt, 1970). One issue relevant to the present exercises concerns the ethics of observation. Is it, for example, ethical to observe people without their consent? Does it constitute an invasion of privacy or is it the case that because pedestrian behaviour occurs within the public domain, invasion of privacy is not relevant? A further problem with the observational method is the reliability of the observations made. One way of improving reliability is to use more than one individual to observe the behaviour in question. How could the reliability of their observations be assessed? What other devices could be used to improve observer reliability?

The observational method does, however, have distinct advantages in certain kinds of research. For example, this method enables behaviour to be studied without influencing it. One way in which the experimental method may influence results is through 'demand characteristics'. (See also the practical exercise on 'Experimenter Bias Effects' in the Experimental Method section of this Manual.) What difficulties might demand characteristics create if pedestrian behaviour were to be studied experimentally? Some psychologists have suggested that the laboratory study of behaviour causes it to become unrecognizably different from its naturally occurring form. This may seem to be an extreme view, but it is relevant to a consideration of the advantages and disadvantages of the observational method. How could this view be examined specifically in relation to pedestrian behaviour?

Bibliography

General background references

GOFFMAN, E. (1972) *Relations in Public*. Harmondsworth: Penguin.

HIRSCH, V. (1970) *A Study of Pedestrian Behaviour*. New York: City University of New York.

HUTT, S.J. and HUTT, C. (1970) *Direct Observation and Measurement of Behaviour*. Illinois: Charles C. Thomas.

MORRIS, D. (1967) *The Naked Ape*. London: Jonathan Cape.

RYAVE, L.A. and SCHENKEIN, J.N. (1974) Notes on the art of walking. In R. Turner (Ed.) *Ethnomethodology*. Harmondsworth: Penguin.

Specific Background References

COLLETT, P.R. and MARSH, P.E. (1981) Patterns of public behaviour: Collision avoidance on a pedestrian crossing. In A. Kendon (Ed.) *Nonverbal Communication, Interaction and Gesture*. The Hague: Mouton Press.

KENDON, A. and FERBER, A. (1973) A description of some human greetings. In R.P. Michael and J.H. Crook (Eds) *Comparative Ecology and Behaviour in Primates*. London: Academic Press.

STILITZ, I.B. (1970) Pedestrian congestion. In D. Cantor (Ed.) *Architectural Psychology*. London: Institute of British Architects.

WOLFF, M. (1973) Notes on the behaviour of pedestrians. In A. Birenbaum and E. Sagar (Eds) *People in Places: The Sociology of the Familiar*. New York: Praeger.

Journal articles

HENDERSON, L.F. and LYONS, D.J. (1972) Sex differences in human crowd motion. *Nature*, 240, 353–355.

JENNI, D.A. and JENNI, M.A. (1976) Carrying behaviour in humans: Analysis of sex differences. *Science*, 194, 859–860.

KEMP, J.F. (1973) Behaviour patterns in encounters between ships. The *Journal of Navigation*, 26, 417–423.

KNOWLES, E. (1972) Boundaries around social space: Dyadic responses to an invader. *Environment and Behaviour*, 4, 437–445.

PRACTICAL 9

A survey of conservatism

Jeremy J. Foster
Manchester Polytechnic

Abstract

A small scale survey is used to test the hypothesis that subgroups of a population differ in their responses on a scale measuring conservatism. The particular hypothesis suggested is that students specializing in different disciplines differ in their conservatism scores, but this practical exercise can be readily modified if students from different specialisms are not available. The practical is likely to prompt discussion of sampling from a target population and how to obtain a representative sample, of the reliability and validity of attitude scales, and of the reasons why different subgroups show different attitude scores.

Materials and Equipment

For this study, access to at least three distinct groups of about 20 people each is needed. A convenient procedure is to use groups of students specializing in different subjects. For example, one group of Business Studies students, one of Social Sciences students and one of Physics students would be adequate. Each participant will need a copy of the modified 'Conservatism Scale' reproduced in *Appendix 1*.

The study can be conducted with a separate group of investigators for each group of participants. The modified 'Conservatism Scale' takes about five minutes to complete, and groups of respondents can fill it out simultaneously. Investigators have to identify the subgroup of respondents they are to study, collect the responses to the scale, and then collate the data. This can be done in one two-hour session. Alternatively, it can be spread over two sessions, the first being used to introduce the topic and identify the subgroups. In the second session investigators report the data they obtained, collate it and carry out the statistical analysis.

Introduction and Hypotheses

General experience might suggest that students from different disciplines have different personality styles. In the higher education sphere, for example, accountancy students may seem conventional while social science students may appear outlandish in attitude as well as dress; natural sciences students seem to lie somewhere between these two. A subjective impression like this is often misleading, but there are some lines of evidence suggesting that there may be fundamental differences between people studying in different disciplines.

Personality and academic specialization

Most psychological theories of the way in which people choose jobs see vocational choice as a function of personality. Super (1957) proposed that occupational choice is a process of implementing one's self-concept: one looks for a job that will allow one to use one's skills and fulfil one's interests. Holland (1985) claimed that vocational

103

choice reflects predominant life-style. He distinguished six personality orientations: motor, intellectual, supportive, conforming, persuasive and aesthetic. According to this theory, jobs can be divided into similar categories, and an important aspect of making a wise choice of occupation is to match one's personality orientation with the characteristics of the job.

Choosing A-level subjects or a particular degree course has some similarities to choosing an occupation: there is a range of alternatives from which to select and most people probably choose subjects or degree courses which reflect their abilities and interests. Therefore, A-level or degree specialization might also be related to personality.

In the educational sphere there has been some interest in the non-intellectual factors related to academic success in higher education. (See also Practical 15 on 'Approaches to Study and Academic Performance'.) Entwistle *et al.* (1971) reported that the relationship between personality and academic achievement varied according to the discipline being studied: 'Neuroticism correlated positively with the criterion for engineers and linguists and negatively for pure scientists and for students taking social studies' (p. 265).

Attitudes

Attitude was defined by Allport (1935) as a 'mental and neural state of readiness. . .exerting a directive or dynamic influence upon the individual's response to all objects and situations with which it is related'. An attitude is a hypothetical construct, that is, something we assume to be present although we cannot observe it directly. The evidence for attitudes comes from consistencies in opinions. For instance, if you regularly and consistently say that you approve of going to church, of studying Christian writings, and of attending Christian religious events, it might be said that you have a positive attitude toward Christianity.

The study of attitudes has been one of the central concerns of social psychology. Two major issues have been the way in which attitudes can be measured and the relation of attitudes to behaviour. This second issue has been studied because it was believed that attitudes motivated behaviour and so it could be expected that people would behave in a way consistent with their attitudes. For example, one would expect the person with a positive attitude to Christianity to go to church. However, it was found that the relationship between expressed attitudes and behaviour was not as close as might have been predicted. Some people who expressed a positive attitude towards an issue or organization did not do anything practical about it, and some people behaved in a way that was contrary to their expressed attitudes. This led to considerable discussion about why this should be so. (This topic will not be considered further here, but it features in almost all social psychological discussions of attitudes, for example, Stahlberg and Frey (1988).)

Much work has been done on measuring the strength of people's attitudes so that a person who scores 50, for example, is known to have a stronger attitude than someone who scores 30. Various techniques have been developed (Stahlberg and Frey (1988) provide a brief summary), but the most common ones involve presenting people with a set of contentious statements about a topic and asking them whether they agree or disagree. In the Likert method, people are given statements such as 'I find regular prayer a rewarding part of my life' and asked to indicate whether they agree or disagree. (A five-point scale is commonly used.)

It has been found that people's attitudes tend to be consistent: someone who is liberal-minded is likely to disapprove of censorship and public executions, and approve of animal welfare and progressive educational methods. This is not to say that all liberal-minded people have these views, but most liberal-minded individuals will share some of them. Attitudes go together to form ideologies. (In this sense, liberal-mindedness and conservatism, which we shall look at in a moment, do not have any political meaning: people can be conservative-minded without being supporters of a Conservative political party.)

Measuring conservatism

Conservatism in this non-political sense involves a set of attitudes; so, it can be measured using attitude scales on different issues such as abortion, socialism, capital punishment. But there are a number of technical difficulties in devising attitude scales (see Wilson and Nias, 1973), and Wilson and Patterson (1968) developed a more convenient method of measuring conservatism. They simply asked people to indicate whether they approved or disapproved of such things as Sunday observance and abortion. This approach stimulated a great deal of research (Wilson, 1973) and substitutions have been made for some of the original items (Wilson, 1975).

Kirton (1978) proposed an abbreviated form of the scale (now out-of-date), containing 30 items rather than the original 50. He deleted items which showed skewed response patterns (that is, everyone tended to give the same response), or which showed only a low correlation with the overall scale scores. On the Kirton version of the conservatism scale, respondents indicate whether they are in favour of, opposed to, or noncommittal about, each item. Approving a 'pro-conservative' item counts for two points, and opposing a 'non-conservative' item also counts for two points. All 'noncommittal' responses count for one point. The maximum possible is 60 points, and Kirton found that the mean score of a group of 286 respondents was 28.1 (SD 11.9). He reported that there are three factors underlying the overall score on the abbreviated scale: religiosity, control/ punitiveness and liberality.

Using a statistical technique called factor analysis, a number of researchers have examined the dimensions underlying the responses to the conservatism scale. Joe (1984) identified three dimensions: religious, sexual, moral control. Green *et al.*, (1988) found a consistent underlying theme of fundamental religious conservatism.

In this practical, we shall use an abbreviated form of the Conservatism Scale (see *Appendix 1*), consisting of 20 items, and based on the findings of Joe (1984). He reports the results of a factor analysis of the results of the conservatism scale, and 18 of the items in *Appendix 1* are included in his table of results. One item, 'evolution theory', has been dropped, and two have been altered: 'pot parties' has been changed to 'smoking pot' and 'co-ed dorms' has been translated into 'mixed-sex halls of residence'.

Sampling.   In most surveys, the researcher takes a sample of the target or parent population, and asks questions of the sample. The results are then extrapolated to the wider population – you will be familiar with opinion polls that take the responses of about 1,000 people and then draw conclusions about the popularity of political parties in the country as a whole. The problem, of course, is how far one is justified in generalizing from the sample to the wider population. There are two factors which are important. The first is the size of the sample: the larger it is, the more confidence one can have in the results if the second condition is met. The second condition is that the sample must be representative of the parent population. If 90% of the parent population have telephones, then 90% of the sample should have telephones. (This is one reason why a survey of the general population based only on telephoning respondents has some unreliability built in to it. The 10% of the population who do not have telephones may well be different from the other members of the population; they may be less well-off or more likely to be pensioners. Therefore, what is true of telephone-owners may not be true of non-telephone owners).

There are various ways of selecting a sample to make it representative of the population. The simplest method is random sampling, where all members of the population have an equal chance of being included in the sample and participants are selected by a random procedure. To achieve a random sample, a list of all members of the target population is needed so that sample members can be selected by a truly random procedure such as choosing numbers from a random number table.

Fundamental to the conducting of a survey is the defining of the population to which you wish to generalize the findings. If you wanted to draw some conclusions about British 18-year-olds, you would need a representative sample of that large population. If you are interested in drawing conclusions about students in your school or college, you need a sample which is representative of that (smaller) parent population. Even this may be difficult to obtain: you will require a list of all the students so you can select participants at random, and then you need to obtain the co-operation of those chosen to be in the sample.

For this practical, students need to identify the populations they wish to compare on conservatism, and then obtain a sample of each. If it is feasible, they can test the hypothesis that students specializing in different disciplines vary in their conservatism. Alternatively, some testable hypothesis such as 'students under 21, between 21 and 30, and over 30 differ in terms of their conservatism', or 'managers, clerical workers and shop-floor workers have different conservatism scores' could be generated. If at all possible, data should be collected from three subgroups.

It should be borne in mind that the results from the sample are only a reliable indication of the conservatism of the subgroup if the sample is representative. Investigators should try to obtain a random sample, but if this is not possible, they may have to rely on an 'availability sample', where they test whoever they can find.

Hypotheses

The hypothesis is that students from different disciplines vary in their scores on the modified 'Conservatism Scale'. (As explained previously, this hypothesis may need to be modified depending on the availability of different subgroups of people.) The null hypothesis is that there will be no difference between the subgroups' scores on the modified 'Conservatism Scale.'

Procedure

If this exercise is being carried out in a class of psychology students, students could form small groups, each concentrating on obtaining data from one of the subgroups being studied. The main task is to recruit a sample from each target population (for example, first year students of Fine Art, of Business Studies and of Sociology).

All participants should be given a copy of the modified 'Conservatism Scale' (*Appendix 1*), and asked to complete and return it. (The response rate will be much higher if investigators wait for them to fill it in.) Investigators should make sure that participants do not put their names on the Scale, but do fill in their age, gender and the subgroup of which they are a member. If students from different HE courses are being compared, this will be the discipline they are studying.

Some respondents may say they do not understand what some of the terms mean; if this happens, they should be given clear, impartial definitions (which can be obtained from a dictionary). Participants should be thanked and debriefed if required.

Results

The first task is to score the responses on the conservatism scale. Care should be taken over the scoring: it is easy to get confused and make mistakes. Investigators should begin by taking the following numbered items:

2   4   7   8   10   12   13   14   17

Every 'Yes' response scores two points.

Then the other items should be taken:

1   3   5   6   9   11   15   16   18   19   20

Every 'No' response scores two points.

For all items, a '?' response scores one point.

The total score for each participant should then be calculated. The maximum possible is 40.

In addition to knowing which subgroup they belonged to, investigators should have three items of data for all participants: their age, their sex and the conservatism score. The results should be tabulated,

107

Table 1. Responses from the conservatism survey

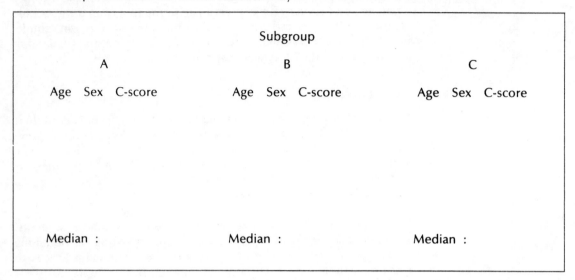

Subgroup								
A			B			C		
Age	Sex	C-score	Age	Sex	C-score	Age	Sex	C-score
Median :			Median :			Median :		

as shown in *Table 1*. The median score should be calculated for each subgroup. (Since this version of the 'Conservatism Scale' has not been standardized, the scores may not be normally distributed and so it is safer to use the median rather than the mean.) To present the results graphically, students could plot a histogram of the median response of each subgroup.

Although much of the past research using the conservatism scale has employed parametric statistical analysis, it is simpler to use non-parametric analysis. This also has the advantage of not assuming that the data comes from an underlying normal distribution. Assuming students have collected responses from at least three subgroups, the appropriate non-parametric test is the Kruskal–Wallis anova. A-level students should use a series of Mann–Whitney tests.

To apply the Kruskal–Wallis test, complete *Table 2*. Rank all the C-scores in a single series, giving one to the lowest score, and put these values in the columns headed Rank-value. Add the rank values for each subgroup to find the Rank Totals (T) for each subgroup of participants. For each subgroup, calculate T^2 and then divide by n, the number of people in the subgroup. Add these values to find the sum of T^2/n. Multiply the sum by $12/(N(N+1))$, where N is the total number of participants you had. From the result, subtract $3(N+1)$ to obtain H. Look up the significance of H in the tables for chi-square, with df=C-1 (that is, one less than the number of subgroups you have).

Discussion

Does the data support the hypothesis? If the value of H is statistically significant, it can be concluded that there is a difference between the conservatism scores of the subgroups studied. If students look at the medians of each subgroup, they will be able to see which scored higher and which lower.

In discussing the results, one issue to consider is whether the

Table 2. Table of rank values from the conservatism survey

			Subgroup				
	A			B			C
C-score	Rank-value		C-score	Rank-value		C-score	Rank-value

Total (T):
    T^2:
    T^2/n:

Total (T):
    T^2:
    T^2/n:

Total (T):
    T^2:
    T^2/n:

Sum of (T^2/n) =

$H = [12/(N(N + 1)) \times \text{Sum of } (T^2/n)] - 3(N + 1)$

df = C − 1 where C is the number of subgroups.

samples were representative of their parent populations. Investigators may well have found it difficult or impossible to obtain random samples. Are there any features of the participant groups, therefore, which makes one cautious about accepting the data as representative? (For example, if participants were students who were in a class on Monday morning at 9.30 a.m., are these perhaps the more highly-motivated students?)

The second issue concerns the psychometric quality of the modified 'Conservatism Scale': is it both reliable and valid? Students may be familiar with the concepts of reliability and validity as applied to psychometric instruments. Reliability has a number of meanings, including whether the test gives the same result if it is given twice to the same respondents (test-retest reliability). Another type of reliability is whether all the items in a test measure the 'same' thing: do the responses to the various items correlate with the overall score? This is known as item homogeneity.

Validity refers to whether the test measures what it claims to measure: is the driving test really a test of driving competence? Does the modified 'Conservatism Scale' really measure conservatism? There are a number of methods for establishing whether a test is valid. One procedure, used by Wilson and Patterson (1968) in their original research, is to see whether the instrument has concurrent validity. This means taking two groups that are known to differ on the feature being measured, and seeing whether they score differently on the test. It would be expected that people who belong to right-wing political organizations would score higher on conservatism than people in left-wing organizations.

The version of the 'Conservatism Scale' used in this practical is a slight modification of previous versions. Although students may have doubts about some of the items, the overall scale has been investigated so frequently that one can assume it to be both reliable and valid. However, students will have noticed that four items are concerned directly with religious belief: they might like to consider whether having such beliefs is necessarily part of conservatism.

Investigators may have found some items caused problems, in that participants were unsure of their meaning. They may also have found that some participants wanted to qualify their responses, for example, 'I am against capital punishment, except for rapists' (or 'murderers of policemen', or some other special group). The scale does not allow these nuances to be shown.

There is one aspect which is open to debate – the scale is transparent, and respondents are likely to see what is being assessed and how a false impression can be produced by answering the questions in particular ways. If someone wishes to mislead the investigator and appear more or less conservative than they really are, it is probably simple for them to do so. This is one reason why it is worth waiting while the participants complete the questionnaire: they are more likely to treat it seriously than if they take it away and sit round with their friends filling it in over a coffee.

Assuming that students found some difference between the subgroups studied, and feel that the sample of participants was reasonably representative, they may wish to discuss why they think the differences arose, and suggest how they could test any speculations empirically. Finally, students may like to suggest how this area of research could be developed further to shed more light on the differences in people's attitudes, and the causes and consequences of this.

Bibliography

General background references

STAHLBERG, D. and FREY, D. (1988) Attitudes I: Structure, measurements and functions. In M. Hewstone, W. Stroebe, J-P. Codol and G.M. Stephenson (Eds) *Introduction to Social Psychology*. Oxford: Blackwell.

WILSON, G.D. (Ed.) (1973) *The Psychology of Conservatism*. London: Academic Press.

Specific background references

ALLPORT, G.W. (1935) Attitudes. In G.M. Murchison (Ed.) *Handbook of Social Psychology*. Clark University Press.

HOLLAND, J.L. (1985) *Making Vocational Choices*. Englewood Cliffs: Prentice Hall.

SUPER, D.E. (1957) *The Psychology of Careers*. New York: Harper and Row.

WILSON, G.D. (1975) *Manual for the Wilson–Patterson Attitude Inventory*. London: NFER.

WILSON, G.D. and NIAS, D.K.B. (1973) The need for a new approach to attitude measurement. In G. Wilson (Ed.) *The Psychology of Conservatism*. London: Academic Press.

Journal articles

ENTWISTLE, N.J., NISBET, J., ENTWISTLE, D. and COWELL, M.D. (1971) The academic performance of students: predictions from scales of motivation and study methods. *British Journal of Educational Psychology, 41,* 258–267.

GREEN, D.E., REYNOLDS, N.S., WALKEY, F.H. and MCCORMICK, I.A. (1988) The conservatism scale: in search of a replicable factor structure, *Journal of Social Psychology, 128,* 507–516.

JOE, V.C. (1984) Factor analysis of the conservatism scale. *Journal of Social Psychology, 124,* 175–178.

KIRTON, M.J. (1978) Wilson and Patterson's conservatism scale: a shortened alternative form. *British Journal of Social and Clinical Psychology, 17,* 319–323.

WILSON G.D. and PATTERSON, J.R. (1968) A new measure of conservatism. *British Journal of Social and Clinical Psychology, 7,* 274–279.

Appendix 1. CONSERVATISM SCALE (modified)

Based on the findings of Joe (1984).

Identification number . . . . . .   Date . . . . . .

Age . . . . . .   Sex: M F

Which of the following do you favour or believe in? There are no right or wrong answers. Do not discuss, just give your first reactions by circling the appropriate answer – yes, no, or '?' for don't know. Please answer all items. Thank you for your help.

1. Premarital virginity	Yes ? No
2. Patriotism	Yes ? No
3. Nudist camps	Yes ? No
4. Bible truth	Yes ? No
5. Striptease shows	Yes ? No
6. Legalized abortion	Yes ? No
7. Church authority	Yes ? No
8. Sabbath observance	Yes ? No
9. Birth control	Yes ? No
10. Censorship	Yes ? No
11. Divorce	Yes ? No
12. Divine law	Yes ? No
13. Chaperones	Yes ? No
14. Capital punishment	Yes ? No
15. Working mothers	Yes ? No
16. Fibs (white lies)	Yes ? No
17. Conventional clothes	Yes ? No
18. Mixed-sex halls of residence	Yes ? No
19. Smoking pot	Yes ? No
20. Hippies	Yes ? No

PRACTICAL 10

Gender differences in the aggressive behaviour of schoolchildren

Mike Cardwell
Filton College, Bristol

[*Readers are reminded of the particular ethical problems involved in schoolchildren acting as participants in psychological investigations. Legal requirements for the protection of children place restrictions on the people who are allowed access to children in schools. Furth= ermore, parental consent may be necessary before studying those under 16 years of age in school. It is strongly recommended that the advice of the headteacher be sought well in advance of conducting any study.*]

Abstract

The aim of this observational exercise is to investigate whether the gender differences in the frequency of aggression typically found in the free-play behaviour (that is, uncontrolled or unstructured re-creational behaviour) of pre-school children would also be evident in the behaviour of older children in the more confined setting of the school classroom. The exercise also seeks to establish whether there are gender differences in the *types* of aggression shown by boys and girls, testing the hypothesis that although boys may show more physical aggression, girls may express more verbal aggression.

Materials
and Equipment

Behaviour coding sheets will be needed for this investigation (see *Appendix 1*). One sheet should be used for each observational period for each child. Investigators should record information about the child's age and gender, and give scores for physical and verbal aggression displayed by the child over the observational period. Note that in this exercise, *verbal* aggression is defined as any vocalization with intention to hurt or abuse another child, not accompanied by smiling or laughing, while *physical* aggression is defined by such actions as hitting, kicking, pinching, wrestling, pushing or pulling. A stopwatch is ideal for accurate recording of the time periods of observation, although an ordinary watch which measures elapsed time in seconds will also do.

The study should take place in a primary school, with children aged from 4 to 11. Whilst there is no minimum number of children needed, common sense would dictate a useful minimum for comparison of six females and six males. Please note that teachers' and parents' permission *must* be sought. If a number of observers are contributing to the same investigation, it is important that they all study children of the same age, unless it is intended that cross-age comparisons be made.

Introduction
and Hypotheses

Observational studies of the aggressive behaviour of pre-school children have tended to show more frequent aggressive acts in boys than in girls (Bardwick, 1971; Maccoby and Jacklin, 1974). These supposed gender differences are usually examined by observing children in free-play situations: very few attempts have been made to duplicate this type of research outside the free-play situation, nor to examine the existence of gender differences in aggression in older children. One such attempt was carried out by Archer and Westeman (1981), and this present study is, in part, a replication of their research. Archer and Westeman carried out an observational study in the classroom, observing equal numbers of boys and girls aged six and eleven. The children were observed individually in their school classrooms for eight five-minute periods, over several weeks. Archer and Westeman found significant gender differences in physical aggression at age eleven, but not at age six. What was particularly interesting about their findings was that, although boys showed more *physical* aggression at age eleven, girls showed more *verbal* aggression. These results should be regarded with some caution, however, as previous research by Whiting and Edwards (1973) had found significant gender differences in verbal aggression, with *boys* being the more generally aggressive in free-play situations. Archer and Westeman suggested that such gender differences are likely to be situation-specific. They also found that there was a higher incidence of same-gender aggressive interactions than of opposite-gender aggressive interactions (this was true for both the six-year-olds *and* the eleven-year-olds). The obvious explanation for this is that both genders interact more with their own gender than with the opposite gender. However, there was little difference in the frequency of cross-gender aggressive acts initiated by boys and girls, which contradicted previous findings by Maccoby and Jacklin (1974) that boys are somehow reluctant to direct aggressive acts towards girls.

This present exercise is designed to answer the following questions:

First, are these reported gender differences found in the classroom, that is, are they evident in the behaviour of *older* children, and in situations other than free-play?

Second, are there gender differences in the types of aggression displayed?

Bardwick (1971) has suggested that although boys engage in more physical aggression, girls display more of other types of aggression, such as verbal aggression and interpersonal rejection. This implies that there is no difference in the underlying aggression motivation of boys and girls, only in the way that the aggression is expressed. This view is challenged by some other researchers (Maccoby and Jacklin, 1974) but analysis of the studies used in their review does seem to indicate the existence of a stronger gender difference in physical aggression, with boys being more aggressive, than in verbal aggression. Later studies (Maccoby and Jacklin, 1980; Parke and Slaby, 1983) have also cast doubt on the 'verbally aggressive girls' idea, and have found boys to be more aggressive in both physical *and* verbal aggression. Observational studies have found that these gender differences appear at around the age of 18 months (Fagot and Hagan,

1982), and various explanations have been put forward to account for these gender differences. The consistency of these gender differences across different cultures is taken as strong evidence for the influence of biology in aggression, although there is still considerable uncertainty as to how a gender-linked biological system for aggression might operate. Swedish research (Olweus, 1980) among adolescents found a relationship between levels of the hormone testosterone and aggression. Boys with high levels of testosterone rated themselves as more aggressive and more likely to respond aggressively when provoked. The influences of socialization on aggression are wide-ranging. Some researchers have found that boys aged between one- and three-years old receive more attention for their aggressive behaviour than do girls, and that this attention is sometimes positive, thus reinforcing the aggressive behaviour (Fagot and Hagan, 1982). Research on the effects of the media on aggressive behaviour has always been controversial, and although there are many critics of this view, most recent research does seem to suggest a causal effect in the television-aggression debate. Eron (1982) found that although TV violence affected both boys *and* girls, boys were still more aggressive. It is obviously difficult to separate the effects of biology and experience. Some individuals may well be more aggressive than others as a direct result of their biological makeup, but differences in behavioural aggression may not become apparent unless these individuals are exposed to environments which provoke aggressive responses, that is, where there is clearly an interactive effect. Research by Parke and Slaby (1983), found that boys were far more likely to retaliate to an attack or threat than were girls, and that this retaliation was more likely to be physical.

The aim of this investigation, therefore, is to test the hypotheses that boys and girls are different in terms of the frequency and type of their aggressive responses. Unlike most research in this area, this study will test these hypotheses in the more confined setting of the classroom, rather than in the playground where the nature of male and female games tends to predetermine appropriate or inappropriate behavioural responses.

Hypotheses

1. There will be a significant gender difference in the incidence of aggressive behaviours in a classroom setting.

2. Boys will show a significantly higher incidence of physically aggressive behaviours in a classroom setting than will girls.

3. Girls will show a significantly higher incidence of verbally aggressive behaviours in a classroom setting than will boys.

For each of the hypotheses stated, the null hypothesis states that there will be no significant gender differences in the incidence of aggressive behaviours, either physical or verbal, under classroom conditions, with any observed differences being due to chance factors. The appropriate level of significance for this study should be $p \leq 0.05$.

Procedure

Investigations involving children place clearly defined ethical responsibilities on the investigator, and *Appendix 1* to this *Manual* should be read for clarification of these.

Arrangements (not least of all, school co-operation) may decide the most appropriate age group to study, but the investigation works just as well for younger schoolchildren as it does for older. The intention is that the investigation should be carried out in a classroom situation, rather than in a free-play situation, therefore a situation where children are interacting fairly freely would be ideal. (Teachers will advise on this.) Ideally, observations should be made over a series of visits to the school, for two main reasons. Firstly, a period of acclimatization to the children is necessary, so that the presence of a stranger does not unduly influence their behaviour. This will allow unobtrusive observations to take place. Secondly, several unobtrusive visits allow more observations, and therefore a more appropriate number of children can be studied over a larger number of observational periods. If this investigation is being carried out as a group project, then each member of the group could study a smaller number of children over more observational periods, and the results combined. Ideally, equal numbers of boys and girls should be used for the investigation, with each observer aiming to observe an equal number of boys and girls, rather than one observer concentrating on boys and another on girls. This minimizes possible gender differences due to socioeconomic class, geographical area and so on, by ensuring that the boys and girls used for comparison are not different in some other important way which might contribute to their aggressive behaviour. Whilst it is difficult to isolate specific socialization experiences which might account for differences in aggressive behaviour, it is wise to minimize these by careful control procedures.

The observational procedure to be used is a type of event sampling, in which the time period during which observations are to be made is divided into intervals, for example 10- or 15- second intervals. If a scorable behaviour (that is, a display of physical or verbal aggression) occurs during this period, it is recorded: the presence or absence of the behaviour is the only aspect recorded, not the number of times it occurs. Thus, if during a 15-second period the behaviour occurs six times, it is entered in the score sheet only once. Therefore, the number of times the behaviour occurs in each time period is irrelevant. It is only the presence or absence of the behaviour which is important. The time period for observing each child in the class will depend on a number of constraints, most notably the time that investigators are allowed for the study. It is suggested that each child is observed for a five-minute period, so that there are twenty 15-second time periods in each observational period, and as each behaviour can be recorded once in each period, there will be a maximum score of 20 per item for each five-minute period. If circumstances allow, and further visits are possible, then a number of five-minute observations can be made of each child. How many will depend on the circumstances of the visit, and the co-operation of the school.

Results

When all the observations have been completed, the data can be combined from all participants and presented in a data summary

Table 1. Number of 15-second periods in which behaviour occurred, expressed as mean per child over ? × 5 minute samples

Behaviour category	Boys (n =)	Girls (n =)
Displays physical aggression (total)		
Displays verbal aggression (total)		
Total aggressive acts:		

table. Each child will yield a number of scores for each five-minute observational period. The mean of these can then be taken to give an average total for each child. For example, if a child is observed over three five-minute periods, their maximum possible verbal aggression score is 60 (comprised of twenty 15-second periods multiplied by three). If the child scored 14 for verbal aggression in the first five-minute period, 7 in the second, and 12 in the third, their total verbal aggression score would be 33, and their mean verbal aggression score 11. This can then be added to scores from the other children used in the study and presented as in *Table 1*.

If there is a large difference in the number of boys and girls used in the study, the figures can be converted into percentages of the maximum score possible for a more meaningful comparison.

These results can also be presented in the form of simple bar charts, so that visual analysis can take place. Does there appear to be any gender difference in the overall incidence of aggression? Is there any gender difference in the incidence of physical aggression or in the incidence of verbal aggression? Which gender appears the more aggressive for each of these types of aggressive behaviour?

In order to test whether there is a significant difference between the genders for the three conditions (total aggressive acts, physically aggressive behaviour, verbally aggressive behaviour), it is necessary to carry out statistical tests. As each child will yield a total score for aggressive behaviour under each condition (all aggressive behaviours, physical aggression, verbal aggression), we can compare the scores of each gender by examining the rank positions of males and females by using Mann–Whitney U tests. These convert the data into a rank order, effectively ordinal data, thus enabling comparisons to be made between the genders for each prediction. Remember also that the participants are only very roughly matched in terms of age and, perhaps, socioeconomic background, so an independent design test has been used. If we had been more strenuous in our matching efforts, we might have used the Wilcoxon test instead. The first hypothesis is two-tailed, and the latter two are one-tailed, and this should be taken into consideration when using statistical tables to interpret the results of each test.

Discussion

The outcome of the statistical tests will determine whether the null hypotheses are to be retained or rejected for each of the investigative

117

hypotheses. It will be possible, then, to compare the results with those of Archer and Westeman (1981), and Maccoby and Jacklin (1974).

The nature of this type of research raises a number of questions relating to methodology. Could these differences between the genders be a reflection of consistent patterns of aggression within the genders, or alternatively, might they be due to a few individuals behaving aggressively? Individual differences within the genders could be a very important factor.

Most studies in this area have concentrated on measuring physical aggression, the demonstration of which is fairly obvious even to the casual observer. Observing verbal aggression is a far trickier exercise, given its often more subtle form. What sort of problems might be encountered in the measurement of verbal aggression, and how might an investigator attempt to overcome them? It is possible that previous studies which found higher overall levels of aggressive behavior in males (for example, Blurton-Jones, 1972), may not have made distinctions between physical and verbal aggression. Indeed, Smith and Green (1975) combined both aspects in their operational definition of 'aggressive behaviour'.

If pupils from more than one school are observed, there is the possibility of variables being confounded by background and situation, or by the constraints placed by individual teachers. Aggressive behaviour, as acknowledged by Archer and Westeman (1981) is often situation-specific, and its expression within a particular situation may have a developmental history which is unknown to the observer.

As in every observational study, there is the possibility of participant reactivity, in that children may react to the presence of the observer by responding either in a more inhibited or more exhibitionist manner. To overcome such problems is a skill in itself, so consideration should be given to how this study might have been improved in that respect, and how future studies in the area might be carried out more successfully.

It may well be the case that no significant gender differences are found in either the total scores for aggressive behaviour, or in the specific types of physical and verbally aggressive behaviour. Might this be a true reflection of the non-existence of gender differences in this area, or might there be another explanation for the findings? If significant gender differences are found, can these successfully be attributed to higher levels of aggression in one or other of the genders, or might their manifestation be more appropriately attributed to some other factor?

This research might be usefully extended in many different ways, to take account of such factors as intra- and intersexual aggression and age differences in aggressive behaviour. It is possible, as suggested by Archer and Westeman (1981), that most aggressive interactions are intrasexual, simply because children spend more time interacting with their own gender, and that boys are not, as might be thought, particularly reluctant to behave aggressively to girls. What are the implications of research such as this? Does it serve any useful educational purpose, such as in the area of classroom management?

Bibliography

General background references

BEE, H. (1989) *The Developing Child*. 6th edn. New York: Harper and Row.
MUSSEN, P.H., CONGER J.J., KAGAN, J. and HUSTON A.C. (1990) *Child Development and Personality*. New York: Harper and Row.

Specific references

BARDWICK, J.M. (1971) *Psychology of Women*. New York: Harper and Row.
BLURTON-JONES, N.G. (1972) Categories of child–child interaction. In N. Blurton-Jones (Ed.) *Ethological studies of Child Behaviour*. London: Cambridge University Press.
BLURTON-JONES, N.G. and KONNER, M.J. (1973) Sex differences in the behaviour of London and Bushman children. In R.P. Michael and J.H. Crook (Eds) *Comparative Ecology and Behaviour of Primates*. London and New York: Academic Press.
FAGOT, B.I. and HAGAN, R. (1982) *Hitting in toddler groups, correlates and continuity*. Paper presented at the annual meeting of the American Psychological Association, Washington, D.C.
MACCOBY, E.E. and JACKLIN, C.N. (1974) *The Psychology of Sex Differences*. Stanford, California: Stanford University Press.
PARKE, R.D. and SLABY, R.G. (1983) The development of aggression. In E.M. Hetherington (Ed.) *Handbook of child psychology; Socialization, personality and social development*. Vol. 4. New York: Wiley.

Journal articles

ARCHER, J. and WESTEMAN, K. (1981) Sex differences in the aggressive behaviour of schoolchildren. *British Journal of Social Psychology, 20*, 31–36.
ERON, L.D. (1982) Parent–Child interaction, television violence and aggression in children. *American Psychologist, 37*, 197–211.
MACCOBY, E.E. and JACKLIN, C.N. (1980) Sex differences in aggression. A rejoinder and reprise. *Child Development, 51*, 964–980.
OLWEUS, D. (1980) Familial and temperamental determinants of aggressive behaviour in adolescent boys: A causal analysis. *Developmental Psychology, 16*, 644–666.
SMITH, P.K. and GREEN, M. (1975) Aggressive behaviour in English nurseries and play groups: Sex differences and responses of adults. *Child Development, 46*, 211–214.
WHITING, B. and EDWARDS, C.P. (1973) Cross-cultural analysis of sex differences in the behaviour of children aged 3 through 11. *Journal of Social Psychology, 91*, 171–188.

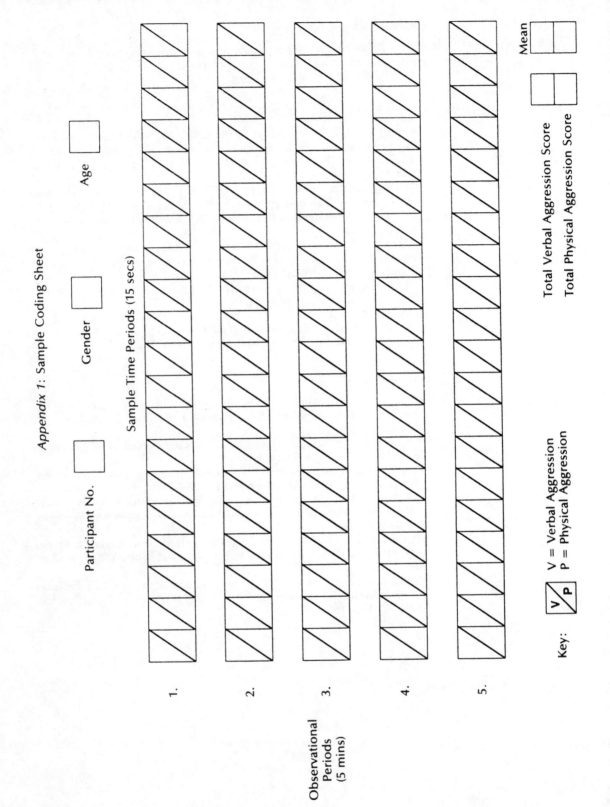

Appendix 1: Sample Coding Sheet

Participant No. ☐   Gender ☐   Age ☐

Sample Time Periods (15 secs)

1.

2.

Observational
Periods
(5 mins)   3.

4.

5.

Key: ☐V/P☐   V = Verbal Aggression
              P = Physical Aggression

Total Verbal Aggression Score ☐☐
Total Physical Aggression Score ☐☐   Mean ☐☐

PREFACE TO THE CORRELATIONAL METHOD

Paul Humphreys
Worcester College of Higher Education

It is important to recognize that correlation is not a research method in the sense that observation and experimentation are research methods. Whilst the experimental and observational methods generate data, the correlational method does not; it is a way of treating or analysing data which have been gathered by other means. However, this is not to say that data cannot be specifically gathered for the purpose of a correlational investigation. Laboratory studies, time-sampling observations and psychometric tests are all ways of gathering data for a correlational study. The practical exercises in this section use a variety of methods to generate data which can then be analysed using the correlational techniques outlined below.

The relationship between two variables

Given what has been said above, it could be argued that the correlational method is inferior to the observational and experimental methods. This argument is, however, fallacious, since the correlational method is both an invaluable and widely used method of investigation. Part of its appeal lies in the fact that it can be used to analyse data generated by other means. Its main appeal however, is that instead of being a simply descriptive method (like many observational studies) or a method seeking to determine whether two or more groups of participants differ in some way (as with the experimental method), the correlational study aims to summarize the relationship between two or more naturally occurring, non-manipulated and measurable variables.

In order to conduct a correlational analysis, paired measurements are required. In some cases, individual participants can provide these. Suppose, for example, that a researcher wished to determine the relationship between children's ability at English and their ability at Maths. The data for each child could be provided in the form of a score, rank or category indicating their ability in the two subjects, thus providing paired measurements. In other cases, *logical pairs* are used for correlational analysis with each pair providing a score, rank or category. For example, a researcher may be interested in assessing the relationship between the intelligence levels of monozygotic twins. Here, both twins would provide an I.Q. test score that would form a logical pair, and, along with pairs of scores provided by other monozygotic twins, could be used to assess the relationship.

To illustrate further the utility of the correlational method, let us return to the example concerning the relationship between children's ability at English and their ability at Maths. The commonly held belief is that these are 'ability opposites', so that children who are good at one almost invariably tend to be poor at the other. In order to examine the relationship between English ability and Maths ability, data could be gathered from teachers' records of performance (providing that ethical guidelines were adhered to), or arrangements could be made for tests in English and Maths to be carried out on a class (or classes) of children.

Independent and dependent variables

As has been noted, the aim of the correlational method in this example is to determine whether any relationship exists between two sets of scores (or 'variables'). In other methods of investigation it is important to make a distinction between independent and dependent variables. With the correlational method, however, this distinction loses its usefulness: a correlational analysis can examine the relationship between two dependent variables (or measures of behaviour) or between an independent and a dependent variable. In some cases, each participant will provide two scores, whilst in other cases a single score will be provided by each member of a logical pair. The correlational method does not require the distinction between an independent and dependent variable to be made.

A perfect positive correlation

To illustrate the correlational method in action, we shall return to the example of the relationship between children's ability at English and Maths. For the sake of simplicity, it will be assumed that a class of ten children have each been ranked according to their ability at English and Maths such that in each case a rank of 1 indicates the best performance and a rank of 10 the worst. For each pupil, A–J, their respective ranks are as illustrated in *Table 1*.

Table 1. Hypothetical data obtained in a correlational study

STUDENT	ENGLISH SCORE (rank)	MATHS SCORE (rank)
A	1	1
B	2	2
C	3	3
D	4	4
E	5	5
F	6	6
G	7	7
H	8	8
I	9	9
J	10	10

Note that it would be extremely unlikely to actually obtain the data presented in the *Table*. Notwithstanding this caution, they demonstrate a very clear kind of relationship between the two sets of rankings. Thus the child who is ranked top in English is also ranked top in

Maths, the child who is ranked second in English is also ranked second in Maths, and so on, all the way down to the child ranked bottom in English who is also ranked bottom in Maths. In this (admittedly artificial) case the scores on one variable are exactly related to the scores on the other. In those circumstances when a rise or fall in the value of one characteristic is associated with a corresponding rise or fall in the other, the correlation between them is said to be *direct* or, more commonly, *positive*. When the rise or fall on the two variables are exactly related, the correlation is said to be *perfect*. The correlation between the two variables in this example can therefore be described as *positive* and *perfect*.

A perfect negative correlation

Suppose, however, that a class of children ranked according to their ability at English and Maths produced the data illustrated in *Table 2*. In this case, the opposite of the first example can be observed. Now, the child who is ranked top in English is ranked bottom in Maths and vice versa. This relationship is just as strong as that in the first example but now the variables are related in what is called an *inverse* or, more commonly, *negative* manner. In those circumstances where a rise in one variable is accompanied by an *exact* corresponding fall in the other, the correlation is said to be *negative* and *perfect*.

Table 2. Hypothetical data obtained in a correlational study

STUDENT	ENGLISH SCORE (rank)	MATHS SCORE (rank)
A	1	10
B	2	9
C	3	8
D	4	7
E	5	6
F	6	5
G	7	4
H	8	3
I	9	2
J	10	1

No correlation

A third extreme possibility is illustrated in *Table 3*. In this case, there appears to be no systematic relationship at all between a child's ability at English and his or her ability at Maths. Thus, some children who are ranked highly for English are also ranked highly for Maths, whilst others ranked highly for English have a medium or low rank for Maths.

Scattergrams

One way to illustrate the strength of a relationship between two variables is pictorially, in the form of a scattergram. In constructing a

Table 3. Hypothetical data obtained in a correlational study

STUDENT	ENGLISH SCORE (rank)	MATHS SCORE (rank)
A	1	10
B	6	9
C	2	2
D	4	1
E	3	6
F	5	5
G	7	8
H	8	3
I	9	4
J	10	7

scattergram, the data obtained for one variable are plotted against the corresponding data for the other variable. Consider, for example, the model data presented in *Table 3*. Ability at English (in terms of rank order) can be plotted on the *x*, or horizontal, axis and ability at Maths (in terms of rank order) can be plotted on the *y*, or vertical, axis. Child A can be represented by placing an 'x' where a line drawn vertically from point 1 on the *x-axis* intersects with a line drawn horizontally from point 10 on the *y-axis*. Child B can be represented by placing an 'x' where points 6 and 9 intersect and so on until all the children are represented on the scattergram. In the case of this example, where it was suggested that there was no systematic relationship between the two variables, the completed scattergram looks like that in *Figure 1*.

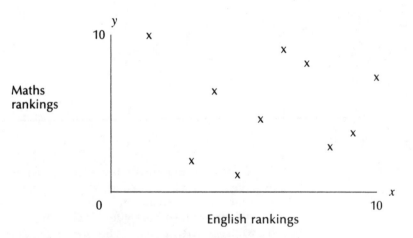

Figure 1. Scattergram of near-zero correlation.

A perfect and positive correlation, however, produces a scattergram which looks like that in *Figure 2*. A perfect and negative correlation produces a scattergram like that in *Figure 3*.

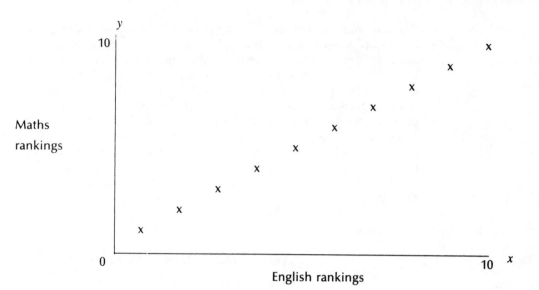

Figure 2. Scattergram of perfect positive correlation.

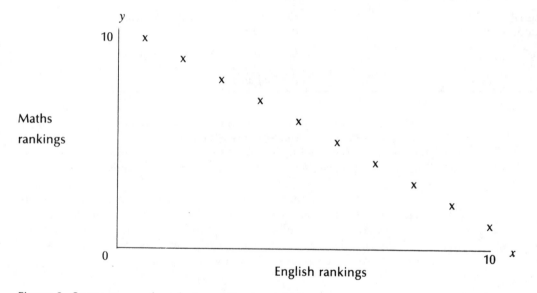

Figure 3. Scattergram of perfect negative correlation.

A range of correlational techniques

Scattergrams offer one way of illustrating the strength of a correlation between two variables. However, a more convenient way to describe the strength of a relationship is numerically, using what is called a *correlation coefficient*. There are a number of techniques for determining a correlation coefficient for a given set of paired measurements. The most commonly employed methods are those devised by

Pearson and Spearman. Pearson's product-moment correlational method is employed with interval/ratio level data. As its name suggests, Spearman's rank order method is employed with ordinal level data. All of the practical exercises presented in this section use either Pearson's or Spearman's method, and descriptions of the computational procedures involved in these tests can be found in most statistical textbooks (for example, Coolican, 1990; Heyes *et al.*, 1986; Miller, 1984).

The methods devised by Pearson and Spearman are not, as has been noted, the only correlational techniques available. *Table 4* lists some other correlational techniques together with the level of measurement they are suited to.

Table 4. Some correlational techniques

TEST NAME	LEVEL OF MEASUREMENT OF VARIABLES
Contingency Coefficient (C)	Both variables *categorical*
Kendall's 'tau'	Both variables *ordinal*
Goodman and Kruskal's 'gamma'	Both variables *ordinal*
Multi-serial Correlation Coefficient	One variable *interval/ratio* and one *ordinal*
Eta	One variable *interval/ratio* and one *categorical* or one variable *ordinal* and one *categorical*

Despite the numerous correlational techniques available, it should be noted that Pearson's and Spearman's techniques are not only the most commonly employed techniques but are also amongst the most computationally straightforward. Both methods produce a correlation coefficient which varies between -1 and $+1$. The mathematical sign ($-$ or $+$) which appears in front of the correlation coefficient indicates the *direction* of the relationship. A '+' sign indicates a direct or positive correlation whilst a '−' sign indicates an inverse or negative correlation. The value of the correlation coefficient indicates the *strength* of the correlation as shown in Figure 4.

```
    −1.0            −0.5            0            +0.5           +1.0
 PERFECT      ------------------------NONE-----------------------PERFECT
 NEGATIVE                                                        POSITIVE
```

Figure 4. Relationship between value of correlation coefficient and strength of correlation.

Prediction

Many students have difficulty in appreciating that a correlation coefficient of -0.9, say, is just as strong as a correlation of $+0.9$. One way to illustrate their similarity is to consider the issue of *predictability*.

The correlation coefficient for the data presented in *Table 1* is, as calculated by Spearman's method, +1.0. Imagine that, for some reason, the data relating to the pupils' ability at English has been mislaid and only the data relating to their ability at Maths remains. For the purposes of writing a report a teacher asks you how well a given child has performed at English. Suppose the child in question is child C. Given that child C was ranked third in Maths, and given that the correlation coefficient for the relationship between English and Maths is +1.0, you could predict (with complete accuracy in this case, since the correlation is perfect) that the child also came third in English.

In the case of *Table 2* which, by Spearman's method produces a correlation coefficient of −1.0, a child who was third from the top in English could confidently be predicted to be third from bottom in Maths since this correlation is a perfect one, albeit negative. However, in the case of *Table 3* where the correlation coefficient is almost 0 (in fact it is −0.02), it would be impossible to predict a child's performance in one subject from a knowledge of his or her performance in the other subject.

This indicates a very important link between correlation and prediction. The stronger the correlation between two variables, the greater the accuracy when we want to predict performance on one variable from a knowledge of performance on the other, irrespective of whether the relationship is positive or negative. Some examples drawn from actual research will serve to illustrate this point further. Sainsbury and Barraclough (1968) correlated the suicide rates of foreign-born US residents with the suicide rates of their countries of birth. The correlation coefficient obtained was +0.87. Thus, given a number of individuals born in different countries, we would be able to predict, with a high degree of certainty, which of them would be most likely to commit suicide.

In a different vein, Wankowski (1973) has reported that the correlation between success at A-level (as measured in terms of grade points) and success at degree level (as measured by degree class) is only +0.37. With such a low correlation coefficient we would not be able to predict with much confidence how well a student would do at degree level given that we knew how well he or she had performed at A-level.

Coefficient of determination

By squaring the correlation coefficient, the *coefficient of determination* is obtained. In the case of the correlation coefficient reported by Sainsbury and Barraclough (1968), the coefficient of determination is +0.76. The coefficient of determination tells us that knowledge of one variable allows us to predict the other variable in such a way that we can account for 76% of the total variance in the two variables. However, the correlation reported by Wankowski (1973) yields a coefficient of determination of only +0.14, indicating that knowledge of one variable allows us to predict the other variable in such a way that we can account for only 14% of the total variance in the two variables.

Statistical significance

Although a correlation coefficient indicates the strength of the relationship between two variables, it says nothing about the statistical significance of a relationship. In the *Preface to the Experimental Method*, the concept of statistical significance was introduced. The point was made that, in the behavioural sciences, we can never deal with absolutes or certainties, only probabilities. In an experiment, for example, we can never be absolutely certain that an independent variable has caused a change in a dependent variable since there is always the possibility that chance factors have operated to produce an apparent effect. Tests of statistical significance provide us with an indication of the likelihood of an effect being due to the operation of chance factors. If the result of a test indicates that the probability of an effect being due to chance is less than 5%, then by convention we conclude that the independent variable probably did affect the dependent variable, and the effect is therefore said to be statistically significant.

The same rationale applies to correlational investigations. A correlation coefficient is a descriptive measure of the strength of a relationship between two variables, and does not indicate whether the relationship is statistically significant. In testing for the statistical significance of a correlation, it is usually assumed initially that there is no correlation at all between the variables in question. Using published statistical tables appropriate to the test conducted, the probability of obtaining by chance a correlation of the size obtained is determined. If the probability is less than 5%, the null hypothesis of no correlation is rejected, and we conclude that the relationship is unlikely to be due to the operation of chance factors.

It should be emphasized that an inferential test for the significance of a correlation makes no comment on the strength of a relationship. Strength is indicated by the correlation coefficient. Thus, two variables such as A-level performance and degree level performance may be weakly related (recall that the correlation coefficient reported by Wankowski was only +0.37), but this relationship may be statistically significant. In other words, although the correlation between the two variables is weak it is unlikely to be due to the operation of chance factors alone. Although its weakness indicates that one variable is not a particularly good predictor of the other, it is better than chance alone.

Factors influencing statistical significance

Four factors, other than the size of the coefficient itself, influence the significance of a relationship:

1. The number of pairs of scores. This factor is important because small numbers of pairs can produce 'fluke' outcomes. For example, if only three children were studied, it is likely that there would be an apparently strong relationship between English and Maths scores, but one which was actually due to chance factors operating. If a very large number of children had been studied, it would be most unlikely that chance alone would produce a high correlation coefficient.

2. The significance level that has been selected. A 1% significance level will be much more demanding than a 5% significance level.

3. Whether a one-tailed or a two-tailed hypothesis is being tested.

4. The correlational test used. Parametric tests (such as Pearson's product-moment method) are more sensitive than non-parametric tests (such as Spearman's rank order method). This is indicated by the relevant tables for the tests. Thus, non-parametric tests require slightly higher correlation coefficients for a given number of observations than do parametric tests before statistical significance can be claimed.

A significant correlation does not imply causality

It is important to emphasize that a significant correlation does *not* indicate that changes in one variable are responsible for, or the cause of changes in the other. Yudkin (1957), for example, reported the existence of a strong positive correlation between the number of TV licences purchased between 1930 and 1956 and the number of deaths due to coronary artery disease during the same period. However, on the basis of this it would be ridiculous to suggest that deaths from heart attacks caused other people (perhaps relatives) to go and purchase a TV licence. In this case, the variables may be strongly correlated but the relationship between them is purely *accidental* or spurious.

Another example of the fallacy of assuming that the correlation between two variables indicates that one of them is *causally* affecting the other is the significant relationship between smoking and lung cancer. The significant correlation has been suggested as 'proof' that smoking causes lung cancer. However, on the basis of the correlation alone it would be just as legitimate (or illegitimate) to conclude that lung cancer causes people to smoke. It could be, as some would argue, that the relationship between smoking and lung cancer is spurious and caused by some other, as yet unknown, variable. For example, an unusual personality type might predispose a person to both smoke and develop lung cancer. Nonetheless, the relationship between smoking and lung cancer does exist; non-smokers are less likely to develop lung cancer.

At best, then, a significant correlation suggests that it might be useful to design a study to examine the possible causal relationship between the two variables. In the case of the smoking–lung cancer relationship, the existence of a causal link could only be confirmed through a study of cause and effect; that is, an experiment. Such an experiment has not been performed on humans, but it has been reported that there is a causal link between the two variables in dogs. Dogs, however, are not human beings and hence any generalization is dangerous. The inclusion of this example, however, is merely to illustrate a point, and should not be taken in any way as an endorsement of smoking.

Non-linear relationships

A few final points concerning the correlational method should be made. First, the most commonly used tests of the strength of a relationship can be employed only when the relationship is *linear* (that is, when the data are related in a straight-line fashion). However, it is possible for two variables to be related in a non-linear manner. For instance, if we were to measure the relationship between the number of people in a group and the group's efficiency in solving problems, a curvilinear relationship would probably be obtained. Initially, adding members to a very small group would add to its efficiency as each new member contributed solutions to the problems (a case of 'many hands make light work'). After a certain point, however, adding new members would not increase the group's efficiency and adding yet more members would decrease efficiency due to communication difficulties (a case of 'too many cooks spoil the broth'). *Figure 5* illustrates such a relationship.

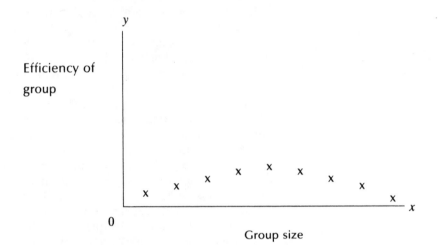

Figure 5. Scattergram of a curvilinear relationship.

Note the strength of the relationship, illustrated by the orderliness of the pattern of 'x's. The strength of the relationship is best illustrated by considering the predictability of one variable by a knowledge of the other. If it was known how many members were in the group, an accurate prediction of the group's efficiency in solving problems could be given. However, if the correlation coefficient for this relationship was calculated using, say, Spearman or Pearson's method, a value of approximately 0 would be obtained. At first sight this does not make sense, since it was argued earlier that a correlation coefficient of around 0 does not allow any sort of accurate prediction to be made.

The reason for this apparent anomaly is that Spearman's and Pearson's methods are only appropriate when the relationship in question is linear. The first part of a curvilinear relationship would produce a very high positive correlation and the second part would produce a very high negative correlation. The net effect of this would be that the two high correlations would cancel each other out giving a value of around 0! There are a variety of sophisticated methods that allow the correlation coefficient for a curvilinear relationship to be computed, but they are beyond the scope of this *Manual*. Nonetheless,

130

the possibility of curvilinear correlations between variables should always be borne in mind.

Multiple correlation

A second point concerns the emphasis that has been placed throughout this *Preface* on the idea that the correlational method examines the relationship between two variables. In some cases, however, a researcher may be interested in the relationship between three or more variables. In this case, a *multiple correlational analysis* is necessary. Alternatively, a researcher may be interested in the relationship between two variables when the effect of a third variable related to them both is controlled for. In this case a *partial correlational technique* is called for.

There are techniques for assessing partial and multiple correlations but, as with curvilinear relationships, they are beyond the scope of this book. However, Long's exercise (*The Basis of People's Fear of Animals*) in this section does introduce the concept of partial correlation in a simple and concise way and suggests an appropriate source for those interested in discovering more about partial and multiple correlational techniques.

Summary

I began by pointing out that strictly speaking the correlation is not a 'method' as it does not generate data; rather it is a technique for data analysis. Data may be gathered (by data generating methods such as observation, surveys and psychometric tests) specifically for analysis, or archival data may be used. Whichever particular test of correlation is used, the analysis measures the relationship between pairs of scores. Relationships may be direct/positive (whereby high scores on one variable are associated with high scores on the second variable), or inverse/negative (whereby high scores on one variable are associated with low scores on the other). The correlation coefficient is a score between 0 (indicating no relationship whatsoever) and 1 (indicating a perfect relationship). A '+' (plus) coefficient indicates a direct relationship, while a '−' (minus) coefficient indicates an inverse relationship. The measures of correlation I have dealt with in this *Preface* measure only linear (that is, straight-line) relationships, but there are other more sophisticated tests which measure non-linear relationships. A visual indication of the strength of a relationship (linear or non-linear) may be gained by plotting a scattergram which shows the intersection points of the pairs of scores.

Correlation coefficients are descriptive measures of the strength of relationship between two variables, but they can be translated into an inferential measure by consulting an appropriate statistical significance table. This will tell the researcher whether it is probable that the relationship is a genuine one (either strong or weak), or whether it is likely to have been due to chance.

One of the major advantages of the correlation is that it can enable us to predict one variable simply from knowledge of the other. The stronger the coefficient is (that is, the closer it is to 1), the greater will be the predictive accuracy of the 'unknown' variable.

References

COOLICAN, H. (1990) *Research Methods and Statistics in Psychology*. London: Hodder and Stoughton.

HEYES, S., HARDY, M., HUMPHREYS, P., and ROOKES, P. (1986) *Starting Statistics in Psychology and Education*. London: Weidenfeld and Nicolson.

MILLER, S. (1984) *Experimental Design and Statistics*. London: Methuen.

SAINSBURY, P. and BARRACLOUGH, B. (1968) Differences between suicide rates. *Nature, 220*, 1252.

WANKOWSKI, J.A. (1973) *Temperament, Motivation and Academic Achievement*. Birmingham: University of Birmingham.

YUDKIN, J. (1957) Diet and Coronary Thrombosis: Hypothesis and Fact. *The Lancet, 273(II)*, 155–162.

The basis of people's fear of animals

Martyn Long
Norfolk College of Arts and Technology

Abstract

Understanding the reasons why some people are afraid of certain types of animal has long been of interest to clinical psychologists. Several explanations have been proposed for the basis of this fear. One view proposes that humans have an innate 'preparedness' to perceive and learn from certain animal characteristics. An alternative approach suggests that humans learn whether animals may be harmful. This could be the result of direct experience, socialization, and the degree to which the animal differs from those already known.

This practical exercise is based upon issues in learning theory and the genesis and treatment of common animal phobias. It investigates whether it is the perceived harmfulness of animals or their appearance which is the strongest factor relating to fear of them. The adequacy of competing theoretical perspectives is discussed together with the implications of the data for the treatment of animal phobias. Some methodological issues relating to the exercise are also considered.

Materials and Equipment

The only materials needed for this exercise are three separate questionnaires on which participants are asked to rate the ugliness, the harmfulness and their own fear of 29 animals and insects. The questionnaires can be found in the Appendix and a sufficient number of these should be photocopied in advance.

A total of 30 participants should complete all three questionnaires, taking a total of five minutes for each participant. The exercise could be conducted by a single investigator or, if carried out in class, students could administer the questionnaires to a smaller number of participants and then pool the data for subsequent analysis. If the latter approach is adopted, the whole exercise, including analysis of the data, could be completed within two hours.

Introduction and Hypotheses

In an original study, Bennett-Levy and Marteau (1984) demonstrated that people's fear of a range of small animals was strongly correlated with the animals' appearance. In particular, the amount of fear expressed related to the extent of the animals' difference from the human form, such as skin texture or number of limbs. These findings are important since they appear to confirm that there may be a readiness to learn fear, which Seligman (1971) has termed 'preparedness', and that it is species-specific, implying a possible genetic basis for conditioning.

Bennett-Levy and Marteau's study has implications for the treatment of classical animal phobias: phobias of animals whose forms differ greatly from that of the human form should be more easily developed and more difficult to treat. The researchers propose that animal phobias may best be approached by first tackling key differences such as sliminess. In this case, Bennett-Levy and Marteau suggest that treatment could start with the presentation of wet soap or porridge to desensitize the phobic. Once this had been achieved, therapy would continue using gradual presentation (either imaginary or *in vivo*) of the animal.

A brief review of the background literature on the subject of the development and treatment of animal phobias is presented in Bennett-Levy and Marteau's (1984) article. Gross (1987), Roth (1990) and Atkinson *et al.* (1990) all give good coverage of the basic ideas behind learning theory, and its subsequent modifications to take account of species-specific behaviours such as 'preparedness'. They also cover the more recent integrated cognitive approaches. These approaches propose that what we learn is an expectation of the association between the conditioned stimulus and unconditioned stimulus (in classical conditioning) and between the response and its outcome (in operant conditioning), rather than a simple stimulus–response strengthening. These authors also cover theoretical approaches to the basis of phobias, and the treatment of phobias by behavioural techniques. Gross, in particular, relates the treatment of phobias to developments in learning theory, placing them in context and using the study conducted by Bennett-Levy and Marteau.

In their research, Bennett-Levy and Marteau tried but failed to control for the perceived harmfulness of the animals they used as their stimulus material. The researchers acknowledged this shortcoming and noted from informal questioning of participants that the most feared animal (the rat) was in fact also seen as potentially harmful. A close inspection of the data reported by Bennett-Levy and Marteau also shows that certain animals with forms most discrepant from the human form (such as the slug, which was rated highest for ugliness) had fear ratings which were below the median.

This finding might be accounted for in terms of other perceived characteristics such as how slowly or quickly the animal moved, since Bennett-Levy and Marteau found that in general, the faster moving animals were more likely to feared. An alternative explanation, however, is that fear of a particular animal is generated primarily by its perceived harmfulness. This may itself be the result of knowledge and/or experience of the animal as well as its general 'strangeness'. In this sense, strangeness means the extent to which the animal differs from the general form of animals we are familiar with (and not just how different it is from the human form).

This explanation suggests that fear of unusual animals would increase with cognitive development; that is, with the initial establishment of the common categories of animal features. For example, as young children become familiar with four-legged animals, such as dogs and cows, they will see animals with more or fewer legs, such as spiders and snakes, as being strange. Fear would then decrease when knowledge and experience were extended to the less common forms. This might account for the peak and subsequent decline of various phobias which have been demonstrated at specific ages (Agras *et al.*, 1969).

Bennett-Levy and Marteau also found that although men and women were similar in their perceptions of the features of animals (namely 'ugliness', 'sliminess', 'speediness' and 'suddenness of move-ment'), women were significantly more fearful of ten particular animals than men were. These included jellyfish, cockroaches, ants and moths. Although a sex-linked genetic basis for this could be proposed, a simpler explanation could lie in different socialization processes for the development and expression of fear of animals in males and females.

If it is possible to show that an adult is more prepared to develop fear of certain types of animals, then this could be explained by either an inherited or a learnt perspective. The inherited perspective would propose that people are genetically predisposed to fear certain animals due to our evolutionary history; the learnt perspective would propose that people learn what the normal forms of animals are, and are therefore prepared to fear unusual forms. Bennett-Levy and Marteau see their own data as specifying the mechanism of innate tendencies as proposed by Seligman (1971).

A direct investigation of the involvement of perceived harmfulness could throw light on the relevance of these alternative approaches. If perceived harmfulness correlates more strongly with fear than any other factor, this would be consistent with it being the principal factor causing fearfulness. This would support the experiential approach, assuming that it is unlikely that harmfulness could be genetically encoded for every possible animal. If perceived strangeness also correlates strongly with perceived harmfulness, then this too would be consistent with the experiential model. Finally, if the effects of perceived harmfulness could be removed, the approach outlined above would suggest that the relationship between fear and strangeness would still exist, but at a much reduced level.

Hypotheses

The present exercise aims to test the following three hypotheses:

1. There is a significant positive correlation between perceived fear and the perceived harmfulness of a range of animals and insects.

2. There is a significant positive correlation between perceived harmfulness and perceived strangeness of a range of animals and insects.

3. There is a significant positive correlation between perceived fear and strangeness of a range of animals and insects, even when the effects of perceived harmfulness have been controlled for.

For each of these one-tailed hypotheses, the null hypothesis predicts that there will not be any significant correlation between the factors studied, and that any relationship observed will be due to the operation of chance factors.

Procedure

In this practical exercise, three variables will be investigated for a range of animals and insects: perceived fear, perceived harmfulness, and perceived strangeness. All three variables will be assessed by having participants rate 29 animals and insects on simple three-point scales. On the first two scales participants will be required to indicate how afraid they are of each of the 29 animals and insects and how harmful they think each of them is. In order to draw comparisons with the original study of Bennett-Levy and Marteau, perceived strangeness will be assessed by having participants rate how 'ugly' they find certain animals.

In the original investigation by Bennett-Levy and Marteau, two separate groups of participants were used to provide ratings. The first group rated animals and insects for four perceived characteristics: ugliness, sliminess, speediness, and suddenness of movement. The second group rated the animals according to how afraid they were of them and how near they would go to them. The purpose of this design was, presumably, to ensure that one group of ratings was relatively independent of the other.

To repeat Bennett-Levy and Marteau's design in this exercise would require three separate groups of participants, but this may be difficult. An alternative design is suggested, therefore, which involves one group of participants rating all three variables. This automatically removes any difficulty of non-matching groups, but it does raise problems of order effects. The most likely problem with this technique is that once a participant has rated an animal on one variable, this decision might directly generalize to ratings on the other two variables. For example, if a participant first rates a rat according to how afraid of it he or she is, the negative set generated in the participant's mind might then lead them to rate the perceived harmfulness (or strangeness) of the rat higher than if the harmfulness (or strangeness) variable had come first. In order to overcome this, ratings of the variables for each animal and insect should be separated as far as possible by having participants complete the ratings for each variable in turn.

If participants complete the three questionnaires in the same order, there is still the danger that completion of the first questionnaire will have an effect on the completion of the others. Participants may remember specific items and be biased by them (as in the example), or be influenced by practice or fatigue effects. To counterbalance and cancel these effects, questionnaires should be administered in all possible orders of presentation. With three questionnaires there are six possible orders of presentation, and these are shown in *Table 1*.

As *Table 1* illustrates, complete counterbalancing will only be achieved if the total number of participants is a multiple of six. In their original study, Bennett-Levy and Marteau used a very large number of participants. The purpose of this was to obtain stable differences in the average ratings of the different animals and insects

Table 1. Possible orders of presentation for the three questionnaires

Participant no.	ORDER OF PRESENTATION		
	First	Second	Third
1	Strangeness	Harmfulness	Fear
2	Strangeness	Fear	Harmfulness
3	Harmfulness	Strangeness	Fear
4	Harmfulness	Fear	Strangeness
5	Fear	Strangeness	Harmfulness
6	Fear	Harmfulness	Strangeness

since, as is the case in this exercise, the raw data were collected using a relatively insensitive three-point scale. In the present exercise it is suggested that 30 participants should give the necessary stability to the means. Investigators can, of course, increase the number of participants to ensure that the ratings are more reliable, but it should be remembered that the total number of participants must be a multiple of six in order to ensure complete counterbalancing.

Note that the order of presentation of the animals and insects to be rated could also be randomized on each occasion, but this may seem excessively cumbersome. However, the lists presented in the *Appendix* have been randomized for the main variable of fear as found in Bennett-Levy and Marteau's study. This will reduce any simple bias from this, or other factors, as an order effect.

Investigators should introduce the topic to each participant in a way which will reassure them about what they are expected to do. The following instructions, which should minimize any bias effects, are suggested:

> Thank you for helping me. This is an investigation into how people perceive a range of small animals and insects. I would like you to complete three separate questionnaires. The questionnaires have the same animals and insects on them, but different characteristics to rate them for. You can complete the questionnaires in your own time and should simply note down what you feel. The results will be kept confidential as I will be using a code for identification rather than your name.

> After participants have completed the questionnaires, they should be debriefed as to the purpose of the investigation. In particular, they should be informed that animal phobias are relatively common. If participants express any concern over their pattern of responses, this should be discussed with them. Investigators should consider what course of action they would take if a participant showed an unusually high level of fear ratings for the animals and insects on the questionnaires.

Results

The initial analysis of the data involves computing the mean values provided by the participants for each of the 29 animals and insects on the fear, harmfulness and strangeness variables. Once the mean values have been computed they should be ranked from highest to lowest on each variable. The ranked data could be summarized as illustrated in *Table 2*.

Table 2. Suggested method of summarizing the ranked mean values generated by the exercise

Stimulus	Ranking of Strangeness	Ranking of Harmfulness	Ranking of Fear
JELLYFISH			
SQUIRREL			
ANT			
↓			
COCKROACH			

In order to examine the hypothesis that there will be a significant positive correlation between the perceived fear and harmfulness of a range of animals and insects, a scattergram should be drawn. Since this exercise examines changes in perceived characteristics, using a range of fear-provoking animals and insects, fear can be taken as the independent variable and should therefore be plotted on the x-axis. The data generated are almost certainly not normally distributed since most animals are not feared. Additionally, it would be safest to assume that the data are at the ordinal level as the means are based on ratings. An appropriate inferential statistical test to use is a Spearman rho correlation. A significant correlation, based on a one-tailed test, will support the hypothesis stated.

The predicted significant positive correlation between the perceived harmfulness and the strangeness of a range of animals and insects can also be assessed initially by means of a scattergram. In this case, harmfulness can be treated as the independent variable and plotted on the x-axis, since it is assumed that harmfulness has the major effect. The statistical significance of the predicted positive correlation can also be assessed using Spearman's rho.

The third hypothesis predicted a significant positive correlation between perceived fear and perceived strangeness of some animals and insects even when the effects of perceived harmfulness had been controlled for. In order to assess this prediction, a scattergram should first be drawn with fear plotted on the x-axis. A Spearman's rho test should then be carried out to look at the degree of relationship between perceived fear and strangeness.

In order to assess the third hypothesis directly, the effects of perceived harmfulness need to be controlled for. One way to do this is to remove each of the animals and insects which has an average harmfulness rating of two or more. The data points which remain can then be plotted on a scattergram and a further Spearman's rho conducted. The influence of harmfulness in the correlation between fear and strangeness could also be cancelled out by calculating the following correlation coefficient (indicated as $r_{12.3}$). This is a first-order partial correlation derived from Guildford and Fruchter (1978, p. 332):

$$r_{12.3} = \frac{r_{12} - (r_{13})(r_{23})}{\sqrt{(1 - r_{13}^2)(1 - r_{23}^2)}}$$

where r_{12} is the initial correlation between fear and strangeness, r_{13} is the initial correlation between fear and harmfulness, and r_{23} the initial correlation between strangeness and harmfulness.

From a theoretical point of view, a crucial feature will be whether the correlation between fear and harmfulness is greater than the correlation between fear and strangeness. These two correlations can be directly compared for the significance of the difference between them by using a test for correlations which are themselves correlated. Guildford and Fruchter (1978, p. 164) offer the following formula:

$$t_d = (r_{12} - r_{13}) \sqrt{\frac{(N - 3)(1 + r_{23})}{2(1 - r_{23}^2 - r_{12}^2 - r_{13}^2 + 2r_{23}r_{12}r_{13})}}$$

t_d is the value of 't' for the difference between the two correlation coefficients, and t is calculated for a one-tailed test since the direction of the difference has been predicted. Degrees of freedom (df) are given by N (the number of pairs) $-$ 3. Note that with the above formula r_{12} is the correlation between fear and harmfulness, r_{13} the correlation between fear and strangeness, and r_{23} the correlation between harmfulness and strangeness.

A further critical feature will be whether the correlation between fear and strangeness is significantly reduced when the effects of harmfulness have been removed. The significance of the difference between the two correlations can also be assessed using the method presented in Guildford and Fruchter.

Discussion

It is important when interpreting the results not to infer that correlations point to a particular causation. They can, however, be more consistent with one particular model or theory and can add weight to it when coupled with other evidence.

The first point to consider concerns the two major theories underlying this exercise. Compare the predictions derived from these theories and the results obtained and discuss which way the evidence points. Additionally, how could a direct effect of strangeness on fear (even with the effects of harmfulness removed) be accounted for?

Bennett-Levy and Marteau infer from their findings that perceived characteristics and discrepancy from the human form contribute to a preparedness to be fearful of certain animals and insects. Does this inference seem likely to be true on the basis of the results obtained in this exercise? Bennett-Levy and Marteau also adopt the view that the basis of the preparedness is innate or inbuilt. Does the data generated in the exercise throw any light on this?

It may be possible to construct a more complete explanation for the process of the development of fear. This involves an interactive approach, whereby the perceived strangeness of animals initially comes about as people first develop generalized expectancies for the perceived characteristics of common animals and their behaviour (dangerous or otherwise). Unusual characteristics would lead to an inability to predict the animal's behaviour and therefore the animal might be dangerous. (As Harlow (1949) has shown, learning sets can themselves be learnt.)

The perception of an animal's harmfulness might come from direct knowledge of that animal and/or its possession of unusual features. Is there any other evidence which could be used to support this approach? The change in fear which occurs over time (Agras *et al.*, 1969) could be considered, as could the sex difference in fear ratings reported by Bennett-Levy and Marteau (1984). Whatever overall model is arrived at, it is important to examine the extent to which it allows the generation of fear for specific animals with different combinations of ugliness and harmfulness to be accounted for, and the extent to which the model is capable of explaining individual participant's scores. Another issue worth discussing concerns the implications of the data for general learning theories. Has a general cognitive approach been vindicated or is there still a possible role for a biological preparedness in humans and animals?

Bennett-Levy and Marteau believe that their findings have implications for the treatment of animal phobias. As noted in the Introduction to this exercise, they suggest that phobics should first be desensitized to the perceptual characteristics of the phobic object. The example given by Bennett-Levy and Marteau is that in the case of fear of a slimy creature (such as a jellyfish), treatment might start with the presentation of wet soap or porridge before proceeding to the gradual presentation of the animal. The alternative approach, assuming the greatest role for cognitive factors, would be to desensitize to a form which retains its overall identification, but reduces harmful and un-usual characteristics. In the case of a jellyfish phobia for instance, this could initially involve the use of a cloth toy jellyfish (a type of approach which is commonly used). Which of these approaches is more likely to be successful and how could a difference in success between the approaches be empirically established?

The questionnaires used should also be discussed. Participants were asked to rate animals and insects for their 'ugliness' even though the variable was called 'strangeness'. Would it have been better for them to rate the discrepancy of the animals and insects from the human form, or to have rated the unusualness of their appearance? Would it have been better to base the fearfulness questionnaire on a more operational defini-tion of fear such as the participant's willingness to approach a given animal or insect? Can a similar point be made with respect to the harmfulness variable? It is worth discussing whether questionnaires are the best vehicle for an exercise such as this, especially those which use a relatively crude three-point scale. Would it be better to use a real-life setting and if so, how could this be undertaken?

It is also worth mentioning the ethical issues which arise in an exercise such as this. For example, was it right not to tell participants about the specific purpose of the exercise before they completed the questionnaires? What about any participants who had high fear ratings, and/or expressed concern about their fears? It might also be of interest, if it is possible, to look at a group of people who have already been identified as clinically phobic (Bennett-Levy and Mar-teau consider this). Why might this be an interesting modification, and what would be the ethical considerations? For example, is it actually better to use phobic patients, assuming that research in this area might benefit them in the future?

A whole host of more general questions could be discussed. For example, was the exercise a good test of the alternative theoretical approaches and did the hypotheses formulated adequately distinguish between them? Are there any better hypotheses that could have been formulated? Was the overall design adequate, or is the use of a single group of participants likely to have biased the results? If three groups of participants were to be used, how could the possibility of one group being more afraid of animals be controlled for? In order to remove the effects of harmfulness from the correlation between fear and strangeness, the more ugly creatures were removed from the analysis. This may have reduced the range for strangeness if some of the more harmful animals were also the more ugly ones. Could this have reduced the correlation between fear and strangeness and made the effect of strangeness appear less than it really was? The partial correlation coefficient does overcome this if it is carried out.

Bibliography

General background references

ATKINSON, R.L., ATKINSON, R.C., SMITH, E., BEM, D. and HILGARD, E. (1990) *Introduction to Psychology*. New York: Harcourt Brace Jovanovich.

GROSS, R.D. (1987) *Psychology*. London: Edward Arnold.

ROTH, I. (Ed.) (1990) *Introduction to Psychology*. Milton Keynes: The Open University.

Specific background references

AGRAS, W., SYLVESTER, D. and OLIVEAU, D. (1969) The epidemiology of common fears and phobias. *Comprehensive Psychiatry, 10*, 151–156.

GROSS, R.D. (1990) *Key Studies in Psychology*. London: Hodder and Stoughton. Chapter 13.

GUILFORD, J. and FRUCHTER, B. (1978) *Fundamental Statistics in Psychology and Education*. Sydney: McGraw-Hill.

Journal articles

BENNETT-LEVY, J. and MARTEAU, T. (1984) Fear of animals: What is prepared? *British Journal of Psychology, 75*, 37–42.

HARLOW, H. (1949) Formation of Learning Sets. *Psychological Review, 56*, 51–56.

SELIGMAN, M. (1971) Phobias and Preparedness. *Behaviour Therapy, 2*, 307–320.

Appendix

This is a questionnaire about how UGLY you find certain animals. Please put a circle round the number which best describes your feelings on this:

	Not ugly	Quite ugly	Very ugly
Jellyfish	1	2	3
Squirrel	1	2	3
Ant	1	2	3
Baby Seal	1	2	3
Lamb	1	2	3
Spaniel	1	2	3
Cat	1	2	3
Rabbit	1	2	3
Moth	1	2	3
Mouse	1	2	3
Hamster	1	2	3
Slug	1	2	3
Beetle	1	2	3
Butterfly	1	2	3
Rat	1	2	3
Baby Chimp	1	2	3
Lizard	1	2	3
Tortoise	1	2	3
Blackbird	1	2	3
Caterpillar	1	2	3
Ladybird	1	2	3
Grasshopper	1	2	3
Robin	1	2	3
Frog	1	2	3
Spider	1	2	3
Crow	1	2	3
Grass Snake	1	2	3
Worm	1	2	3
Cockroach	1	2	3

Appendix (cont.)

This is a questionnaire about how HARMFUL you think certain animals are. Please put a circle round the number which best describes your feelings on this:

	Not harmful	Quite harmful	Very harmful
Jellyfish	1	2	3
Squirrel	1	2	3
Ant	1	2	3
Baby Seal	1	2	3
Lamb	1	2	3
Spaniel	1	2	3
Cat	1	2	3
Rabbit	1	2	3
Moth	1	2	3
Mouse	1	2	3
Hamster	1	2	3
Slug	1	2	3
Beetle	1	2	3
Butterfly	1	2	3
Rat	1	2	3
Baby Chimp	1	2	3
Lizard	1	2	3
Tortoise	1	2	3
Blackbird	1	2	3
Caterpillar	1	2	3
Ladybird	1	2	3
Grasshopper	1	2	3
Robin	1	2	3
Frog	1	2	3
Spider	1	2	3
Crow	1	2	3
Grass Snake	1	2	3
Worm	1	2	3
Cockroach	1	2	3

Appendix (cont.)

This is a questionnaire about how AFRAID you are of certain animals. Please put a circle round the number which best describes your feelings on this:

	Not afraid	Quite afraid	Very afraid
Jellyfish	1	2	3
Squirrel	1	2	3
Ant	1	2	3
Baby Seal	1	2	3
Lamb	1	2	3
Spaniel	1	2	3
Cat	1	2	3
Rabbit	1	2	3
Moth	1	2	3
Mouse	1	2	3
Hamster	1	2	3
Slug	1	2	3
Beetle	1	2	3
Butterfly	1	2	3
Rat	1	2	3
Baby Chimp	1	2	3
Lizard	1	2	3
Tortoise	1	2	3
Blackbird	1	2	3
Caterpillar	1	2	3
Ladybird	1	2	3
Grasshopper	1	2	3
Robin	1	2	3
Frog	1	2	3
Spider	1	2	3
Crow	1	2	3
Grass Snake	1	2	3
Worm	1	2	3
Cockroach	1	2	3

Assessing the relationship between adults' attitudes towards mental illness

Alison Wadeley,
Filton College, Bristol,
and
Rob McIlveen,
Springwood High School, King's Lynn

Abstract

Understanding the relationship between beliefs about and attitudes towards mental illness is an important concern for community and social psychiatry, as such an understanding could be helpful in the development of techniques for changing attitudes. Norman and Malla (1983) reported findings concerning adolescents' beliefs about mental illness, and the purpose of this exercise is to look at the extent to which their findings generalize to an adult population.

Six two-tailed hypotheses concerning the relationship between beliefs about mental illness and attitudes towards it are examined, using procedures based on those employed by Norman and Malla. Participants are asked to read vignettes (short fictitious case descriptions) developed by Star (1955), describing a mentally healthy individual and a paranoid schizophrenic, and then answer nine questions about the individual described. The central discussion points arising from the exercise concern the similarities and differences between the correlations obtained in this exercise and those reported by Norman and Malla. Other discussion points consider possible extensions to the exercise, methodological issues arising, and the practical applications and implications of the results obtained.

Materials
and Equipment

The materials required for this exercise are two questionnaires. Investigators should ensure they have a sufficient number of copies of these to supply to participants. The first questionnaire contains a vignette describing a person who might be diagnosed as a paranoid schizophrenic, and participants are required to answer nine questions concerning the individual described. The second questionnaire contains a vignette describing a mentally healthy person and participants are required to answer the same nine questions concerning this person's behaviour.

The nature of the exercise requires that participants, who should number at least 20, must have reached the age of 18 and be male students in further or higher education. This constraint is necessary due to the way in which the vignettes have been constructed (see the Procedure section). Each participant should be able to complete the two questionnaires within ten minutes. The data could be collected by a single investigator, or several investigators could each administer the questionnaire to a smaller number of participants and then pool the data for subsequent analysis. The analysis of the data obtained can be completed within a two-hour period.

145

Introduction and Hypotheses

Lay people's attitudes towards mental illness have long been of interest to psychologists and others in the mental health professions. Nearly 40 years ago Star (1955) reported a national study of the American public's attitudes towards mental illness. The report indicated that there were three interrelated characteristics which the public perceived as being indicative of mental illness. These were:

1. A breakdown in intellect . . . a loss of reason.
2. A loss of self-control, usually to the point of dangerous violence against others, and certainly to the point of being not responsible for one's acts.
3. Behaviour which is inappropriate, that is, neither reasonable nor expected under the particular circumstances in which the person finds him or herself. (Star, 1955, p. 5)

Other early studies (for example, Nunnally, 1961) indicated that although public information about mental illness was not highly structured, a strong 'negative halo' was associated with the mentally ill. Thus, the mentally ill were indiscriminately considered to be 'all things bad'. In Nunnally's view, 'the average man generalizes to the point of considering the mentally ill as dirty, unintelligent, insincere and worthless' (1961, p. 233). Nunnally attributed the public's negative attitude to a lack of information about mental illness, and a failure to observe and learn about mental illness in daily life.

Since the pioneering work of Star and Nunnally, a number of researchers have examined attitudes towards mental illness and in particular how these attitudes have been affected by different types of education programmes. Useful comment and reviews of the relevant literature can be found in Arieti (1987) and Bootzin and Acocella (1984). A more general discussion concerning the concepts of mental disorder and illness can be found in Gross (1987).

One way of investigating attitudes towards mental illness is through the use of standardized case descriptions of behaviour which might be diagnosed as mental illness. Star (1955) was the first to devise fictitious case descriptions illustrating different types of mental disorders as conceived by the mental health professions. The 'Star vignettes' depict the type of person who might be diagnosed as having one of six mental disorders: paranoid schizophrenia, simple schizophrenia, alcoholism, anxiety neurosis, juvenile character disorder, and compulsive phobia. Star's vignettes were verified by a number of psychiatrists who generally agreed that they did accurately portray the type of behaviour which would correspond to the six diagnostic categories identified by Star. The vignettes have subsequently been used in a number of studies, and their use has become common in research assessing public attitudes towards mental illness. Yamamoto and Dizney (1967) also used the idea of vignettes, and give the following example of schizotypal personality disorder:

> *Here is a brief description of a young man. Imagine that he is a respectable student attending your school. He is very quiet, he does not talk much to anyone – even in his own family. He has never participated in any kind of student activities and does not seem to*

want to do so. He acts like he is afraid of people, especially women his own age. He does not like to go out with anyone and, whenever someone comes to visit his family, he stays in his own room until they leave. He just stays by himself and day-dreams all the time, and shows no interest in anything or anybody.

As Brockman *et al.* (1979) have suggested, vignettes have the advantage of allowing participants to react to concrete situational behaviours under circumstances that allow a great measure of experimental control.

Another method of assessing the public's attitudes towards mental illness is through the use of Social Distance Scales. These are sociometric instruments for measuring the degree of closeness a person would willingly accept to other people of various groups, in this instance the mentally ill. The participant is given a number of statements and asked to agree or disagree with each of them. Examples of such statements (taken from Bentz and Edgerton, 1971, p. 31) include:

1. *I would not hesitate to work with someone who had been mentally ill.*

2. *I would be willing to share a room with someone who had been mentally ill.*

3. *I would strongly discourage my children from marrying anyone who had been mentally ill.*

4. *I can't imagine myself falling in love with a person who had been mentally ill.*

Like Star's vignettes, the use of Social Distance Scales allows researchers to make comparisons across time with respect to attitudes towards the mentally ill. For example, Aviram and Segal (1973) compared data spanning a fourteen-year period between 1957 and 1971. Amongst other things, the results of the study indicated a quite dramatic change in the attitudes of the American public, such that attitudes became significantly more accepting towards the mentally ill.

Much of the research conducted using Star's vignettes and Social Distance Scales has looked at specific factors influencing attitudes towards the mentally ill. One characteristic that has been extensively researched is gender, although the results obtained have not been consistent. Thus, some researchers (for example, Brockman and D'Arcy, 1978) have found no differences in the reactions of men and women towards the mentally ill, whilst others (for example, Farina *et al.*, 1978) have shown that women are more accepting of former mental patients than men are.

As interesting as such studies are in indicating that different groups in society hold different views, they say little about the relationship between the various components of attitudes towards the mentally ill within a given population. A large body of research has suggested that if this relationship can be understood, then effective techniques for changing attitudes can be developed (Rokeach, 1968). It has also been suggested that such knowledge could be useful in determining whether attitudes will be stable and/or related to behaviour (Norman, 1975).

With respect to attitudes towards the mentally ill, Rabkin (1974) has suggested that a greater level of understanding could be achieved if the various attitudes held by people were first separated out and then examined for the presence of relationships between them. A similar argument was advanced by Norman and Malla (1983). As they noted, there is considerable controversy as to whether educational mental health campaigns should emphasize a medical (that is, *physically* caused) or psychosocial (that is, *psychologically* caused) model of mental illness. Although this debate implies that public beliefs about the causes (aetiology) of mental illness have some influence on other beliefs, such as the method by which the mentally ill should be treated, Norman and Malla pointed out that there was little, if any, evidence to indicate how strong such relationships were.

Consequently, Norman and Malla set out to examine the relationship between beliefs about the causes of mental illness, proper method of treatment, perceived prognosis, and preferred level of social distance towards the mentally ill. (For the purposes of this practical, these are the only beliefs we will examine, but it should be noted that they also assessed adolescents' belief in medical treatment, belief in psychosocial treatment, and anticipated prognosis.) In Norman and Malla's study, 413 Canadian adolescents were asked to complete questionnaires based on six vignettes devised by Star (1955). These six vignettes were made up of three types of behaviour attributed to either a male or female target person. The three types of behaviour were intended to describe a mentally healthy person, a paranoid schizophrenic, and a person manifesting a schizotypal personality disorder.

Several significant relationships emerged. First, the perceived severity of mental disorder was positively related to attributions to physical causes, and negatively related to social acceptability. Second, beliefs in psychosocial aetiology and psychosocial treatment were positively correlated with optimistic beliefs about prognosis. Finally, belief in the appropriateness of psychosocial treatment was related to greater acceptance of the mentally ill, whereas belief in medical treatment was negatively related to social acceptance. Although the correlations obtained were not always high (ranging from -0.9 to $+0.30$), they were significant beyond the 0.01 level.

As noted, the data presented by Norman and Malla were based upon an adolescent population – Canadian schoolchildren with a modal age of 16. As the researchers have remarked, adolescence has been shown to be a critical stage in the development of attitudes towards politics, religion and morality, and may be a discrete phase in the development of attitudes towards mental illness. The post-adolescent period may bring an increase in a person's ability to see more subtle similarities and dissimilarities between the self and others from different groups. These changes could affect a person's ability to empathize with people displaying disturbed behaviour and, in turn, influence attitudes towards mental illness.

If such post-adolescent changes do occur, then it is clearly important to look at the extent to which the findings obtained by Norman and Malla generalize to other age groups. The aim of the present exercise is to examine the relationship between the components of attitudes towards mental illness in a male adult student population. Four attitudinal components will be assessed. These are:

1. Perception of behaviour as indicative of mental illness.

2. Belief that mental illness has a physical cause (or aetiology).

3. Belief that mental illness has a psychosocial cause (or aetiology).

4. Preferred social distance.

Hypotheses

[Six hypotheses are presented here, but students may wish to simplify the exercise by reducing the number of hypotheses examined.]

Each of the components will be correlated with the others, giving a total of six correlations. Since there is no previous research on which to base a prediction, two-tailed hypotheses will be advanced. The six two-tailed hypotheses are:

1. Perception of behaviour as indicative of mental illness is correlated with the belief that mental illness has a physical cause.

2. Perception of behaviour as indicative of mental illness is correlated with the belief that mental illness has a psychosocial cause.

3. Perception of behaviour as indicative of mental illness is correlated with preferred social distance.

4. Belief that mental illness has a physical cause is correlated with the belief that mental illness has a psychosocial cause.

5. Belief that mental illness has a physical cause is correlated with preferred social distance.

6. Belief that mental illness has a psychosocial cause is correlated with preferred social distance.

For each of these six two-tailed hypotheses, the null hypothesis predicts that no significant correlation will be observed, and that any correlation found between the variables will be a result of the operation of chance factors.

Procedure

The procedure is modelled on that used by Norman and Malla (1983), although there are some important differences. Before describing the procedure to be followed, it is first necessary to say something about the stimulus material that will be used.

Appendix 1 contains a vignette based on one originated by Star (1955) which describes a person behaving in a way characteristic of paranoid schizophrenia. *Appendix 2* contains a modified version of Star's vignette describing a mentally healthy person. Both Appendices contain an identical questionnaire. The questionnaire is introduced to participants as being designed to measure opinions about mental illness and the mentally ill, and consists of nine questions derived from Norman and Malla (1983).

The first question asks the participant to rate the extent to which he or she believes the person described in the vignette to be mentally ill. This question measures the 'Perception of behaviours as indicative of mental illness' attitudinal component. The second question asks the participant to indicate the extent to which he or she thinks that the person's behaviour is the direct result of physical causes, such as the condition of the brain and nervous system, and/or what has been inherited from the parents. This question is designed to assess the 'Belief that mental illness has a physical cause' attitudinal component.

Questions 3 and 4 are designed to assess the 'Belief that mental illness has a psychosocial cause' attitudinal component. Question 3 asks the participant to rate the extent to which he or she believes the person's behaviour to be the direct result of present life circumstances, such as home life, relationships in school or college, relationships with friends and so on. Question 4 asks the participant whether the person's behaviour is the direct result of past experience, that is, what happened to him and how he felt as a child. The remaining five questions are designed to assess 'Preferred social distance'.

It should be noted that both vignettes describe the target person as male; this is different to the methodology employed by Norman and Malla. In their study, participants were given vignettes describing both males and females. However, the researchers reported that the gender of the target person had no significant effect on the ratings provided by participants. Therefore, in order to simplify the design, males only have been used as the target person. The use of both genders could, however, form an interesting extension to this exercise (see Discussion).

Prior to conducting the exercise, a sufficient number of copies of *Appendices 1* and *2* should be made. Each participant will be required to complete a questionnaire for both the mentally healthy person and the paranoid schizophrenic person. However, the participant should *not* be told of the psychiatric label given to the individual described in the vignette (nor does this appear anywhere on the questionnaire). Since all participants will complete both questionnaires, some control for order of presentation is necessary. This can be achieved by means of counterbalancing: half of the participants should receive *Appendix 1* followed by *Appendix 2* whilst the other half should receive *Appendix 2* followed by *Appendix 1*. Investigators are strongly advised to staple the questionnaires together in the preferred sequence, and to ensure that an even number of participants take part in the exercise.

As was noted in the Introduction to this exercise, the evidence concerning the influence of gender as a characteristic in attitudes towards mental illness is mixed, with some studies reporting gender differences and others failing to report such differences. By using only members of one gender as participants, the possibility that gender will act as a confounding variable is eliminated. Again, however, this could form an interesting extension to the present exercise (see Discussion).

It is also important to note that the questionnaires do not ask participants to identify themselves by name. The assurance of anonymity should be stressed to participants since this is more likely to elicit honest answers from them. The only demographic information collected is the participant's age. Participants should be informed that investigators are conducting a psychological investigation into attitudes towards mental illness, and asked if they would be willing to complete two questionnaires. Once the participant has completed the questionnaires, he should be thanked and debriefed as to the purpose of the exercise. Participants should be given the opportunity to see the final results of the exercise if they so desire.

Results

For each item appearing on the questionnaire, participants will have provided a rating on the 7-point scale. The 'Perception of behaviour as indicative of mental illness' attitudinal component is measured in Question 1. High ratings will indicate a greater belief that the behaviour displayed is indicative of mental illness. 'Belief in physical causes' is assessed in Question 2. Again, each participant's ratings will vary between 1 and 7, with higher ratings indicating a greater belief in physical aetiology.

The 'Belief in psychosocial causes' attitudinal component is measured in Questions 3 and 4. In Norman and Malla's (1983) study, the responses to these questions correlated sufficiently highly to justify combining them into a single scale of psychosocial aetiology. Participant's responses to Questions 3 and 4 should therefore be added together to provide an overall rating ranging from 2 to 14, with higher ratings indicating a greater belief in psychosocial aetiology.

Questions 5 to 9 assess 'preferred social distance'. Norman and Malla reported an average intercorrelation of 0.66 between these five scales and judged this to be high enough to justify combining them into a single social distance scale. The ratings from these five scales should therefore be added together to provide an overall rating ranging from 5 to 35, with higher ratings indicating greater social acceptance of the person described in the vignette.

The scoring system for this exercise is summarized in *Table 1*.

Table 1. Scoring system employed in the exercise

Attitude Component	Questions	Possible Range of Ratings
1. Perception of behaviour as indicative of mental illness	1	1–7
2. Belief in physical causes	2	1–7
3. Belief in psychosocial causes	3 and 4	2–14
4. Preferred social distance	5–9	5–35

Initially, only the ratings for each participant's responses to the paranoid schizophrenic vignette should be calculated, as indicated in *Table 1*. These should then be collated and displayed as illustrated in *Table 2*. Once this has been done, each participant's responses to the mentally healthy vignette should be collated and displayed in the same way.

Table 2. Suggested method of collating participants' ratings on the questionnaire

Participant no.	Gender	Attitude Component			
		1	2	3	4
1					
2					
3					
4					
etc.					
MEAN (or MEDIAN)					
S.D. (or RANGE)					

Before assessing the correlations between the four attitudinal components, a preliminary analysis of the vignettes is necessary in order to determine whether or not the differences between them produce significant results in terms of the ratings of mental illness perceived to be present. The one-tailed prediction which can be made here is that the paranoid schizophrenic vignette will receive significantly higher ratings than the mentally healthy vignette. In order to test this hypothesis, the ratings provided by each participant in response to Question 1 should be examined, using an appropriate test for differences.

The test chosen will depend on a number of factors. The debatable factor here is whether the questionnaire can be seen as forming an equal-interval scale. This question is an important one to answer, since it will also determine the descriptive statistics employed: that is, whether the mean or median, and standard deviation or range, are used as measures of central tendency and dispersion repectively.

If the questionnaire can be seen as forming an equal-interval scale, then a parametic test such as the related 't' would be appropriate provided that all other requirements for using this test are met. If they are not, or if the questionnaire is seen as constituting an ordinal level of measurement, then a non-parametric test such as the Wilcoxon or the sign test would be more appropriate. In Norman and Malla's study, the paranoid schizophrenic vignette received a mean rating of 4.7, and the mentally healthy vignette a mean rating of 1.5, a difference which was statistically highly significant ($p < 0.001$).

On the assumption that the difference between the two vignettes is statistically significant, the six two-tailed hypotheses advanced earlier can be tested. Initially only the participants' responses to the paranoid schizophrenic vignette should be used. Note that for each hypothesis a preliminary assessment can be made by constructing a scattergram which will provide some information about the direction and magnitude of the relationship present. Statistical testing of the correlations can be made using Pearson's method (if the data are judged to be at the interval level and all the necessary requirements for using this test are met) or Spearman's method (if the assumptions are not met or the questionnaire is judged to provide only ordinal level data).

HYPOTHESIS 1: 'Perception of behaviour as indicative of mental illness is correlated with the belief that mental illness has a physical cause.' This hypothesis can be assessed by correlating ratings on Question 1 with ratings on Question 2. A significant positive correlation suggests that the more a behaviour is seen to be an indicator of mental illness, the more likely it is to be attributed to physical causes. A significant negative correlation suggests that the more a behaviour is seen to be an indicator of mental illness, the less likely it is to be attributed to physical causes. Norman and Malla reported a significant positive correlation amongst their sample of participants.

HYPOTHESIS 2: 'Perception of behaviour as indicative of mental illness is correlated with the belief that mental illness has a psychosocial cause.' This hypothesis can be examined by correlating ratings on Question 1 with the combined ratings provided for Questions 3 and 4. A significant positive correlation suggests that the more behaviour is seen as an indicator of mental illness, the more likely it is to be attributed to psychosocial causes. A significant negative correlation suggests that the more behaviour is seen as an indicator of mental illness, the less likely it is to be attributed to psychosocial causes. Norman and Malla found no significant correlation, positive or negative, between these two variables.

HYPOTHESIS 3: 'Perception of behaviour as indicative of mental illness is correlated with preferred social distance.' This hypothesis can be assessed by correlating ratings on Question 1 with the combined ratings provided for Questions 5 to 9 inclusive. A significant positive correlation suggests that the more behaviour is seen as an indicator of mental illness, the closer the preferred social distance desired with that person. A significant negative correlation suggests that the more behaviour is seen as an indicator of mental illness, the greater the preferred social distance required with that person. A significant positive correlation would, at the least, be unexpected. Much more likely is a negative correlation, an outcome which would replicate Norman and Malla's finding.

HYPOTHESIS 4: 'Belief that mental illness has a physical cause is correlated with belief that mental illness has a psychosocial cause.' This hypothesis can be assessed by correlating ratings on Question 2 with the combined ratings provided for Questions 3 and 4. A significant positive correlation would be surprising, and suggest that the more it is believed that mental illness has a physical cause, the more it is believed that it also has a psychosocial cause. If anything, a negative correlation is more likely, suggesting that the more it is believed that mental illness has a physical cause, the less it is believed that it has a psychosocial cause. Norman and Malla reported a non-significant correlation of only 0.03 on these variables with their sample.

HYPOTHESIS 5: 'Belief that mental illness has a physical cause is correlated with preferred social distance.' This hypothesis can be examined by correlating the ratings on Question 2 with the combined ratings provided for Questions 5 to 9 inclusive. A significant positive correlation indicates that the greater the belief that mental illness has a physical cause, the closer the preferred social distance. A significant negative correlation indicates that the greater the belief in a physical aetiology of mental illness, the greater the preferred social distance. Norman and Malla reported no correlation whatsoever between these two variables.

HYPOTHESIS 6: 'Belief that mental illness has a psychosocial cause is correlated with preferred social distance.' This hypothesis can be examined by correlating the combined ratings provided for Questions 3 and 4 with the combined ratings provided for Questions 5 to 9 inclusive. A significant positive correlation indicates that the greater the belief that mental illness has a psychosocial cause, the closer the preferred social distance. A significant negative correlation indicates that closer preferred social distances are related to the lack of belief that mental illness has a psychosocial cause. Norman and Malla reported a non-significant correlation (-0.07) between these two variables.

The correlations between the four attitudinal components for the paranoid schizophrenic vignette should be presented in a correlation matrix as shown in *Table 3*. Correlation coefficients for the participants' ratings on the mentally healthy vignette should also be computed and presented as in *Table 3*. These correlations are worth examining since, in a sense, they act as controls and allow some sort of additional assessment to be made of the size of the correlations obtained for the paranoid schizophrenic vignette. Indeed, an argument could be made for the correlations obtained for the attitudinal components for the mentally healthy vignette constituting a null hypothesis against which to test the size of the correlations obtained for the paranoid schizophrenic vignette. There are tests to determine whether two correlation coefficients differ significantly from each other, but these are beyond the scope of this manual. Nonetheless, a comparison between correlations across vignettes could form an interesting discussion point.

Table 3. Correlation matrix for the 6 hypotheses

Perception of Mental Illness	Perception of Mental Illness	Belief in Physical Aetiology	Belief in Psychosocial Aetiology
BELIEF IN PHYSICAL AETIOLOGY	HYPOTHESIS 1		
BELIEF IN PSYCHOSOCIAL AETIOLOGY	HYPOTHESIS 2	HYPOTHESIS 4	
PREFERRED SOCIAL DISTANCE	HYPOTHESIS 3	HYPOTHESIS 5	HYPOTHESIS 6

Discussion

As Norman and Malla (1983, p. 49) have noted, 'the growth of community and social psychiatry has necessitated a greater understanding of various aspects of public beliefs about and attitudes toward mental illness'. The central discussion point of the present exercise must therefore be the extent to which this exercise has produced significant correlations between attitudinal components. What do these correlations (or lack of them) suggest, and how might they influence the development of strategies designed to educate the public about mental illness? Would such campaigns be more effective if they emphasized the psychosocial aspects of mental illness in order to encourage acceptance of the mentally ill, for example, or would it be better to present the medical aspects in such a way that they encouraged more positive aspects about the mentally ill?

The answers to questions such as these would indeed be useful to mental health campaigns, since, as Norman and Malla have noted, it is important to influence beliefs and attitudes about the mentally ill in the direction of greater social acceptability. Equally important is the issue of whether, and why, adults' attitudes are similar or dissimilar to those expressed by adolescents. Is the possibility of changes in attitude from adolescence to post-adolescence plausible in the light of the data obtained? For example, judging by the results obtained, is it still reasonable to suggest that changes from adolescence to adulthood can affect people's ability to empathize with people displaying disturbed behaviour and, in turn, influence their attitudes toward mental illness? If attitudes between adolescents and adults are dissimilar, does this suggest that mental health campaigns should stress different aspects of mental illness to the two populations? Would this be a practical exercise?

As was noted in the Introduction to this exercise, Nunnally (1961) has suggested that the public's information about mental illness is not highly structured. Is there any evidence of apparent incongruities in the data obtained in this exercise? What implications would such incongruities have for those devising educational campaigns concerning the mentally ill? Instead of presenting a primarily medical or primarily psychosocial model of mental illness, could a shift in public attitudes towards greater social acceptance of the mentally ill benefit from a 'multi-model' approach to mental illness (see the points mentioned in the previous paragraph)?

Several important methodological issues also arise from this exercise. For example, in addition to the two vignettes used here, Norman and Malla also employed a third, describing behaviour typical of schizotypal personality disorder (this can be found in the Introduction to this exercise). Norman and Malla reported a mean rating of 3.4 on the 7-point scale assessing the extent to which the behaviour was seen as indicative of mental illness. Might this say something about people's conceptions of mental illness? Would the inclusion of the schizotypal personality disorder vignette have been likely to affect participants' responses, and if so how? What other sorts of vignettes would it be interesting to use?

The present exercise also involved participants rating both the mentally healthy and the paranoid schizophrenic vignettes. Although counterbalancing was used to control for order effects, is it possible that using the same participants to assess both vignettes may have led to some of them guessing the aims, and perhaps also the likely hypotheses, of the exercise? How could this have affected their behaviour? What sort of alternative methodology could have been used in this exercise?

A further problem concerns the possibility of 'social desirability' responding to items on the questionnaire. Segal (1978) has reviewed the relevant literature concerning the relationship between attitudes expressed toward the mentally ill and actual behaviours observed. How could the presence of social desirability responding be checked for, and how could its existence be minimized? Could the construction of the questionnaire used in the present exercise have induced a 'set' in participants, particularly with respect to the presentation of Questions 3 to 9 concerning preferred social distance? How could such a possibility be overcome?

Two additional methodological problems are also worth considering. The first concerns the use of vignettes as stimulus material. Despite the fact that vignettes are used extensively in this type of research, and that such use is supported by reviews of their efficacy (for example, Brockman *et al.*, 1979), vignettes may be criticized on the grounds that they lack ecological validity. What alternative stimuli could be used in research of this type? The second methodological issue concerns the level of measurement of the data gathered in this exercise, an issue that is bound up with the type of descriptive statistics presented and the inferential statistical test used. Are the data at the interval level, or do they at best represent an ordinal level of measurement, and why?

The present exercise could be extended to further examine how far the findings reported by Norman and Malla can be generalized. What sorts of questions could be added to the questionnaire in order to elicit adults' views about the treatment and prognosis of mental illness? Norman and Malla have hypothesized that psychosocial factors are perceived as more flexible than medical factors, and therefore recovery is seen as more likely to occur. How could this hypothesis be assessed? Other researchers (for example, Cochrane, 1983; Jones and Cochrane, 1981) have reported the existence of certain stereotypes regarding the mentally ill. How could these findings be used to further assess the public's attitudes towards mental illness?

The present exercise has limited itself to participants of one gender. Norman and Malla looked at differences between the sexes with respect to beliefs about mental illness. They reported that although males and females did not differ with respect to their tendency to perceive particular behaviours as indicative of mental illness, female adolescents showed greater social acceptance of the mentally ill than did males, a finding consistent with that reported by Farina *et al.*, (1978). Norman and Malla also reported that females held a greater belief in the psychosocial aetiology of mental illness. Could it be that the importance females attach to the psychosocial dimensions of mental illness results in their being more concerned than men not to foster the social isolation of the mentally ill? If so, why?

The exercise could be extended to look at the differences between the sexes, but this would seem to require the systematic manipulation of the gender of the target person described in the vignettes as well (recall that the target person in the vignettes employed in the present exercise was described as a male). What sort of design would be needed to assess the role of gender as a characteristic influencing attitudes towards mental illness, and how could the data generated from such a design be analysed?

General background references

ARIETI, S. (1987) *Understanding and Helping the Schizophrenic.* Harmondsworth: Penguin.

BOOTZIN, R.R. and ACOCELLA, J.R. (1984) *Abnormal Psychology.* 4th edn. New York: Random House.

COCHRANE, R. (1983) *The Social Creation of Mental Illness.* New York: Longman.

GROSS, R.D. (1987) *Psychology: The Science of Mind and Behaviour.* London: Edward Arnold.

Specific background references

NUNNALLY, J. (1961) *Popular Conceptions of Mental Health: Their Development and Change.* New York: Holt, Rinehart and Winston.

ROKEACH, M. (1968) *Beliefs, Attitudes and Values.* San Francisco: Jossey-Bass.

STAR, S.A. (1955) *The Public's Ideas About Mental Illness.* Mimeo National Opinion Research Center. Chicago: University of Chicago.

Journal articles

AVIRAM, U. and SEGAL, S.P. (1973) Exclusion of the mentally ill. *Archives of General Psychiatry, 29,* 126–131.

BENTZ, W.K. and EDGERTON, J.W. (1971) The consequences of labelling a person as mentally ill. *Social Psychiatry, 6,* 29–33.

BROCKMAN, J. and D'ARCY, C. (1978) Correlates of attitudinal social distance toward the mentally ill: a review and resurvey. *Social Psychiatry, 13,* 69–77.

BROCKMAN, J., D'ARCY, C. and EDMONDS, L. (1979) Facts or artifacts? Changing public attitudes towards the mentally ill. *Social Science and Medicine, 13A,* 673–682.

FARINA, A., FISHER, J.D., GETTER, H. and FISCHER, E.H. (1978) Some consequences of changing people's views regarding the nature of mental illness. *Journal of Abnormal Psychology, 87,* 272–279.

JONES, L. and COCHRANE, R. (1981) Stereotypes of mental illness: A test of the labelling hypothesis. *International Journal of Social Psychiatry, 27,* 99–107.

NORMAN, R. (1975) Affective-cognitive consistency, attitudes, conformity and behaviour. *Journal of Personality and Social Psychology, 32,* 83–91.

NORMAN, R.M. and MALLA, A.K. (1983) Adolescents' attitudes towards mental illness: relationship between components and sex differences. *Social Psychiatry, 18,* 45–50.

RABKIN, J. (1974) Public attitudes toward mental illness: A review of the literature. *Schizophrenia Bulletin, 10,* 9–33.

SEGAL, S.P. (1978) Attitudes towards the mentally ill: a review. *Social Work, 23,* 211–217.

YAMAMOTO, K. and DIZNEY, H.F. (1967) Rejection of the mentally ill: a study of attitudes of student teachers. *Journal of Counselling Psychology, 14,* 264–268.

Appendix 1. QUESTIONNAIRE

This questionnaire is designed to measure opinions about mental illness and the mentally ill. Please try to answer the questions as honestly as possible. You are not required to identify yourself by name, but it would be very helpful if you could indicate your age:

AGE (to the nearest year) =

Now read the description of the fictitious person below and answer the questions that follow.

Here is a brief description of a young man. Imagine that he is a respectable student attending your school or college. He is very suspicious, doesn't trust anybody and is sure everyone is against him. Sometimes he thinks that people he sees on the street are talking about him or following him. A couple of times he has picked fights with people who don't even know him, because he thought they were spying on him and plotting against him. The other night he began to curse his mother terribly, because he said she was working against him too – just like everybody else.

(Based on material from S.A. Star (1955) *The Public's Ideas About Mental Illness*. Mimeo National Opinion Research Center; University of Chicago.)

Please bear in mind that the questions are not intended as a test of any kind. We merely wish to know your personal opinions concerning them. When you answer, please place a circle around the number that best reflects your opinion. For example, if the questionnaire asked if you saw the person as being 'intelligent' and you saw him as being 'fairly intelligent', you might answer as follows:

Definitely NO	1	2	3	4	⑤	6	7	Definitely YES

---

(1) To what extent do you believe the person described to be mentally ill?

Definitely NO	1	2	3	4	5	6	7	Definitely YES

(2) Do you think that the person's behaviour is the direct result of physical causes, such as the condition of the brain and nervous system, and/or what has been inherited from the parents?

Definitely NO	1	2	3	4	5	6	7	Definitely YES

(3) Do you think that the person's behaviour is the direct result of present life circumstances such as home life, relationships in school or college, relationships with friends, and so on?

Definitely NO	1	2	3	4	5	6	7	Definitely YES

(4) Do you think that the person's behaviour is the direct result of past experiences; that is, what happened to him and how he felt as a child?

Definitely NO	1	2	3	4	5	6	7	Definitely YES

(5) If you knew this person would you speak to him on the street?

Definitely   1   2   3   4   5   6   7   Definitely
  NO   YES

(6) If you knew this person would you have lunch with him?

Definitely   1   2   3   4   5   6   7   Definitely
  NO   YES

(7) If you knew this person would you do school or college work with him?

Definitely   1   2   3   4   5   6   7   Definitely
  NO   YES

(8) If you knew this person would you go to a party at his home?

Definitely   1   2   3   4   5   6   7   Definitely
  NO   YES

(9) If you knew this person would you invite him to a social gathering at your home for an evening?

Definitely   1   2   3   4   5   6   7   Definitely
  NO   YES

(Questions based on material from R.M.G. Norman, A.K. Malla. Adolescents' attitudes towards mental illness: relationship between components and sex differences. *Social Psychiatry, 18*, 45–50. © Springer-Verlag.)

Appendix 2. QUESTIONNAIRE

This questionnaire is designed to measure opinions about mental illness and the mentally ill. Please try to answer the questions as honestly as possible. You are not required to identify yourself by name but it would be very helpful if you could indicate your age to the nearest year:

AGE (to the nearest year) =

Now read the description of the fictitious person below and then answer the questions that follow.

Here is a brief description of a young man. Imagine that he is a respectable student attending your school or college. He accepts both happy and unhappy emotions freely and expresses his feelings and opinions openly. He is easy to get along with and others seek his company, knowing that he is generally pleasant. He plans ahead, thinks clearly, and is usually keen to learn.

(Based on material from S.A. Star (1955) *The Public's Ideas About Mental Illness*. Mimeo National Opinion Research Center; University of Chicago.)

Please bear in mind that the questions are not intended as a test of any kind. We merely wish to know your personal opinions concerning them. When you answer, please place a circle around the number that best reflects your opinion. For example, if the questionnaire asked if you saw the person as being 'intelligent' and you saw him as being 'fairly intelligent', you might answer as follows:

Definitely NO	1	2	3	4	⑤	6	7	Definitely YES

---

(1) To what extent do you believe the person described to be mentally ill?

Definitely NO	1	2	3	4	5	6	7	Definitely YES

(2) Do you think that the person's behaviour is the direct result of physical causes, such as the condition of the brain and nervous system, and/or what has been inherited from the parents?

Definitely NO	1	2	3	4	5	6	7	Definitely YES

(3) Do you think that the person's behaviour is the direct result of present life circumstances such as home life, relationships in school or college, relationships with friends, and so on?

Definitely NO	1	2	3	4	5	6	7	Definitely YES

(4) Do you think that the person's behaviour is the direct result of past experiences, that is, what happened to him and how he felt as a child?

Definitely NO	1	2	3	4	5	6	7	Definitely YES

(5) If you knew this person would you speak to him on the street?

Definitely NO	1	2	3	4	5	6	7	Definitely YES

(6) If you knew this person would you have lunch with him?

Definitely NO	1	2	3	4	5	6	7	Definitely YES

(7) If you knew this person would you do school or college work with him?

Definitely NO	1	2	3	4	5	6	7	Definitely YES

(8) If you knew this person would you go to a party at his home?

Definitely NO	1	2	3	4	5	6	7	Definitely YES

(9) If you knew this person would you invite him to a social gathering at your home for an evening?

Definitely NO	1	2	3	4	5	6	7	Definitely YES

(Questions based on material from R.M.G. Norman, A.K. Malla.Adolescents' attitudes towards mental illness: relationship between components and sex differences. *Social Psychiatry, 18,* 45–50. © Springer-Verlag.)

PRACTICAL 13

Liking for, and familiarity with, male forenames: a partial replication of Colman, Hargreaves and Sluckin (1981)

Rob McIlveen
Springwood High School, King's Lynn

Abstract

This practical exercise examines the nature and extent of the relationship between peoples' familiarity with, and liking for, male forenames. Previous research has indicated that familiarity and liking are sometimes related in a positive monotonic (or straight line) fashion, sometimes in a negative monotonic fashion and sometimes in an inverted-U fashion. A study conducted by Colman, Sluckin and Hargreaves (1981) indicated that familiarity with, and liking for, male forenames were strongly positively correlated. The present exercise attempts to replicate the data reported by Colman and his colleagues.

The primary discussion of the results concentrates on the explanation proposed by Colman and his associates for the occurrence of different types of relationships between familiarity and liking. Other discussion points consider the innovative methodology that has been used in this area of psychological research and the potential practical applications that the findings from such studies have.

Materials
and Equipment

This exercise involves the use of the 100 male forenames employed by Colman, Hargreaves and Sluckin (1981). The names, which can be found in *Appendix 1*, were originally selected from the *Oxford Dictionary of English Christian Names* using a quasi-random sampling procedures; that is, names were selected according to some arbitrary rule (for example, every 10th name) whilst ensuring that the whole book was used. The list includes both very common names, such as John and David, and very rare names, like Balthasar and Gawain. Investigators will need 100 small pieces of card (index cards are suitable) on to which a name can be typed or printed. Ten other small pieces of card are also required. Their purpose is described fully in the Procedure section.

The data generated by participants can be recorded using the score sheets presented in *Appendix 2*. The exercise can be conducted by a single investigator who will obtain ratings from a total of 20 participants, ten of whom will rate the forenames according to their familiarity with them, and ten according to their liking of them. Alternatively, pairs of investigators could work together with one collecting ratings for familiarity and the other ratings for liking. Each participant should be able to complete the ratings within ten minutes. With pairs of investigators working together, data collection and analysis should take no longer than two hours. Single investigators should allow themselves a further hour.

Introduction
and Hypotheses

Studies of the relationship between people's familiarity with things and their liking of them is part of an area of psychology known as experimental aesthetics. Attempts to explain why some things are aesthetically pleasing and others are not have a long history in psychological research, and interesting reviews of both methodological approaches and empirical findings can be found in Boring (1957), Mace (1962) Berlyne (1971, 1974), and Pickford (1972).

One early hypothesis concerning the relationship between familiarity and liking was proposed by Zajonc (1968). In his 'mere exposure' theory, Zajonc proposed that a positive monotonic relationship exists between familiarity and liking for all kinds of stimuli. Although intuitively appealing, this simplistic approach ignored several important stimulus characteristics that can influence liking, such as complexity, discriminability and orderliness. It also failed to account for certain findings (for example, Cantor and Kubose, 1969), which indicated that familiarization with stimuli can reduce liking for them: that is, a negative relationship sometimes exists between familiarity and liking. Nonetheless, a review of the relevant literature conducted by Harrison (1977) generally supported Zajonc's hypothesis, Cantor and Kubose's findings notwithstanding.

Andrew Colman and his Aesthetics Research Group at the University of Leicester have conducted a number of studies looking at the relationship between people's liking for stimuli and their familiarity with them. In an early study, Sluckin *et al.*, (1973) found that young children (aged five) showed a distinct preference for letters presented in a form they were familiar with (Roman alphabet) compared with letters that were less familiar to them (Cyrillic alphabet), a result consistent with Zajonc's hypothesis. However, whilst older children (aged ten) also preferred familiar letters, their preferences were less strong, even though they were more familiar with the letters than the younger children. Sluckin and his colleagues concluded that, at least as far as letters of the alphabet were concerned, liking and familiarity were initially strongly positively correlated but extra exposure could lead to a reduction in liking.

Sluckin and his colleagues' conclusion tentatively hinted at the possibility of an inverted-U relationship between familiarity and liking, a relationship inconsistent with both Zajonc's hypothesis and Cantor and Kubose's experimental findings. However, two later studies confirmed the existence of the inverted-U. In the first, Colman *et al.*, (1975) reported that, whilst children preferred very common two syllable words to uncommon two syllable words, young adults showed a significant preference for uncommon (and likely to be unfamiliar) words over common (and likely to be familiar) words. In the second study, Sluckin *et al.*, (1980) assessed participants' familiarity with, and liking for, 100 emotionally neutral one syllable words, some of which were extremely rare (such as 'crore') and others extremely common (such as 'chair'). The results indicated that the function which properly fitted the familiarity–liking relationship was curvilinear, first rising and then falling.

One criticism that could be made of the stimulus material used in these studies is their lack of ecological validity. Cognizant of this, the

163

Aesthetics Research Group turned their attention to surnames and forenames, both of which possess a considerable amount of psychological and social significance. In one study, Colman, Sluckin and Hargreaves (1981) found that very common and familiar surnames, such as Smith, were not liked very much. However, the same was true for very unfamiliar names such as Bodle. Only those names which were in the middle range of familiarity, such as Burton, tended to be liked. The inverted-U relationship was thus manifested for highly ecologically valid stimuli. Forenames, however, did not produce the inverted-U. Colman, Hargreaves and Sluckin (1981) reported strong positive monotonic relationships between familiarity and liking for both male and female forenames. Thus, names that were rated as being highly familiar, such as David, were also among the most liked, whilst names rated as highly unfamiliar, such as Fulbert, were among the least liked.

Sluckin *et al.*'s (1982) explanation for the sometimes inverted-U and sometimes monotonic relationship between familiarity and liking concerns the nature of the stimuli employed. They argue that, in many studies, initially novel stimuli are used and their familiarity is manipulated by means of repeated exposure. In their own studies, however, naturally occurring stimuli are used with which participants are likely to be differentially familiar as a result of their experiences. Consequently, a much wider range of the familiarity continuum is sampled, compared with studies which manipulate exposure experimentally. The researchers propose that an inverted-U relationship emerges only when a very wide range of the familiarity continuum is sampled.

In support of this position, Sluckin and his colleagues found that when the words used in the Sluckin *et al.* (1980) study were divided into relatively unfamiliar and relatively familiar, liking was positively related to familiarity in the former case and negatively related in the latter case. These outcomes correspond to the findings reported by Zajonc, and Cantor and Kubose respectively. Thus, the positive and negative correlations between liking and familiarity are simply the ascending and descending parts respectively of the inverted-U curve. Moreover, even those studies which indicate that liking is independent of familiarity (e.g. Stang, 1974) can be explained in terms of the inverted-U by proposing that they correspond to the top, approximately flat, part of the curve!

Despite the explanatory power of the inverted-U, there remains the problem of the positive monotonic relationship reported for forenames. Since forenames were used which covered a wide range of the familiarity continuum, it is unlikely that the positive correlation simply represents the ascending part of the inverted-U. Given this, there is clearly some merit in attempting to replicate the data reported by Colman, Hargreaves and Sluckin (1981). The findings that emerge can then be compared with those reported by Colman and his colleagues and discussed in terms of the explanation they have proposed for the relationship between liking of, and familiarity with, forenames.

Hypotheses

In this exercise, only male forenames will be examined. On the basis of Colman and his colleagues' findings, it may be predicted that a significant positive correlation between familiarity with, and liking for, male forenames will be found. The null hypothesis predicts that there will be no significant relationship between the two variables and that any relationship observed is due to the operation of chance factors.

Procedure

Since this is a replication study, the design and methodology of this exercise duplicates that employed by Colman, Hargreaves and Sluckin (1981). Before the exercise begins, investigators should first type or print each of the 100 male forenames presented in *Appendix 1* on to separate pieces of card. Ten further pieces of card should also be prepared. Five of these will be used for the ratings of familiarity with the male forenames and five for the ratings of liking of these same names.

The five cards that will used for the familiarity ratings should be labelled:

'Very uncommon names in my experience'

'Quite uncommon names in my experience'

'Names which are neither common nor uncommon in my experience'

'Quite common names in my experience' and

'Very common names in my experience ', respectively.

The five cards that will be used for the liking ratings should be labelled:

'Names I dislike'

'Names I rather dislike'

'Names I neither like nor dislike'

'Names I rather like' and

'Names I like'.

Participants could be asked to rate the male forenames for both familiarity and liking. However, one disadvantage of this design is that participants might generate their own hypotheses and expectations concerning the relationship between familiarity and liking. Alternatively, or additionally, participants' judgements of their familiarity with a name might influence judgements concerning their liking of it (and vice versa).

For these reasons, the 20 participants who will generate the data in this exercise should be randomly assigned to a condition in which they either rate their familiarity with the forenames or their liking of them. Thus, ten participants will rate the names for their familiarity with them and ten for their liking of them. If the exercise is conducted in such a way that participants are discouraged from talking about their experiences to one another, none of the participants will know that familiarity and liking are the two variables under investigation. The data produced will therefore be unaffected by any hypotheses or expectations that participants might generate. This methodology also eliminates the possibility of ratings of familiarity and liking mutually influencing one another.

Depending on which condition the participant has been allocated to, the five cards that will form the rating scale should then be laid out on a table. The cards should be laid out from left to right in the order least familiar/liked–most familiar/liked. The 100 cards containing the male forenames should be shuffled to randomize the order in which participants are exposed to the stimulus material, and then stacked in a deck. Each participant should be tested individually and requested to sort the names into the five piles. Participants should also be requested to try to put roughly equal numbers of cards into each pile if possible. (The purpose of this is to try to influence people to use the whole scale and to counter the occasional tendency to concentrate on the two extreme or middle (neutral) positions.)

Once the cards have been sorted into the piles the results can be transferred to the score sheet presented in *Appendix 2*. For participants in the familiarity condition, scoring should take place in the following way:

'Very uncommon' scores 0

'Quite uncommon' scores 1

'Neither common nor uncommon' scores 2

'Quite common' scores 3

'Very common' scores 4

For participants in the liking condition, scoring should take place as indicated below:

'Dislike' scores 0

'Rather dislike' scores 1

'Neither like nor dislike' scores 2

'Rather like' scores 3

'Like' scores 4

When all the ratings have been transferred to the score sheet, the 100 cards should be shuffled again and the next participant's ratings collected and recorded. When all 20 participants have rated the male forenames, the data can be analysed and the relationship between familiarity and liking assessed.

Results

The first task is to compute the mean liking and familiarity ratings for each of the 100 male forenames by computing the sum of the ratings provided by participants and dividing this by the number of participants providing those ratings. *Appendix 2* contains a column headed 'Mean Rating' and the computed values should be placed in this column. The 100 mean ratings for familiarity and liking can then be plotted in a scattergram. The ratings will, of course, range from a minimum of 0 ('Dislike' or 'Very uncommon') to a maximum of 4 ('Like' or 'Very common').

In keeping with the scattergrams presented by Colman, Hargreaves and Sluckin (1981), familiarity should be plotted on the *x*-axis and liking on the *y*-axis. It should be noted that each of the data points in Colman and his associates' study was based on 20 participants in each condition, whereas in the present exercise the points are based on only ten participants in each condition. Nonetheless, even with only ten participants, the data points can be regarded as fairly stable.

Overall means and standard deviations for the familiarity and liking ratings could also be computed for comparison with the data presented by Colman, Hargreaves and Sluckin. For familiarity they reported a mean value of 1.86 with a standard deviation of 1.09, whilst for the liking ratings the mean value was 1.76 with a standard deviation of 0.76.

In order to assess the significance of the relationship between familiarity and liking, a Pearson's product–moment correlational test can be used provided that all the assumptions for using this parametric test have been met. Since it has been predicted that a positive correlation between familiarity and liking will be observed, a one-tailed test can be used. Degrees of freedom (df) are equal to $N-2$. In this case $N-2 = 98$. If the assumptions for using Pearson's method are not met, then a suitable non-parametric test of correlation should be used. An appropriate test would be that of Spearman, though ranking 100 names first for familiarity and then for liking could be time consuming.

For male forenames, Colman and his colleagues reported a correlation which was significant beyond the 0.001 level. Furthermore, four of the five most-liked names (David, Peter, Richard and John) were also among the most familiar, whilst two of the five least-liked names (Balthasar and Fulbert) were also among the five least familiar. The researchers additionally reported that none of the most familiar or best-liked names received an average or below average mean rating on the other variable, nor did any very unfamiliar or strongly disliked names receive an average or above average mean rating on the other variable. The data produced in this exercise could be examined for their similarity with those presented by Colman, Hargreaves and Sluckin.

Discussion

The most likely outcome of the present exercise is that the data produced have replicated the findings reported by Colman and his colleagues, and a highly significant positive correlation between familiarity with, and liking for, male forenames has been obtained. The point at issue is how this linear correlation can best be explained, given the strong evidence for the existence of an inverted-U relationship between familiarity and liking.

Sluckin *et al.* (1982) distinguish between two classes of naturally occurring stimuli. The first (Class A) consists of those stimuli where frequency of exposure depends largely on voluntary choice. Into this category fall male and female forenames. What other sorts of stimuli would fall into this category? The second (Class B) consists of those stimuli where frequency of exposure is virtually beyond voluntary control. Surnames fall into this category because, unlike forenames, they are not usually chosen at will. What other sorts of stimuli could be placed in this category?

The categories into which forenames and surnames fall can be used to explain the different type of relationship between familiarity and liking that has been observed for them. Stimuli like surnames can become so common in a culture that they pass the peak of the familiarity-liking curve and hence, for them, an inverted-U relationship is observed. Forenames, however, are prevented from reaching the peak of the curve since voluntary choice will reduce the frequency of exposure to people when a name begins to decline in popularity. In other words, whilst liking is a function of familiarity for some stimuli, for forenames the causal relationship is partly reversed: the best liked names are given most frequently to newborns and hence tend to become more familiar.

When a forename begins to become common, it often becomes less frequently chosen by people. Thus, no forenames are so frequently given that they pass the peak of the inverted-U curve. Colman and his colleagues have termed this explanation the Preference–Feedback hypothesis. This hypothesis would be supported if it could be shown that cyclical fashions in forenaming practices exist. Is there any evidence to suggest the existence of cyclical vogues? The work of Seeman (1972) could be useful in this context. *The Times* newspaper publishes annually lists showing the popularity of boys' and girls' names, taken from an analysis of entries in its 'Births' column. This too could be useful in the search for cyclical vogues in forenaming practices.

It is also worth discussing the extent to which other Class A stimuli fit in with the Preference–Feedback hypothesis and whether the hypothesis can explain the differences in speed with which certain fashions wax and wane in a culture. An alternative approach in this regard could be to consider the parameters of the inverted-U curve.

Colman and Sluckin (1976) have suggested that the peak of liking tends to occur earlier with stimuli that are subjectively simple, highly discriminable and predictable. This embraces things which have an almost instant appeal but which soon become boring. What examples are there of such instantly appealing yet quickly boring stimuli? Do they possess the characteristics suggested by Colman and Sluckin? With stimuli that are subjectively complex, poorly discriminable and unpredictable, the peak of liking is suggested to occur later. Here, liking develops more slowly but turns out to be more durable. What stimuli are there which 'grow on people' and continue to last? Do they possess the characteristics suggested above?

Colman and his colleagues do not suggest that familiarity is the only factor which determines liking, although they do believe that it is an important one. As Colman, Hargreaves and Sluckin (1981, p. 3) note, 'preferences for forenames are influenced by unique aspects of personal experience'. Has the present exercise generated any data where, say, a forename rated as highly familiar received a very low rating on the liking scale? Could social stereotyping be useful in explaining the occurrence of such apparently contradictory data and if so, how?

Colman and his colleagues have also looked at the relationship between familiarity and liking for forenames using Australian participants, and report similar, highly significant correlations. However, although there were no differences in the size of correlations between the Australian and English samples with respect to female forenames, the correlation for the English sample's rating of male forenames was higher than that of their Australian counterparts. It has been suggested that this may be due to 'the greater stereotyping of male than female names and the more centralized character of the mass media in England than in Australia'. What do Colman and his colleagues mean by this, and how could their suggestion be examined empirically?

Many aesthetic judgement studies have assessed participants' preferences before and after exposing them to the chosen stimuli. In the present exercise, participants' preferences were tested once only. What practical advantage does a single testing session offer to investigators? Another novel design feature of the Aesthetic Research Group's studies is the use of subjective rather than objective measures of familiarity. Other researchers have manipulated familiarity by systematically varying the number of exposures to a stimulus. In Colman's methodology the number of exposures is not known but can range from zero to millions. What sorts of advantages does this give compared with objective measures of familiarity such as word counts?

As well as the theoretical importance of the data, there are numerous practical applications of the Aesthetic Research Group's findings. How could advertisers and record company executives, say, use the Preference–Feedback hypothesis and the inverted-U relationship to their advantage? Could it even be the case that such people are actually (unknowingly perhaps) applying theoretical concepts? Apart from advertisers and record company executives, who else could potentially benefit from a knowledge of the theoretical basis of the liking–familiarity relationship?

Bibliography

General background references

BERLYNE, D.E. (1971) *Aesthetics and Psychobiology*. New York: Appleton-Century-Crofts.

BERLYNE, D.E. (Ed.) (1974) *Studies in the New Experimental Aesthetics*. New York: Halsted Press.

BORING, E.G. (1957) *A History of Experimental Psychology*. New York: Appleton-Century-Crofts.

MACE, C.A. (1962) Psychology and aesthetics. *British Journal of Aesthetics*, 2, 3–16.

Specific background references

COLMAN, A.M. and SLUCKIN, W. (1976) Everyday likes and dislikes: the psychology of human fancy. *New Society*, 38, 123–125.

HARRISON, A.A. (1977) Mere exposure. In L. Berkowitz (Ed.), *Advances in Experimental Social Psychology*. New York: Academic Press.

PICKFORD, R.W. (1972) *Psychology and Visual Aesthetics* Hutchinson Educational.

ZAJONC, R.B. (1968) Attitudinal effects of mere exposure. *Journal of Personality and Social Psychology*, 9, Monograph Supplement 2, Part 2, 1–21.

Journal articles

CANTOR, G.N. and KUBOSE, S.K. (1969) Preschool children's ratings of familiarized and nonfamiliarized visual stimuli. *Journal of Experimental Child Psychology*, 8, 74–81.

COLMAN, A.M., HARGREAVES, D.J. and SLUCKIN, W. (1981) Preferences for Christian names as a function of their experienced familiarity. *British Journal of Social Psychology*, 20, 3–5.

COLMAN, A.M., SLUCKIN, W. and HARGREAVES, D.J. (1981) The effect of familiarity on preference for surnames. *British Journal of Psychology*, 72, 363–369.

COLMAN, A.M., WALLEY, M. and SLUCKIN, W. (1975) Preferences for common words, uncommon words and non-words by children and young adults. *British Journal of Psychology*, 66, 481–486.

SEEMAN, M.V. (1972) Psycho-cultural aspects of naming children. *Canadian Psychiatric Association Journal*, 17, 149–151.

SLUCKIN, W., COLMAN, A.M. and HARGREAVES, D.J. (1980) Liking words as a function of the experienced frequency of their occurrence. *British Journal of Psychology*, 71, 163–169.

SLUCKIN, W., COLMAN, A.M. and HARGREAVES, D.J. (1982) Some experimental studies of familiarity and liking. *Bulletin of The British Psychological Society*, 35, 189–194.

SLUCKIN, W., MILLER, L.B. and FRANKLIN, H. (1973) The influence of stimulus familiarity/novelty on children's expressed preferences. *British Journal of Psychology*, 64, 563–567.

STANG, D.J. (1974) Methodological factors in mere exposure research. *Psychological Bulletin*, 81, 1014–1025.

Acknowledgment. Dr. A.M. Colman's help and advice are gratefully acknowledged.

Appendix 1. MALE FORENAMES USED BY COLMAN, HARGREAVES AND SLUCKIN (1981)

ABRAHAM	GODWIN
ADRIAN	GORDON
ALAN	GRAHAM
ALBERT	GUNTER
ALEXANDER	GUY
ALFRED	HAMISH
ALWYN	HAROLD
ANDREW	HENRY
ARCHIBALD	HERBERT
ARNOLD	HERMAN
BALTHASAR	HORACE
BARNABUS	HOWARD
BASIL	HUGH
BENJAMIN	IVOR
BERNARD	JACK
BRIAN	JAMES
BRUCE	JASON
CECIL	JEROME
CEDRIC	JOHN
CHARLES	JONATHON
CLARENCE	JOSEPH
CLEMENT	JULIAN
CLIVE	JULIUS
COLIN	KELVIN
CONRAD	KEVIN
CONSTANTINE	LAMBERT
CYRIL	LEONARD
DANIEL	LOUIS
DAVID	LUCIAN
DENIS	MANFRED
DEREK	MATTHEW
DONALD	NIGEL
DOUGLAS	OSWALD
DUNCAN	PATRICK
DUNSTAN	PETER
EDGAR	PHILIP
EDWARD	RALPH
EDWIN	RAYMOND
ERNEST	REYNOLD
EUGENE	RICHARD
EUSTACE	ROGER
FRANK	SEBASTIAN
FREDERICK	SELWYN
FULBERT	SIDNEY
GABRIEL	SIMON
GAWAIN	STEPHEN
GEOFFREY	THEODORE
GEORGE	TIMOTHY
GERALD	TOBY
GODFREY	WILLIAM

APPENDIX 2: SCORE SHEET FOR FAMILIARITY RATINGS (P1 = Participant 1)

Male Forename	P1	P2	P3	P4	P5	P6	P7	P8	P9	P10	Mean Rating
ABRAHAM											
ADRIAN											
ALAN											
ALBERT											
ALEXANDER											
ALFRED											
ALWYN											
ANDREW											
ARCHIBALD											
ARNOLD											
BALTHASAR											
BARNABUS											
BASIL											
BENJAMIN											
BERNARD											
BRIAN											
BRUCE											
CECIL											
CEDRIC											
CHARLES											
CLARENCE											
CLEMENT											
CLIVE											
COLIN											
CONRAD											
CONSTANTINE											
CYRIL											
DANIEL											

Male Forename	P1	P2	P3	P4	P5	P6	P7	P8	P9	P10	Mean Rating
DAVID											
DENIS											
DEREK											
DONALD											
DOUGLAS											
DUNCAN											
DUNSTAN											
EDGAR											
EDWARD											
EDWIN											
ERNEST											
EUGENE											
EUSTACE											
FRANK											
FREDERICK											
FULBERT											
GABRIEL											
GAWAIN											
GEOFFREY											
GEORGE											
GERALD											
GODFREY											
GODWIN											
GORDON											
GRAHAM											
GUNTER											
GUY											
HAMISH											
HAROLD											
HENRY											
HERBERT											

Male Forename	P1	P2	P3	P4	P5	P6	P7	P8	P9	P10	Mean Rating
HERMAN											
HORACE											
HOWARD											
HUGH											
IVOR											
JACK											
JAMES											
JASON											
JEROME											
JOHN											
JONATHON											
JOSEPH											
JULIAN											
JULIUS											
KELVIN											
KEVIN											
LAMBERT											
LEONARD											
LOUIS											
LUCIAN											
MANFRED											
MATTHEW											
NIGEL											
OSWALD											
PATRICK											
PETER											
PHILIP											
RALPH											
RAYMOND											
REYNOLD											
RICHARD											

Male Forename	P1	P2	P3	P4	P5	P6	P7	P8	P9	P10	Mean Rating
ROGER											
SEBASTIAN											
SELWYN											
SIDNEY											
SIMON											
STEPHEN											
THEODORE											
TIMOTHY											
TOBY											
WILLIAM											

SCORE SHEET FOR LIKING RATINGS

Male Forename	P1	P2	P3	P4	P5	P6	P7	P8	P9	P10	Mean Rating
ABRAHAM											
ADRIAN											
ALAN											
ALBERT											
ALEXANDER											
ALFRED											
ALWYN											
ANDREW											
ARCHIBALD											
ARNOLD											
BALTHASAR											
BARNABUS											
BASIL											
BENJAMIN											
BERNARD											

Male Forename	P1	P2	P3	P4	P5	P6	P7	P8	P9	P10	Mean Rating
BRIAN											
BRUCE											
CECIL											
CEDRIC											
CHARLES											
CLARENCE											
CLEMENT											
CLIVE											
COLIN											
CONRAD											
CONSTANTINE											
CYRIL											
DANIEL											
DAVID											
DENIS											
DEREK											
DONALD											
DOUGLAS											
DUNCAN											
DUNSTAN											
EDGAR											
EDWARD											
EDWIN											
ERNEST											
EUGENE											
EUSTACE											
FRANK											
FREDERICK											
FULBERT											
GABRIEL											
GAWAIN											

Male Forename	P1	P2	P3	P4	P5	P6	P7	P8	P9	P10	Mean Rating
GEOFFREY											
GEORGE											
GERALD											
GODFREY											
GODWIN											
GORDON											
GRAHAM											
GUNTER											
GUY											
HAMISH											
HAROLD											
HENRY											
HERBERT											
HERMAN											
HORACE											
HOWARD											
HUGH											
IVOR											
JACK											
JAMES											
JASON											
JEROME											
JOHN											
JONATHON											
JOSEPH											
JULIAN											
JULIUS											
KELVIN											
KEVIN											
LAMBERT											
LEONARD											

Male Forename	P1	P2	P3	P4	P5	P6	P7	P8	P9	P10	Mean Rating
LOUIS											
LUCIAN											
MANFRED											
MATTHEW											
NIGEL											
OSWALD											
PATRICK											
PETER											
PHILIP											
RALPH											
RAYMOND											
REYNOLD											
RICHARD											
ROGER											
SEBASTIAN											
SELWYN											
SIDNEY											
SIMON											
STEPHEN											
THEODORE											
TIMOTHY											
TOBY											
WILLIAM											

PRACTICAL 14   # Locus of control and stress: an investigation into the relationship between perceptions of controllability of events and levels of reported stress

Mark Lauder
South Devon College

Abstract

This exercise is concerned with investigating the relationship between people's beliefs about the control they have over events in their lives and the stress they report experiencing. The hypothesis to be tested is that the less control a person believes he/she has over events, the greater the level of reported stress. The reliability and validity of the measures used is discussed as well as background theory and research. Relationships between locus of control and factors other than stress are outlined with a view to further studies. Whatever the outcome of the exercise, it is expected that both the problems associated with an investigation of this sort and the implications of the results obtained will be discussed.

Materials and Equipment

This is a correlational exercise involving the use of questionnaires, examples of which can be found in *Appendices 1* and *2*. Participants will need a copy of each questionnaire and instructions on how to complete them.

One of the questionnaires is the *Professional Life Stress Scale* so participants in this exercise will need to be employed adults in professional jobs. The smallest number of participants advisable is 20, but it should be possible to obtain a larger sample, especially if several investigators work as a group and pool the data. Instructing participants, completion of the questionnaires and debriefing participants is likely to take no more than 10–15 minutes per person.

Introduction and Hypotheses

J.B. Rotter's (1966) theory of locus of control was an early application of the principles of social learning theory to the field of personality. It is sometimes called a 'narrow band' theory of personality (Peck and Whitlow, 1975) because its area of concern is more specific and restricted than more comprehensive theories, such as that of Sigmund Freud.

Rotter used the term 'locus of control' to refer to the extent to which a person believed that he or she was in control of life events. He argued that this belief develops as a result of the different patterns of reinforcement that an individual experiences. As a child grows, he or she will find that some actions result in the same or similar consequences, while others do not. Expectations about actions will, therefore, develop. The more an action is followed by similar consequences, the greater the expectation will be that these consequences

179

will occur again; the more varied the consequences, the less the expectation. The child will thus come to distinguish actions resulting in predictable consequences from those that do not, and will generalize across learning situations. Social learning theory would also predict that these general expectations will be influenced by observing others and through instruction.

Thus, individuals will develop a tendency to believe that they are, or are not, in control across many situations. At one extreme, there are people who see their behaviour and the events in their lives as influenced by external events or other people beyond their personal control. They perceive events as being due to factors such as chance, fate or luck. Such people are said to have an external locus of control.

At the other extreme, there are those who see events in their lives as being controlled by internal factors and who believe in their own ability to control and bring about changes in their behaviour and life events. Such people are said to have an internal locus of control. Others occupy a position somewhere between these two extremes.

In order to assess locus of control, Rotter and his colleagues (Rotter *et al.*, 1961) devised the *I–E Scale*. This is a questionnaire which assesses the position of people on the bipolar continuum Internal–External. It consists of 23 pairs of statements with one of each pair expressing an external explanation for an event and the other an internal explanation. The participant ticks the statement in each pair which comes closest to being true. For example, either:

'People's misfortunes result from the mistakes they make.'

or: 'Many of the unhappy things in people's lives are partly due to bad luck.'

Whilst both split-half and test-retest reliability checks of the scale reached acceptable levels ($r = 0.49$ and $r = 0.85$ respectively), its validity has been questioned. It has been suggested that the items in the scale measure not just one single factor, but a number of distinct factors. Gurin *et al.* (1969) identified four factors:

Control ideology – how much control most people in society have.
Personal ideology – how much control one has personally.
System modifiability – how far society's problems can be overcome.
Race ideology – how far the races differ in their perceived/actual control.

In addition, while acknowledging that there is a common theme of internal–external control of reinforcement running through Rotter's questionnaire, Collins (1974) identified four different factors from those proposed by Gurin *et al.*:

The easy/difficult world – beliefs about the complexity of the world we live in.
The just/unjust world – beliefs about the extent to which effort is rewarded.
The predictable/unpredictable world – beliefs about the role of luck/fate in shaping our lives.

The politically responsive/unresponsive world – beliefs about the power the individual has to shape and influence society.

Collins claimed that Rotter's scale forces participants to choose between an I and E statement and this may make it difficult to respond appropriately. For instance, in the example given earlier, the participant may believe that people's misfortunes do indeed result from the mistakes they make (that is, internal on factor 1 – the easy/difficult world) and, at the same time, believe that many of the unhappy things in people's lives are partly due to bad luck (that is, external on factor 3 – the predictable/unpredictable world). Collins felt that if participants may be external with respect to one factor and internal with respect to another, there may be a number of different types of internals and externals depending on which factors they give external or internal endorsement.

In addition, he claimed that the forced choice approach of Rotter's scale could produce misleading results. Often a participant may believe both statements, or neither, yet may obtain the same score as someone who believes one statement but not the other.

It has also been suggested (for example Joe, 1971) that the questionnaire is open to 'socially desirable responses' whereby people answer untruthfully in order to present themselves in a favourable light. Many of the internal statements may be construed as more socially desirable than the external statements.

Since Rotter devised the scale, a number of different tests have been constructed to measure locus of control in adults and in children (Lefcourt, 1982). Appendix 2 contains an adaptation of Rotter's original scale which overcomes some of the problems outlined and it is the scale which will be used in this exercise. Notice that there is no longer a forced choice between two statements although the actual statements remain the same.

In spite of criticisms, a great deal of research has been carried out using I–E scales, and Internality/Externality have been shown to be significantly correlated with a large number of other variables.

Behavioural correlates.   Externals have been found to be generally less competent than internals in their performance on a number of tasks. They are less active in solving mental problems (Lefcourt, 1976) and less attentive to relevant cues when skill is demanded (Lefcourt and Wine, 1980). They are more likely to prefer tests of chance to tests of skill (Kahle, 1980) and are likely to make lower estimates of their success even when their actual success is no less than that of internals (Benassi *et al.*, 1979).

Externals are more likely than internals to be suicidal (Strickland, 1974), experience illness (Kobosa, 1979) and smoke cigarettes (Coan, 1973). They have also been found to engage in less physical exercise (Walker, 1973). Externals are less willing than internals to join in civil rights work (Gore and Rotter, 1963) and participate less frequently in the feminist movement (Pawlicki and Almquist, 1973).

Individual differences.   Women tend to be more external than men but this difference has not been found in adolescents. Internality seems to increase with age, particularly around 15 years (Baldo *et al.*, 1975).

Personality correlates. Using a 'self acceptance' questionnaire and Rotter's I–E scale, Lombardo *et al.* (1975) found that, compared with internals, externals have a greater discrepancy between 'real self' and 'ideal self'. The degree of this discrepancy is an indicator of maladjustment, as found in other studies (for example, Truax *et al.*, 1968). Thus, externality correlates with emotional instability, poor social adjustment, anxiety and neuroticism. Externals tend to feel more anger and perceive others to be less friendly (Holmes and Jackson, 1975). Rotter (1970) found that externals tend to be more suspicious, dogmatic and authoritarian and Scheidt (1973) found that they were more likely to believe in paranormal phenomena. Phares (1978) found externals to be less persuasive, and Goodstadt and Hjelle (1973) found that they rely less on persuasion than on coercion in personal relationships. Internals are less likely than externals to conform when there is pressure to do so (Crowne and Liverant, 1963).

In contrast, internals are more independent, achieving and dominant (Rotter, 1970). They express more contentment with life (Naditch *et al.*, 1975) and experience less debilitating anxiety (Strassberg, 1973) and depression (Lefcourt, 1976). Internals are also found to be more psychosocially mature. Baldo *et al.* (1975) found that externals have been less successful in resolving Eriksonian crises such as autonomy, initiative, independence and identity.

These examples illustrate the range of research stimulated by Rotter's work. Introductory textbooks which examine this topic provide many other examples (for example, Brown, 1986; Deaux and Wrightsman, 1988; Rosenhan and Seligman, 1989; Sugarman, 1986). They also examine the usefulness of the concept of locus of control and may suggest further studies which could be conducted. In this exercise, attention will be focused on one area, namely the relationship between locus of control and level of perceived stress.

Many of the studies cited suggest a connection between externality and maladjustment. For instance, Kobosa's (1979) study compared a group of highly stressed executives, who became ill, with a similar group who did not. She found that one of the characteristics which best distinguished one group from the other was locus of control. Internals seemed to be more 'hardy' than externals. Brown (1986) has suggested that life events are stressful in as much as they are perceived to be uncontrollable. Johnson and Sarason (1978) used Rotter's scale and devised a new scale (the *Life Events Scale*) and found that externals were more likely to have life events related to psychiatric illness, especially depression and anxiety.

In a related analysis of depression, Seligman (1973) has suggested that depression is caused by 'learned helplessness'. He based his analysis on a series of experiments in which dogs who were given electric shocks which they were powerless to avoid subsequently developed symptoms of severe depression. Krantz *et al.* (1974) have suggested a connection between learned helplessness and heart attacks, which are often associated with high levels of stress. In a reformulation of the theory of learned helplessness, Abramson *et al.* (1978) proposed that it is not simply the expectation of uncontrollability that causes depression, but the attributions that a person makes. Sufferers of depression attribute failure to personal, global and persistent causes while attributing success to external, unstable, specific causes. These, and other findings, strongly support a connection between locus of control and stress. This exercise seeks to investigate further this connection.

Hypotheses

The hypothesis to be tested in this exercise is that there will be a positive correlation between internality/externality and perceived stress such that greater externality will be associated with higher levels of reported stress. This is a one-tailed hypothesis based on findings from previous research. The null hypothesis is that there will be no relationship between internality/externality and reported stress, and that any relationship found will be due to chance.

Procedure

First, investigators will need to decide on the number and type of participants to be approached and how they are to be selected. A total of at least 20 men and women will be needed, preferably more, and they must be in employment. It is unlikely that random sampling will be possible so the sample will probably be selected opportunistically from the defined population. Each participant will need a copy of *Appendices 1* and 2. (The stress scale in *Appendix 1* is not sensitive enough to provide an accurate measure of stress, but it is sufficient to give a general impression.)

One of the main problems with questionnaires, especially when they deal with such sensitive issues as stress, is that people may not answer questions truthfully. There are two reasons for this. The first, which was discussed earlier, concerns 'socially desirable responses'. To minimize this it is usual to reassure participants that their responses will be anonymous. The second reason is that people may try to fulfil the expectations of the investigator (as far as it is possible to identify them). This is more difficult to deal with, especially since it is not desirable to deceive participants about the purpose of the study. In this exercise, honest and fairly general instructions should suffice. For example:

> I/we are trying to find out why some people feel more stress than others. I/we would be very grateful if you could help me/us by taking part in this investigation and filling in two questionnaires.

Participants should then be shown the questionnaires and informed that it will not be necessary for them to give their names. If the participant agrees to proceed, the next instruction can be given:

> Please complete both questionnaires. There is no need to think too hard before responding as your first response will be most helpful. You will find brief, written instructions at the beginning of each questionnaire.

Spaces for information on age, gender, occupation, or any other variables of interest suggested by the background literature, may also be included in the questionnaires if the investigators wish to test the influence of these variables. Once questionnaires have been completed, investigators should offer to explain the purpose of the exercise and the expected findings in more detail, and any questions raised by the participant should be answered. The participant should then be thanked for taking part.

Results

The first task is to tabulate raw data. An example of how this could be laid out is provided in *Appendix 3*. The two questionnaires are scored as follows:

THE I–E SCALE.

Internal statements – 2, 3, 5, 7, 9, 11, 12, 13, 14, 15, 16, 20.
External statements – 1, 4, 6, 8, 10, 17, 18, 19.

Participants will have indicated the extent to which they agree or disagree with each statement. A score between 1 and 6 should be given to each response as follows:

Internal statements – 1 (agree very much) to 6 (disagree very much).
External statements – 6 (agree very much) to 1 (disagree very much).

Thus, a low score indicates internality while a high score indicates externality. Total scores can range from 20 to 120.
The statements allocated to Collin's four factors are:

Easy/difficult world – 1, 4, 6, 10, 17.

Just/unjust world – 7, 9, 11, 14, 20.

Predictable/unpredictable world – 3, 5, 12, 15, 18.

Politically responsive/unresponsive world – 2, 8, 13, 16, 19.

PROFESSIONAL LIFE STRESS SCALE

Items 1 to 22 are are scored as follows:

1. a) 0 b) 1 c) 2 d) 3 e) 4
2. Score 1 for each 'yes' response
3. Score 0 for 'more optimistic', 1 for 'about the same', 2 for 'less optimistic'
4. Score 0 for 'yes' and 1 for 'no'
5. Score 0 for 'yes' and 1 for 'no'
6. Score 0 for each 'yes' response and 1 for each 'no' response
7. Score 0 for 'yourself' and 1 for 'someone else'
8. Score 2 for 'very upset', 1 for 'moderately upset' and 0 for 'mildly upset'
9. Score 0 for 'often', 1 for 'sometimes' and 2 for 'only occasionally'
10. Score 0 for 'no' and 1 for 'yes'

11. Score 2 for 'habitually', 1 for 'sometimes' and 0 for 'only very occasionally'
12. Score 0 for 'mostly', 1 for 'sometimes' and 2 for 'hardly ever'
13. Score 0 for 'yes' and 1 for 'no'
14. Score 0 for 'yes' and 1 for 'no'
15. Score 0 for 'yes' and 1 for 'no'
16. Score 2 for 'often', 1 for 'sometimes' and 0 for 'very rarely'
17. Score 0 for 'most days', 1 for 'some days' and 2 for 'hardly ever'
18. Score 0 for 'yes' and 1 for 'no'
19. Score 0 for 'yes' and 1 for 'no'
20. Score 1 for 'a' and 0 for 'b'
21. Score 0 for 'exceeding your expectations', 1 for 'fulfilling your expectations' and 2 for 'falling short of your expectations'
22. Score 0 for '5', 1 for '4' and so on down to 4 for '1'

With this scale, a high score denotes a high level of stress, while low scores denote lower levels. The minimum possible score is 0 and the maximum possible is 60.

The raw data tables are likely to be extensive. For this reason, a summary table of results using descriptive statistics, such as measures of central tendency and spread should be presented in the main body of the report. Raw data can then be placed in an Appendix.

The next task is to plot pairs of results in the form of a scattergram where the horizontal axis is used for locus of control and the vertical axis for perceived stress scores. Strictly speaking, one should rank the locus of control data, then the perceived stress data, and then plot pairs of ranks. The scattergram will enable investigators to see if there is a positive correlation, as predicted in the hypothesis.

Further analysis should be carried out using a non-parametric test of correlation, suitable for ordinal data, such as Spearman's rho. Pearson's product–moment correlation coefficient, which is a parametric test, is not suitable here as the level of measurement does not reach the required standard. The calculated value of rho should be interpreted using the appropriate statistical table using a probability level of ≤ 0.05 and bearing in mind that the hypothesis is one-tailed.

If data have been collected on other variables, such as gender, age and occupation of participants, further analyses may be carried out: for example, age could be correlated with locus of control. A further possibility is to test for differences between the sexes, or different occupational groups, on any of the measures taken. A suitable test in this case would be the Mann–Whitney U-test. Scores relating to the four factors suggested by Collins may also be extracted and each factor correlated with the stress scale scores. Tests of difference could also be incorporated here, again comparing the sexes or occupational groups.

Discussion

The exact form of the discussion will vary according to the focus of the exercise and the outcome of the statistical analysis. However, the following points may be helpful.

How do the results compare with those of similar studies? Do they support the hypothesis and do they agree with the findings of Johnson and Sarason (1978) and those of other researchers? If the results differ, in what way do they contradict previous findings?

Whether or not evidence is supportive, it is important to consider the implications of this for the underlying theories. If the hypothesis is supported, how does this fit in with the suggestions and theories offered in the Introduction? For instance, could Seligman's theory of learned helplessness be used to explain the results? Other studies linking lack of control of events to stress (such as Brady's (1958) study on ulcers in executive monkeys) could be cited along with appropriate criticisms.

If the null hypothesis is retained, it will be necessary to consider whether other factors could have affected the outcome. Some reservations about the measurement of locus of control, and the use of questionnaires in general, were raised in the Introduction. It follows from this that the results are likely to obscure a more complicated pattern of inter-relationships between a number of factors. For example, it is possible that happy-go-lucky people feel less stress, or that, for certain groups of people, it may be more realistic and beneficial to accept that they are not in control, rather than blame themselves. The validity and reliability of the I–E scale could also be considered. It may be that one of Collins' factors is related to stress, or even that one is positively related, while others show no relationship or a negative relationship.

A close examination of the data may reveal interesting trends. Look for differences in the measures of central tendency and spread and in the pattern of the scattergram. What do these suggest about the findings? It is important to remember that correlation does not imply causation so any factors responsible for a significant correlation could be considered at this point.

It is usual to examine the design of the investigation in order to identify further weak points or limitations and this should be carried out even if the hypothesis was accepted. The reliability and validity of the stress scale should be considered as well as the extent to which participants were honest. Is it possible to generalize the findings from the sample obtained? What improvements and/or modifications could be made to a future study of this kind? Extensions to the investigation could be suggested using background reading for ideas.

Finally, the practical applications of the findings should be discussed. A connection between perceived uncontrollability of events and perceived stress could be important in helping people to deal with stress and stress-related illness. Evidence cited in the Introduction, and resulting from this investigation, may provide some ideas. If there is no evidence of a relationship, the implications of such findings should also be discussed.

Bibliography

General background references

BARON, R. and BYRNE, D. (1987) *Social Psychology: Understanding Human Interaction.* 5th edn. London: Allyn and Bacon, Inc. Chapter 14.
BROWNE, R. (1986) *Social Psychology.* 2nd edn. New York: Free Press.
DEAUX, K. and WRIGHTSMAN, L. (1988) *Social Psychology.* 5th edn. Pacific Grove, California: Brooks/Cole Publishing Company.

FONTANA, D. (1989) *Managing Stress*. Leicester: BPS Books (The British Psychological Society).

GROSS, R. (1987) *Psychology: The Science of Mind and Behaviour*. London: Edward Arnold. Chapter 17.

ROSENHAM, D. and SELIGMAN, M. (1989) *Abnormal Psychology*. 2nd edn. London: W.W. Norton and Company.

SUGARMAN, L. (1986) *Life-span Development: Concepts, theories and interventions*. London: Methuen.

Specific background references

JOHNSON, J.H. and SARASON, I.G. (1978) Life stress, depression and anxiety: Internal–external control as a moderator variable. *Journal of Psychosomatic Research, 22*, 205–208.

LEFCOURT, H.M. (1976; 1982) *Locus of control: Current trends in theory and research*. 1st and 2nd edns. Hillsdale, New Jersey: Lawrence Erlbaum.

PECK, D. and WHITLOW, D. (1975) *Approaches to Personality Theory*. London: Methuen. Chapter 5.

PHARES, E. (1978) Locus of control. In H. London and J. Exner (Eds) *Dimensions of Personality*. New York: Wiley.

ROTTER, J.B. (1970) Some implications of a social learning theory for the practice of psychotherapy. In D.J. Levis (Ed.) *Learning approaches to therapeutic behavior change*. Chicago: Aldine.

Journal articles

ABRAMSON, L., SELIGMAN, M. and TEASDALE, J. (1978) Learned helplessness in humans: Critiques and reformulation. *Journal of Abnormal Psychology, 87*, 32–48.

BALDO, R., HARRIS, M. and CRADALL, J. (1975) Relations among Psychosocial Development, Locus of Control and Time Orientation. *Journal of Genetic Psychology, 126*, 297–303.

BENASSI, V.A., SWEENEY, P.D. and DREVNO, G.E. (1979) Mind over matter: Perceived success at psychokinesis. *Journal of Personality and Social Psychology, 37*, 1377–1386.

BRADY, J.P. (1958) Ulcers in 'executive' monkeys. *Scientific American, 199*, 95–100.

COAN, R.W. (1973) Personality variables associated with cigarette smoking. *Journal of Personality and Social Psychology, 26*, 86–104.

COLLINS, B.E. (1974) Four components of the Rotter Internal–External scale: Belief in a difficult world, a just world, a predictable world, and a politically responsive world. *Journal of Personality and Social Psychology, 29*, 381–391.

CROWNE, D. and LIVERANT, S. (1963) Conformity under varying conditions of personal commitment. *Journal of Abnormal and Social Psychology, 66*, 547–555.

GOODSTADT, B. and HJELLE, L. (1973) Power to the powerless: Locus of control and the use of power. *Journal of Personality and Social Psychology, 27*, 190–196.

GORE, P.M. and ROTTER, J.B. (1963) A personality correlate of social action. *Journal of Personality, 31*, 58–64.

GURIN, P., GURIN, G., LAO, R.C. and BEATTIE, M. (1969) Internal–external control in the motivational dynamics of Negro youth. *Journal of Social Issues, 25*, 29–53.

HOLMES, D.S. and JACKSON, T.H. (1975) Influence of locus of control in interpersonal attraction and affective reactions in situations involving reward and punishment. *Journal of Personality and Social Psychology, 31*, 132–136.

JOE, V. (1971) Review of the internal–external control construct as a personality variable. *Psychological Reports, 28*, 619–640.

KAHLE, L.R. (1980) Stimulus condition self-selection by males in the interaction of locus of control and skill–chance situations. *Journal of Personality and Social Psychology, 8*, 50–56.

KOBOSA, S.C. (1979) Stressful life events, personality and health: An inquiry into hardiness. *Journal of Personality and Social Psychology, 37*, 1–11.

KRANTZ, D.S., GLASS, D.C. and SNYDER, M.L. (1974) Helplessness, stress level and the coronary prone behaviour pattern. *Journal of Experimental Social Psychology, 10*, 284–300.

LEFCOURT, H.M. and WINE, J. (1969) Internal versus external control of reinforcement and the development of attention in experimental situations. *Canadian Journal of Behavioural Sciences, 1*, 167–181.

LOMBARDO, J.P., FANTASIA, S.C. and SOHEIM, G. (1975) The relationship of Internality–Externality, self-acceptance, and self-ideal discrepancies. *The Journal of Genetic Psychology, 126*, 281–288.

NADITCH, M.P., GARGAN, M. and MICHAEL, L.B. (1975) Denial, anxiety, locus of control and the discrepancy between aspirations and achievements as components of depression. *Journal of Abnormal Psychology, 84*, 1–9.

PAWLICKI, R.E. and ALMQUIST, C. (1973) Authoritarianism, locus of control and tolerance of ambiguity as reflected in membership and nonmembership in the women's liberation group. *Psychological Reports, 32*, 1331–1337.

ROTTER, J.B. (1966) Generalized expectancies for interval versus external control of reinforcement. *Psychological Monographs, 30*, 1–26.

ROTTER, J.B., LIVERANT, S. and CROWNE, D. (1961) The growth and extinction of expectancies in chance controlled and skilled tasks. *Journal of Psychology, 52*, 161–177.

SCHEIDT, R.J. (1973) Belief in supernatural phenomena and locus of control. *Psychological Reports, 32*, 1159–1169.

SELIGMAN, M. (1973) Fall into helplessness. *Psychology Today 7, 81*, 43–48.

STRASSBERG, D.S. (1973) Relationships among locus of control, anxiety and valued goal expectations. *Journal of Consulting and Clinical Psychology, 2*, 319–328.

STRICKLAND, B.R. (1974) *Locus of control and health related problems*. Paper presented at the meeting of the Inter-American Congress of Psychology, Bogota, Colombia, December 1974.

TRUAX, C.B., SCHULLDT, W.J. and WARGO, D.J. (1968) Self-ideal concept congruence and improvement in group psychotherapy. *Journal of Consulting and Clinical Psychology, 32*, 47–53.

WALKER, T.G. (1973) Behaviour of temporary members in small groups. *Journal of Applied Psychology, 58*, 144–146.

Appendix 1. PROFESSIONAL LIFE STRESS SCALE

For the following questions, please tick the answers you feel apply most to you.

1. Two people who know you well are discussing you. Which of the following statements would they be most likely to use?

   (a) 'X is very together. Nothing much seems to bother him/her.'
   (b) 'X is great. But you have to be careful what you say to him/her at times.'
   (c) 'Something always seems to be going wrong with X's life.'
   (d) 'I find X very moody and unpredictable.'
   (e) 'The less I see of X the better.'

2. Are any of the following common features of your life?

   - Feeling you can seldom do anything right
   - Feelings of being hounded or trapped or cornered
   - Indigestion
   - Poor appetite
   - Difficulty in getting to sleep at night
   - Dizzy spells or palpitations
   - Sweating without exertion or high air temperature
   - Panic feelings when in crowds or in confined spaces
   - Tiredness and lack of energy
   - Feelings of hopelessness ('what's the use of anything?')
   - Faintness or nausea sensations without any physical cause
   - Extreme irritation over small things
   - Inability to unwind in the evenings
   - Waking regularly at night or early in the mornings
   - Difficulty in taking decisions
   - Inability to stop thinking about problems or the day's events
   - Tearfulness
   - Convictions that you just can't cope
   - Lack of enthusiasm even for cherished interests
   - Reluctance to meet new people and attempt new experiences
   - Inability to say 'no' when asked to do something
   - Having more responsibility than you can handle

3. Are you more or less optimistic than you used to be? a) more b) less c) about the same

4. Do you enjoy watching sport? a) No b) Yes

5. Can you get up late at weekends if you want to without feeling guilty? a) No b) Yes

6. Within reasonable professional and personal limits, can you speak your mind to: a) your boss? b) your colleagues? c) members of your family?

7. Who usually seems to be responsible for making the important decisions in your life: a) yourself? b) someone else?

8. When criticized by superiors at work, are you usually: a) very upset? b) moderately upset? c) mildly upset?

9. Do you finish the working day feeling satisfied with what you have achieved: a) often? b) sometimes? c) only occasionally?

10. Do you feel most of the time that you have unsettled conflicts with colleagues? a) No b) Yes

11. Does the amount of work you have to do exceed the amount of time available: a) habitually? b) sometimes? c) only very occasionally?

12. Have you a clear picture of what is expected of you professionally: a) mostly? b) sometimes? c) hardly ever?

13. Would you say that generally you have enough time to spend on yourself? a) No b) Yes

14. If you want to discuss your problems with someone, can you usually find a sympathetic ear? a) No b) Yes

15. Are you reasonably on course towards achieving your major objectives in life? a) No b) Yes

16. Are you bored at work a) often? b) sometimes? c) very rarely?

17. Do you look forward to going into work: a) most days? b) some days? c) hardly ever?

18. Do you feel adequately valued for your abilities and commitment to work? a) No b) Yes

19. Do you feel adequately *rewarded* (in terms of status and promotion) for your abilities and commitment to work? a) No b) Yes

20. Do you feel your superiors actively hinder you in your work? a) No b) Yes

21. If ten years ago you had been able to see yourself professionally as you are now, would you have seen yourself as: a) exceeding your expectations? b) fulfilling your expectations? c) falling short of your expectations?

22. If you had to rate how much you like yourself on a scale from 5 (most like) to 1 (least like), what would your rating be?

Appendix 2. LOCUS OF CONTROL SCALE

Here are some statements that people have made about their attitudes to life. Try to decide how far you agree or disagree with each statement.

	agree very much	agree somewhat	agree slightly	disagree slightly	disagree somewhat	disagree very much
1. Sometimes I feel that I don't have enough control over the direction my life is taking	☐	☐	☐	☐	☐	☐
2. By taking an active part in political and social affairs people can control world events	☐	☐	☐	☐	☐	☐
3. It is impossible for me to believe that chance or luck plays an important role in my life	☐	☐	☐	☐	☐	☐
4. Many times I feel that I have little influence over the things that happen to me	☐	☐	☐	☐	☐	☐
5. Getting people to do the right things depends upon ability; luck has little or nothing to do with it	☐	☐	☐	☐	☐	☐
6. Unfortunately, an individual's worth often passes unrecognized no matter how hard he tries	☐	☐	☐	☐	☐	☐
7. Capable people who fail to become leaders have not taken advantage of their opportunities	☐	☐	☐	☐	☐	☐
8. This world is run by a few people in power, and there is not much the little guy can do about it	☐	☐	☐	☐	☐	☐
9. What happens to me is my own doing	☐	☐	☐	☐	☐	☐
10. Most people don't realize the extent to which their lives are controlled by accidental happenings	☐	☐	☐	☐	☐	☐
11. People's misfortunes result from the mistakes they make	☐	☐	☐	☐	☐	☐
12. There is really no such thing as 'luck'	☐	☐	☐	☐	☐	☐
13. The average citizen can have an influence on government decisions	☐	☐	☐	☐	☐	☐
14. In the long run people get the respect they deserve in the world	☐	☐	☐	☐	☐	☐
15. In my case getting what I want has little or nothing to do with luck	☐	☐	☐	☐	☐	☐
16. With enough effort we can wipe out political corruption	☐	☐	☐	☐	☐	☐
17. Who gets to be the boss often depends on who was lucky enough to be in the right place first	☐	☐	☐	☐	☐	☐
18. Many of the unhappy things in people's lives are partly due to bad luck	☐	☐	☐	☐	☐	☐
19. It is difficult for people to have much control over the things politicians do in office	☐	☐	☐	☐	☐	☐
20. People are lonely because they don't try to be friendly	☐	☐	☐	☐	☐	☐

Appendix 3. EXAMPLE OF RAW DATA TABLE

Participant Number	Locus of Control score	Stress score	Male/ Female	Age	Occupation

PRACTICAL 15

Approaches to study and academic performance

Jeremy J. Foster
Manchester Polytechnic

Abstract

This practical exercise is intended to test the hypothesis that there is a correlation between students' approaches to study and actual academic attainment. Participants complete an 'Approaches to Study Questionnaire' (*Appendix 2*) devised by Entwistle (1981), and their responses are correlated with a score of their academic performance. Discussion points likely to arise from the exercise include the questions of whether training students in approaches to study is likely to improve their academic performance, whether past academic performance can be expressed as a single number, and a consideration of the main factors influencing academic performance.

Materials
and Equipment

For this study access to as large a number of participants as possible is needed, at least 30 and preferably more. If possible, they need to be aged at least 18 and should have taken A-levels, GCSEs, or equivalent examinations. If it is not possible to obtain a group of participants who meet these criteria, ways in which the study could be modified are considered in the Discussion.

Each participant needs a copy of both the 'Personal Details Questionnaire' (*Appendix 1*) and the 'Approaches to Study Questionnaire' (*Appendix 2*), and a paperclip to clip them together once they have been completed.

Introduction
and Hypotheses

Why do people differ in their levels of academic achievement? Why do some students get high marks in their examinations, some do poorly, and others fail altogether? Perhaps the first answer which comes to mind is that people differ in terms of their ability to learn, which is one aspect of what is meant by intelligence. This is by no means the whole answer, however, as the correlation between measured intelligence and academic achievement is not perfect. Many intelligent people do not do well at school (Einstein and Churchill are two examples). What are the other factors leading to academic success?

Research into this topic has been prompted by two main motives. One is the wish to improve allocation of places: if there are more applicants for higher education than there are places, one wants to ensure that the places are given to those who will gain most benefit from them. The second motive is the hope that better counselling can be provided for students in higher education: if students are having difficulties with their work they should be helped to make the best use of their abilities and do as well as they are able. If we understand what helps people succeed, we can advise students on ways of maximizing their chances of doing well.

It is not difficult to suggest factors which may influence a student's success. We shall look briefly at three topics which psychologists have investigated.

Academic success and personality

Personality is a 'fuzzy' concept, impossible to define precisely, and any introductory text will provide an account of the topic. Broadly speaking, personality refers to the stable motivational and behavioural characteristics of individuals which distinguish one person from another. A number of researchers have investigated the hypothesis that personality features are related to academic achievement.

In British research, the personality theory most widely used in studying academic performance is that of Eysenck. This asserts that there are two major personality dimensions: neuroticism and introversion–extraversion. People rated high on neuroticism have easily roused emotions and a tendency to worry and be depressed. Extraverts are sociable, easy-going and impulsive, while introverts are cautious, unsociable and serious. A person's standing in each of these dimensions can be assessed by examining his or her responses to a particular type of questionnaire known as a personality inventory. A version of the inventory is published in one of Eysenck's books (Eysenck and Wilson, 1976). (Descriptions of his theory can be found in many sources, such as Eysenck and Eysenck (1969).)

Neuroticism and end-of-year performance in higher education. Among 139 university first-year students, Entwistle and Entwistle (1970) found that there was a small, non-significant negative correlation ($r = -0.11$, $p > 0.05$) between end-of-year examination performance and neuroticism. There was no correlation ($r = 0.02$, $p > 0.05$) in a group of 118 college of education students. Cowell and Entwistle (1971) also found no correlation ($r = 0.00$) between end-of-year performance and neuroticism among 117 Ordinary National Certificate (ONC) students. In contrast, Entwistle *et al.* (1971) reported a low negative correlation between neuroticism and academic performance among 562 college of education ($r = -0.12$, $p < 0.05$) and 190 polytechnic ($r = -0.17$, $p < 0.05$) students, but not among the university group of 898 students ($r = -0.03$, $p > 0.05$). (It should be remembered that the 'polytechnics' studied then were not the same as polytechnics are now. The present-day polytechnics did not exist when the data was collected, and the colleges used by Entwistle *et al.* would be more accurately described as colleges of technology. The A-level attainment of these students was well below that of the university group, and 30% of them had ONC qualifications.)

Extraversion and end-of-year performance in higher education. Entwistle and Entwistle (1970) reported a significant negative correlation ($r = -0.25$, $p < 0.05$) between extraversion and academic performance for first-year university students, but not for education students ($r = -0.11$, $p > 0.05$). The lack of a correlation in a non-university group was also reported by Cowell and Entwistle in their study of ONC students. Using much larger samples of participants than in the 1970 study, Entwistle *et al.* (1971) supported the notion that there is a difference between the correlations for university and non-university students: extraversion correlated negatively with academic attainment at university (r = − 0.12, p<0.05) and at education college (r = − 0.15, p<0.05), but not among polytechnic students (r = − 0.01, p>0.05).

Personality and previous A-level performance. The previous research examined the relationship between personality attributes and academic performance assessed later, at the end of the year. Some investigations also examined the relation between the personality measures and the students' previous A-level performance. As an example, Entwistle and Entwistle (1970) reported that for 139 university students, A-level grades correlated − 0.10 (p>0.05) with extraversion and + .18 (p<0.05) with neuroticism. For 118 education students the coefficients were both non-significant, being − 0.03 and + 0.11 respectively.

Entwistle *et al.* (1971) reported separate correlations for the two sexes. Among 793 men, A-levels correlated with extraversion − 0.18 (p<0.05) and with neuroticism − 0.03 (p>0.05). For the 857 women, the correlations were − 0.18 (p<0.05) with extraversion, and −0.01 (p>0.05) with neuroticism. The participants included students from different types of institution, and the data show a lack of agreement with the Entwistle and Entwistle (1970) figures. From the larger sample, it would seem that there is a tendency for A-level performance to be related to extraversion but not to neuroticism.

Personality and school performance. The data considered so far were obtained from higher education students. Among 1,293 14-year-old boys and 1,245 14-year-old girls, Entwistle and Welsh (1969) reported very low but statistically significant (p<0.05) correlations between academic attainment and neuroticism (r = − 0.150 for boys; r = − 0.198 for girls). The correlations between academic attainment and extraversion were non-significant (r = − 0.012 for boys and r = 0.048 for girls). (The significance levels are not stated in the article − I have calculated them from the figures supplied.)

Conclusion. Overall, the correlations between personality and academic performance are low. The figures for neuroticism are inconsistent. For extraversion, there is an indication of a small negative relationship with end-of-year performance among university students, but not among other groups. Although Entwistle and Wilson (1977) wrote that 'there is convincing evidence for the overall superiority of introverts', the size of the correlations is disappointing. The figures demonstrate one important point: low correlations can be statistically significant if the number of participants in the survey is large enough. Entwistle *et al.* (1971), for example, had 898 university students in their sample, and on this number a correlation of 0.07 is significant at the 5% level. A correlation of this size has little practical significance, however. So are there other aspects of the students which demonstrate higher relationships with academic performance?

Academic success, study attitudes and habits

Students and their teachers believe that a major factor influencing academic success is the amount of studying done. It is gratifying to both parties to know that there is evidence to support this common sense opinion: Entwistle *et al.* (1971) asked participants to fill in a grid showing how many hours a week they spent studying, and found a positive and significant correlation with end-of-year attainment. On the other hand, it is disappointing to find the correlation was only 0.19. As Entwistle and Thompson (1974) noted, 'Long hours of obsessive, but ineffective, work will rarely lead to academic success' (p. 393). If the time spent studying is not a very good predictor of academic attainment, what other variables might be considered?

The answer has been to look at study habits and attitudes. Early studies used an American questionnaire, but Entwistle and his colleagues constructed their own *Student Attitudes Inventory* (reproduced in Entwistle *et al.*, 1971). This consisted of 47 statements, and the respondents indicated whether they agreed or disagreed with each one. Scores on four subscales were obtained. The Motivation subscale contained items such as 'I enjoy the challenge of a difficult new topic in lectures'. The Study Methods scale had 14 items, such as 'I'm rather slow at starting work in the evenings', while Examination Technique was assessed using items such as 'I rarely seem to do myself justice in exams'. The final subscale, Lack of Distractions, contained items such as 'Money worries have distracted me from my work'. (These items form the basis of the questionnaire used in studies reported in Entwistle and Wilson, 1977).

The correlations between scores on this inventory and academic performance were more substantial than those between performance and personality. Entwistle *et al.* (1971) reported correlations with the A-level grades of their students as +0.23 for women and +0.21 for men. The correlations with end-of-year grades were +0.24, +0.28 and +0.31 among university, education and polytechnic students. The subscale showing the strongest relationship was Examination Technique.

Another approach to student learning derives from the work of researchers such as Marton (Marton *et al.*, 1984), and is based on qualitative methods, rather than the quantitative methods used by Entwistle in the early 1970s. These qualitative methods use semi-structured interviews to obtain an 'empathetic understanding' of the educational experience from the students' viewpoint. A result of this approach was a realization that higher education students differ in terms of what they believe education to be about. Some believe their task is to remember as much as possible of the material they are given, and then reproduce it in the examination. This is referred to as the surface approach. Other students adopt a deep approach, where they 'see themselves as creators of knowledge who have to use their capabilities to make critical judgements, logical conclusions, and come up with their own ideas' (Marton and Saljo, 1984, p. 40).

This concept of approaches to study was pursued in subsequent work. Entwistle and Ramsden (1983) distinguish four study orientations: meaning, reproducing, achieving (or strategic), and non-academic. Ramsden (1984) lists the characteristics of the different orientations:

Meaning orientation
Looks for meaning; interacts actively; links with real life; examines evidence critically and uses it cautiously.
Actively relates new information to previous knowledge.
Interested in learning for its own sake.

Reproducing orientation
Relies on rote learning; conscious of exam demands.
Prefers to restrict learning to defined syllabus and specified tasks.
Anxiously aware of assessment requirements; lacking in self-confidence.
Not prepared to look for relationships between ideas; fact-bound.

Strategic orientation
Actively seeks information about assessment requirements; tries to impress staff.
Qualifications main source of motivation for learning.
Competitive and self-confident; motivated by hope for success.

Non-academic orientation
Fails to plan ahead; not prompt in submitting work.
Little involvement in work set; cynical about higher education.
Over-readiness to generalize and jump to conclusions without evidence.

To assess a student's orientation, Entwistle (1981) devised an inventory shown here in *Appendix 2*. This provides scores on seven subscales, and it is suggested that the best predictor of overall academic success is obtained by calculating a score which combines the subscale scores. (The relevant formula is given in the Results section.)

(Some authors have queried whether the 'Approaches to Study Questionnaire' measures the four orientations identified by Entwistle and Ramsden. For example, Harper and Kember (1989) suggest that the four factors measured by the questionnaire are 'deep', 'surface', 'narrow' and 'goal' orientations. They argue that the way in which the items on the questionnaire are related to the four orientations is rather different from the pattern found by Ramsden and Entwistle (1981). But for this practical, we shall use Entwistle's interpretation of the questionnaire.)

Overall, the research into student academic achievement suggests that the examination of study approaches looks promising. The aim of this practical is to investigate the relationship between the approaches to study and academic attainment (A-level, GCSE, or equivalent examination performance). To achieve this aim, data from participants on the 'Approaches to Study Questionnaire' and on their academic performance will be needed.

How can one assess academic performance?

For this practical, one needs an index of academic performance available at the time the practical is done, so school examination performance should be used. There are drawbacks to this, as will be mentioned in the Discussion, but it is a feasible method of testing the hypothesis.

One immediate problem is the production of a quantitative index of A-level, GCSE, or equivalent examination performance. The conventional procedure is to use a 'points count', where different grades are awarded points: for example, A counts as 5, B counts as 4, and so on. (Although traditionally used, this is clearly very crude, and rather misleading, because the numbers make it appear as if one has an interval scale when one really only has a rank scale.) The suggested 'points count' for use in this practical is detailed in the *Results* section.

Hypotheses

The hypothesis is that there is a positive correlation between scores on the 'Approaches to Study Questionnaire' and academic attainment. The null hypothesis is that any correlation between the two sets of scores is due to chance.

Procedure

Each participant should be asked to complete the 'Personal Details Questionnaire' (*Appendix 1*) and the 'Approaches to Study Questionnaire' (*Appendix 2*). The questionnaires can be administered to groups or individuals. To preserve the privacy of participants, they should be informed that they are welcome to use a pseudonym so that they cannot be identified from their data. (They must use the same pseudonym for both questionnaires!) Investigators may like to have a 'ballot box' into which people put their completed forms, to provide a further guarantee of anonymity.

Results

Scoring the questionnaires

For the 'Personal Details Questionnaire,' points should be awarded for examination performance as shown here:

	A-level	A/S level	GCSE
A	20	12	7
B	18	11	6
C	16	10	5
D	14	9	4
E	12	8	3
F	–	–	2
G	–	–	1

S.C.E. Highers

Grade and Band:	A1	A2	A3	A4	A5	B6	B7	C8	C9	D10	D11
Points:	14	13	12	11	10	9	8	7	6	5	4

[It should be noted that these scales have been simplified for the

198

purposes of this practical and are not intended to reflect the actual points system.]

For the 'Approaches to Study Questionnaire', the subscale to which each item is assigned is shown in *Appendix 3*. Investigators should count up the total score for each subscale (A–G), and calculate the overall score using this formula:

$$T = A + D + C + E + (48 - B - F - G)$$

It will be seen from *Appendix 3* that there are six items for scales A, B and D and three items for the other scales. Therefore the maximum on each of scales A, B and D is 24. For scales C, E, F and G the maximum is 12 on each.

Investigators will have obtained four items of information for each participant: sex, age, index of academic performance, and ASQ score. A table such as that shown in *Table 1* should be completed.

Table 1. Data on participants' academic performance and ASQ

P	Sex	Age	Academic Performance	ASQ score
1				
2				
3				
etc.				
:				
:				

A scattergram of academic performance and ASQ scores should be plotted. Using graph paper, students should plot academic perform-ance scores along the horizontal axis, and ASQ scores on the vertical. For each participant, a point should be marked at the position repre-senting his or her scores on the two variables. Investigators should then calculate the correlation between these two sets of data. As the academic achievement scores are really rank data, the Spearman rank correlation (rho) should be calculated:

$$r_s = 1 - \frac{6\sum d^2}{N(N^2 - 1)}$$

The significance of a correlation coefficient can be tested using the formula:

$$t = \frac{r\sqrt{N - 2}}{\sqrt{1 - r^2}} \quad \text{with df} = N-2$$

If sufficient respondents are available, students can calculate sep-arate correlations for males and females. The ASQ scores for males and females can also be compared, to see whether one sex scores higher than the other, using the Mann–Whitney test. Frequency or bar charts of these groups of data could be interesting and revealing.

If students wish, they can tabulate participants' scores on each subscale separately and examine the relationships between the sub-scale scores. Is there, for example, a negative correlation between scores on scale A (Achieving orientation) and scale B (Reproducing orientation)?

Discussion

The correlation which has been calculated will demonstrate whether or not the hypothesis is supported. The content of the discussion will obviously depend on whether or not a significant relationship was found. If students failed to do so, can they suggest why this might have happened? (Note that the number of respondents available to the investigators is probably far smaller than the number used in the studies described in the Introduction to this practical.)

If a significant, positive correlation was found, the possible implications should be considered. Should ASQ be used as one of the items in selecting students? Can students who obtained a low score be taught better approaches to study? If this were possible, would one expect them to obtain higher academic grades in future? On this point, Entwistle and Waterston (1988) provide a note of caution. They observe that:

> the learning environment has profound effects on studying. . .Any attempts to modify students' study strategies are only likely to be effective if the learning environment is also changed in parallel to ensure that the recommended ways of studying are also perceived by students to pay off within the reward structure of the courses (p. 264).

If tutors reward a reproducing approach to the course material, there is little point in trying to teach students to use the meaning orientation!

One issue worth considering is the fact that the measure of academic performance is retrospective: we have assumed that the ASQ score obtained now is pertinent to the examination performance of months or years ago. It might be interesting to discuss the drawbacks to this aspect of the data.

Another point is the validity of the technique for assessing academic performance. Is an A-level grade B in Physics worth the same as a grade B in Home Economics or History? Should any allowance be made for those who accumulated their qualifications over a number of years, taking one subject per year? Should people who took an examination more than once be awarded a lower number of points than those who passed at the first attempt? What credit should be given for other qualifications?

Entwistle and Wilson (1977) list a number of problems in conducting research into the prediction of student academic performance. Among others, they include: deciding on the general research design; whether to use case studies; whether to compare contrasting groups; whether to use the whole ability range by following up a complete intake of students; and the problems of selecting a representative sample of participants. These are all topics relevant to any discussion of the validity of the results.

This practical can be extended or modified in a number of ways. If the facilities are available, students can assess their participants' personalities (perhaps using the tests in Eysenck 1976), examine the relationship between personality and academic achievement, and compare the findings with the results cited in the Introduction to this practical exercise. Are those with higher academic achievement also higher on extraversion or neuroticism?

If investigators do not have access to respondents with A-level, GCSE or equivalent qualifications, schoolchildren or adults with some other academic background could be used. *Appendix 1* will have to be modified, and students will need to devise a method for scoring academic performance along the lines of the points system suggested in the *Results* section.

School pupils' attitudes to study were investigated by Entwistle and Kozeki (1985) who developed a 120-item questionnaire designed to assess the pupil's standing on 20 dimensions, each represented by six items of the questionnaire. This was completed by 579 Hungarian and 614 British school pupils of both sexes, aged from 13 to 17. Correlations with academic attainment, assessed for British pupils by self-ratings or 'O' level performance, were reported (ibid., Table 4, p. 130). For the British students, the correlations between academic attainment and study orientation ('approaches to studying') were low, but in the expected direction. 'Deep approach' related positively (r from 0.11 to 0.23 for different subgroups), and surface approach negatively (r between −0.13 and −0.23).

The investigation of students' learning processes is a very large field. The book by Marton *et al.* (1984) may be of interest to students. Although it is not very relevant for the report on this practical, it surveys the results of investigations of student learning practices which have used the interview method rather than the more impersonal psychometric/correlation approach adopted here. A useful survey is provided by Entwistle (1981), who describes the different approaches that students adopt when studying. This text provides many further references which could be used in reports.

Bibliography

General background references

EYSENCK, H.J. and EYSENCK, S.B.G. (1969) *Personality Structure and Measurement*. London: Routledge and Kegan Paul.
EYSENCK, H.J. and WILSON, G. (1976) *Know Your Own Personality*. Harmondsworth: Penguin.

Specific background references

ENTWISTLE, N. (1981) *Styles of Learning and Teaching*. Chichester: Wiley.
ENTWISTLE, N. and RAMSDEN, P. (1983) *Understanding Student Learning*. London: Croom Helm.
ENTWISTLE, N.J. and WILSON, J. (1977) *Degrees of Excellence*. London: Hodder and Stoughton.
MARTON, F., HOUNSELL, D. and ENTWHISTLE, N. (1984) *The Experience of Learning*. Edinburgh: Scottish Academic Press.
MARTON, F. and SALJO, R. (1984) Approaches to learning. In F. Marton, D. Hounsell and N. Entwistle (Eds) *The Experience of Learning*. Edinburgh: Scottish Academic Press.

RAMSDEN, P. (1984) The context of learning. In F. Marton, D. Hounsell and N. Entwistle (Eds) *The Experience of Learning*. Edinburgh: Scottish Academic Press.

RICHARDSON, J.T.E., EYSENCK, M.W. and PIPER, D.W. (Eds) (1987) *Student Learning: Research in Education and Cognitive Psychology*. Milton Keynes: SRHE and Open University Press.

Journal articles

COWELL, M.D. and ENTWISTLE, N.J. (1971) The relationship between personality, study attitudes and academic performance in a technical college. *British Journal of Educational Psychology, 41*, 85–90.

ENTWISTLE, N.J. and ENTWISTLE, D. (1970) The relationship between personality, study methods and academic performance. *British Journal of Educational Psychology, 40*, 132–143.

ENTWISTLE, N. and KOZEKI, B. (1985) Relationships between school motivation, approaches to studying and attainment among British and Hungarian adolescents. *British Journal of Educational Psychology, 55*, 124–137.

ENTWISTLE, N.J., NISBET, J., ENTWISTLE, D. and COWELL, M.D. (1971) The academic performance of students: predictions from scales of motivation and study methods. *British Journal of Educational Psychology, 41*, 258–267.

ENTWISTLE, N.J. and THOMPSON, J. (1974) Motivation and study habits. *Higher Education, 3*, 379–396.

ENTWISTLE, N. and WATERSTON, S. (1988) Approaches to studying and levels of processing in university students. *British Journal of Educational Psychology, 58*, 258–265.

ENTWISTLE, N.J. and WELSH, J. (1969) Correlates of school attainment at different ability levels. *British Journal of Educational Psychology, 39*, 57–63.

HARPER, G. and KEMBER, D. (1989) Interpretation of factor analyses from the approaches to studying inventory. *British Journal of Educational Psychology, 59*, 66–74.

RAMSDEN, P. and ENTWISTLE, N. (1981) Effects of academic departments on students' approaches to studying. *British Journal of Educational Psychology, 51*, 368–383.

APPENDIX 1. PERSONAL DETAILS QUESTIONNAIRE

Please answer the following questions about yourself. To preserve anonymity, please do not put your real name, but use a pseudonym.

1 Pseudonym: ....

2 How old are you? ....

3 Which gender are you? ....

4 Please list the A-levels, GCSEs or equivalent examinations you have taken and the grades you obtained:

....
....
....
....
....
....
....

5 Please list any A/S levels you have taken and the grades you obtained:

....
....
....
....
....
....
....

Please clip this questionnaire to your Study Questionnaire and hand them back to the investigator.

Thank you for your help.

APPENDIX 2. APPROACHES TO STUDY QUESTIONNAIRE

(From N. Entwistle (1988) *Styles of Learning and Teaching* London: David Fulton. Reproduced with permission.)

Pseudonym ....
Please answer every item quickly by giving your immediate response. Circle the appropriate number to show your general approach to studying.

4 means 'Definitely agree'
3 means 'Agree with reservations'
1 means 'Disagree with reservations'
0 means 'Definitely disagree'
2 is only to be used if the item does not apply to you or if you find it impossible to give a definite answer

1.	I find it easy to organize my study time effectively.	4	3	1	0	2
2.	I try to relate ideas in one subject to those in others, whenever possible.	4	3	1	0	2
3.	Although I have a fairly good general idea of many things, my knowledge of the details is rather weak.	4	3	1	0	2
4.	I like to be told precisely what to do in essays or other set work.	4	3	1	0	2
5.	The best way for me to understand what technical terms mean is to remember the textbook definition.	4	3	1	0	2
6.	It is important to me to do really well in the courses here.	4	3	1	0	2
7.	I usually set out to understand thoroughly the meaning of what I am asked to read.	4	3	1	0	2
8.	When I am reading I try to memorize important facts which may come in useful later.	4	3	1	0	2
9.	When I am doing a piece of work, I try to bear in mind exactly what that particular lecturer seems to want.	4	3	1	0	2
10.	I am usually cautious in drawing conclusions unless they are well supported by evidence.	4	3	1	0	2
11.	My main reason for being here is so that I can learn more about the subjects which really interest me.	4	3	1	0	2
12.	In trying to understand new ideas, I often try to relate them to real-life situations to which they might apply.	4	3	1	0	2
13.	I suppose I am more interested in the qualifications I will get than in the courses I am taking.	4	3	1	0	2
14.	I am usually prompt at starting work in the evenings.	4	3	1	0	2
15.	Although I generally remember facts and details, I find it difficult to fit them together into an overall picture.	4	3	1	0	2
16.	I generally put a lot of effort into trying to understand things which initially seem difficult.	4	3	1	0	2
17.	I often get criticized for introducing irrelevant ideas into essays or discussions.	4	3	1	0	2
18.	I often find I have to read things without having a chance to really understand them.	4	3	1	0	2
19.	If conditions are not right for me to study, I generally manage to do something to change them.	4	3	1	0	2
20.	Puzzles or problems fascinate me, particularly when you have to work through the material to reach a logical conclusion.	4	3	1	0	2
21.	I often find myself questioning things that I hear in lectures or read in books.	4	3	1	0	2
22.	I find it helpful to 'map out' a new topic for myself by seeing how ideas fit together.	4	3	1	0	2
23.	I tend to read very little beyond what is required for completing assignments.	4	3	1	0	2

24. It is important to me to do things better than my friends, if I possibly can.   4 3 1 0 2
25. Tutors seem to want me to be more adventurous in making use of my own ideas.   4 3 1 0 2
26. I spend a good deal of my spare time in finding out more about interesting topics which have been discussed in classes.   4 3 1 0 2
27. I seem to be a bit too ready to jump to conclusions without waiting for all the evidence.   4 3 1 0 2
28. I find academic topics so interesting, I should like to continue with them after I finish the course.   4 3 1 0 2
29. I think it is important to look at problems rationally and logically without making intuitive jumps.   4 3 1 0 2
30. I find I have to concentrate on memorizing a good deal of what we have to learn.   4 3 1 0 2

APPENDIX 3. APPROACHES TO STUDY QUESTIONNAIRE: SUBSCALE ASSIGNATION FOR ANSWERS

(From N. Entwistle (1988) *Styles of Learning and Teaching* London: David Fulton. Reproduced with permission.)

1.(A) 2.(C) 3.(G) 4.(B) 5.(F) 6.(A) 7.(D) 8.(B) 9.(A) 10.(E) 11.(D) 12.(C) 13.(B) 14.(A) 15.(F) 16.(D) 17.(G) 18.(B) 19.(A) 20.(E) 21.(D) 22.(C) 23.(B) 24.(A) 25.(F) 26.(D) 27.(G) 28.(D) 29.(E) 30.(B)

Scale A assesses **Achieving** orientation – organized study methods and competitiveness

Scale B measures the **Reproducing** orientation – syllabus-boundness, memorization, extrinsic motivation

Scale C is **Comprehension** learning – relating ideas to real life, mapping out subject areas

Scale D is **Meaning** orientation – looking for meaning, motivated by interest in topics

Scale E concerns **Operation** learning – caution in using evidence, interest in logical problems and rationality

Scale F is **Improvidence** – emphasis on facts and details

Scale G is **Globetrotting** – superficial approach, jumping to conclusions, making generalizations without sufficient evidence

There are six items for scales A, B and D and three items for the other scales. So the maximum on each of A, B and D is 24. For C, E, F and G the maximum is 12 on each scale.

Score = A + D + C + E + (48 – B – F – G)

As you can see, scales A, D, C and E are positive, while B, F and G are negative.

APPENDIX 1

Ethical considerations in carrying out psychological research

Alison Wadeley
Filton College, Bristol

Ethical matters were an important consideration in the preparation of this *Manual*, particularly in the selection of suitable practical exercises for readers to carry out. This is not to say that this absolves the reader from considering the ethical standards of any exercise which he or she uses, or adapts, from this book. It is still vital for individual researchers to take responsibility for familiarizing themselves with ethical guidelines and to arrive at a personal conviction that he or she has thoroughly considered the ethical implications of any research project and taken them into account before proceeding.

It is not the intention here to discuss ethical considerations in depth. These are dealt with elsewhere (for example, see Coolican, 1990; Wadeley, 1991). Instead, in keeping with the nature of this book as a manual, some general points will be raised. Further reading about the issue of ethics is strongly recommended – indeed, it is essential for anyone who carries out research in the name of psychology.

So why do psychologists concern themselves with ethics? The term 'ethics' refers to moral principles and rules of conduct and in order that psychologists can maintain high standards in their work, interested bodies have produced documentation to help them. Guidelines issued by the British Psychological Society (1985; 1990) begin with the assertion that psychologists are committed to increasing people's understanding of their own and others' behaviour in order to improve the quality of human life. To achieve this, they need an atmosphere of free enquiry which they must earn by carrying out their work in a way which respects the rights and dignity of all research participants. Psychologists must also consider the importance of maintaining a good reputation for psychology, and recognize that its future may be threatened if people's sympathy is lost.

The BPS guidelines stress that research should be objective, competent and non-wasteful. They go on to expand on ten areas of concern covering: general issues, obtaining consent from participants, the use of deception, debriefing participants, participants' right to withdraw from an investigation, confidentiality, protection of participants from physical or psychological harm, considerations in observational research, giving advice to participants and monitoring colleagues' research. Many of the issues raised in the guidelines are relevant to the exercises recommended in this book.

There is no escape from ethical considerations. They are always present whenever psychological research is carried out, and at whatever level that may be. In many cases there is no clear cut decision about whether the research should proceed. Often it is a matter for serious debate involving weighing up the possible benefits of research in terms of theoretical or practical gains, against the psychological costs to participants and costs in terms of the reputation of psychology.

Consideration of ethical issues should be second nature to anyone involved in psychological research but this is no excuse for complacency. Even the most experienced researchers should look carefully at their research designs and, before proceeding, work through a checklist such as the one which follows.

A checklist for your own research

1. What method are you using and is it the only one suitable for asking the questions you are interested in?
2. Are you qualified and competent to carry out this kind of research?
3. Have you checked your procedures with your tutor or with a colleague qualified to pass judgement?
4. Have you tried the procedure out on yourself or can you carry out a pilot study on a fully informed group of participants, similar to those you will eventually use, in order to obtain their judgement on your procedures?
5. Will the participants experience discomfort and is this really necessary?
6. Do you propose to deceive participants and is this really necessary?
7. Do participants know they can withdraw at any time without penalty?
8. Have you obtained freely given, informed consent from the participants or, if this is not possible, from someone acting on their behalf?
9. Do the participants know that they can withdraw their data and have it destroyed if they so wish?
10. Will the procedure intrude on the participants' privacy and is this really necessary?
11. Will the information gathered remain confidential?
12. Will the participants be debriefed fully at the end of the study?
13. Will your study offend participants in any way and in this really necessary?
14. Will your study create a bad public image for psychology?

In short, it is vital to consider a proposed study from all possible angles and to make strenuous efforts to eradicate any ethical flaws before proceeding. As a general rule, if a researcher is in any doubt about the ethical soundness of a research design, it is safer and more considerate not to proceed. Very often, there are alternatives to unethical procedures or areas of research which are equally engaging without being ethically suspect. This is not to say that it is possible to achieve perfection. Even the best intentioned and best informed psychologist is still only human. A painstakingly careful research design, which seems innocuous to its creator, can still, unexpectedly,

The Basic Rules for Ethical Psychological Research

Reproduced by kind permission of Dr Lesley Cooke and Angela Hughes, Chester College.

cause offence. The guidelines are there to help reduce such occurrences but, in the end, it is for the individual to decide.

References

BRITISH PSYCHOLOGICAL SOCIETY (1985) A code of conduct for psychologists. *Bulletin of the British Psychological Society, 38,* 41–43.

BRITISH PSYCHOLOGICAL SOCIETY (1990) *Ethical Principles for Conducting Research with Human Participants.* Leicester: The British Psychological Society.

COOLICAN, H. (1990) *Research Methods and Statistics in Psychology.* London: Hodder and Stoughton.

WADELEY, A. (1991) *Ethics in Psychological Research and Practice.* Leicester: BPS Books (The British Psychological Society).

APPENDIX 2

Writing up reports in psychology

Rob McIlveen, Alison Wadeley and Paul Humphreys

Write-ups of psychological investigations can vary widely in terms of presentation, and there is no single style which is more 'correct' than any other. However, there are widely accepted standards and conventions which should be followed. Most report write-ups adopt the format outlined here.

TITLE
TABLE OF CONTENTS
ABSTRACT
INTRODUCTION AND HYPOTHESES
METHOD: Design and Overview
           Participants and Experimenters/Investigators
           Apparatus
           Procedure
RESULTS
ANALYSIS OF RESULTS
DISCUSSION
CONCLUSION
REFERENCES
APPENDICES

Note that some teachers like to separate Introduction and Hypotheses whilst others include Analysis of Results under Results. As has been noted, there is no single correct way of writing-up a report, and you should check with your teacher for any idiosyncratic expectations he or she might have with respect to report writing. For A-level Psychology it is suggested that the Title page also include your full name, candidate number, centre name and centre number.

Writing a good report of a practical is not an easy task. In what follows we have presented a model write-up of an experiment concerned with forgetting from short-term memory, though it should be noted that students starting a course in psychology will probably not conduct an investigation as complex as the one presented here. We are not claiming that the write-up is perfect. Very few, including those that appear in academic journals, are. However, the model write-up is an example of what students should aspire to (and we do acknowledge that to students new to psychology the write-up may appear daunting). In the write-up we have included the type of information likely to attract a high grade or examination mark. Adjacent to the report we have offered our own comments to highlight important features of a good practical write-up. Please note that although we refer to Appendices, these have not been included for reasons of space.

TITLE: The title should be concise yet clear enough to give the reader an idea of the investigation's central concerns. 'A Memory Study' would have been too vague whereas 'Testing the Passive Decay Theory of Forgetting from Short-Term Memory using a task similar to that employed by Peterson and Peterson (1959)' would have been far too long.

TABLE OF CONTENTS: The table of contents or 'index' is explicit and covers the main headings of the report. The headings are, of course, given a page number (corresponding to the pagination in the report).

ABSTRACT: This should be a self-contained and brief summary of the main points of the write-up. The abstract is intended to give your reader a clear idea of the work or theory being investigated, why the investigation has been done, and how it was conducted. The abstract should also mention the participants involved (including, if relevant, their gender and age range) and the method by which they were sampled. Also included are the main findings, their statistical significance, and the inferential test used. The abstract normally ends with an indication of how the results have been interpreted and the findings discussed. Note that the abstract is the last part of the report to be written even though it appears at the beginning of the write-up.

INTRODUCTION AND HYPOTHESES: This contains the background to the investigation you are conducting. It begins with a broad statement of the aims of the study and the hypothesis or hypotheses that will be tested. The Introduction continues with a brief review of the relevant background psychological literature, that is, a description of those theories/studies which are central to the topic being investigated. Note that exhaustive reviews, covering every aspect of the investigation's concerns, are not necessary and are actively discouraged.

TITLE

An Experimental Study of Forgetting from Short-Term Memory

TABLE OF CONTENTS

Page Number

ABSTRACT

The present experiment tested the Passive Decay theory of forgetting from short-term memory. According to this theory, memories decay over time unless maintained by repetition or rehearsal. Peterson and Peterson (1959) were the first to present data supporting the Passive Decay theory. This experiment attempted to conceptually replicate the Petersons' findings and hence lend further support to the Passive Decay theory. Thirteen naïve participants, selected by means of opportunity sampling, were required to recall lists of four consonants after delays of 10 and 30 seconds. Rehearsal was prevented by means of an interpolated task during the delay interval. Participants were also required to recall consonants immediately after presentation (0 seconds delay). Analysis of the results by means of independent 't' tests indicated that significantly more consonants were recalled following 0 seconds delay as compared with both 10 seconds delay ($p < 0.0005$, one-tailed) and 30 seconds delay ($p < 0.0005$, one-tailed). A significant difference between recall following 10 seconds delay and 30 seconds delay was also obtained ($p < 0.05$, one-tailed). The results are discussed in terms of the adequacy of Passive Decay theory as an explanation of forgetting from short-term memory. Modifications and implications for further research are also discussed.

INTRODUCTION AND HYPOTHESES

The aim of this experimental study is to investigate forgetting from short-term memory. The experiment examines the Passive Decay theory of forgetting which proposes that, as a result of metabolic processes, memories decay with the passage of time unless maintained by repetition and rehearsal.

The importance of memory cannot be disputed. Without it, organisms could not benefit from past experience and life would consist of momentary episodes bearing little or no relation to one another. The structure of memory has long been of interest to experimental psychologists. Over 100 years ago James (1890) suggested that a distinction could be made between 'primary' memory, lasting for a brief period of time, and 'secondary' memory, lasting for a much longer period of time. Nowadays, the terms short-term memory (STM) and long-term

INTRODUCTION AND HYPOTHESES (Cont.): The introduction continues by developing the rationale underlying the investigation, and flows naturally into the hypothesis or hypotheses which will be tested. Logical organization is crucial here: the introduction should move smoothly from aims to background to hypotheses.

INTRODUCTION AND HYPOTHESES (Cont.): This section concludes with a statement of the specific hypotheses and whether and why they are one- or two-tailed. For each experimental hypothesis the corresponding null hypothesis should be stated together with the minimum probability level at which the experimental hypothesis will be retained.

memory (LTM) are used to describe James' 'primary' and 'secondary' memories respectively.

There has been considerable debate over whether a distinction between the two proposed storage systems can be justified. As Clifford (1991) has noted, data from physiological studies (for example, Duncan, 1949; Hebb, 1949), studies of clinical amnesics (for example, Shallice and Warrington, 1970) and experimental investigations (for example, Murdock, 1962; Glanzer and Cunitz, 1966) strongly support the view that memory is composed of two separate and separable storage systems. Given that there are reasonably good grounds for a STM–LTM distinction, attention can now be turned to the issue of how information is forgotten from the storage systems.

Passive Decay theory has already been briefly described. Two other theories also claim to be able to explain STM forgetting. According to Interference theory, forgetting occurs because memories interfere with one another. Two types of interference have been proposed: 'proactive' in which material previously learnt interferes with material currently being learnt, and 'retroactive' in which the reverse occurs. The Displacement theory of STM forgetting assumes that STM is limited in capacity, and that when capacity is reached new material displaces old material, the latter then being either transferred to LTM or lost from the system completely.

Peterson and Peterson (1959) were interested in the topic of forgetting from STM and wanted to investigate the rate of forgetting from this system when rehearsal was prevented. Their experiment consisted of many trials. On some of these a trigram (that is, three consonants such as XPJ) was presented acoustically and participants had to immediately recall what they had heard. On other trials, however, participants heard a three digit number immediately after the trigram had been presented. Participants were informed that whenever they heard a three digit number they should begin counting backwards in threes out loud until they heard a tone. This interpolated task was designed to prevent rehearsal, and lasted for 3, 6, 9, 12, 15, or 18 seconds. On hearing the tone, participants were asked to try and recall the trigram.

The results indicated that the longer the delay between presentation of the trigram and the requirement to recall it, the poorer the recall; an outcome which lends support to the claims of Passive Decay theory. Since Peterson and Peterson's results have important implications for Passive Decay theory and its application to forgetting from STM, it is important that they are reliable. The aim of the present experiment is to replicate Peterson and Peterson's findings. The experiment is a conceptual rather than a complete replication of the Petersons' experiment, since slightly different stimulus material will be used and recall will be tested using only three delay intervals: 0, 10, and 30 seconds.

Three one-tailed experimental hypotheses will be tested. The hypotheses are one-tailed since the expected direction of the effect is stated. The first hypothesis predicts that recall of verbal material will be poorer when it is delayed by 10 seconds than when it is immediate (that is, delayed by 0 seconds). The null hypothesis for this experimental hypothesis is that there will not be a difference in the recall of verbal material, and that any difference observed will be due to the operation of chance factors. The second hypothesis predicts that recall of verbal material will be poorer when it is delayed by 30 seconds than when it is immediate (that is, delayed by 0 seconds). The null hypothesis predicts that there will be no significant difference in the recall of verbal material, and that any difference observed will be due to the operation of chance factors. The third hypothesis is that recall of verbal material will be poorer when it is delayed by 30

METHOD: The purpose of this section is to inform the reader precisely how the investigation was undertaken. The method section has several sub-sections, and there are no hard and fast rules about what details go where. However, the most important thing to remember is that the reader should be given enough detail to enable the investigation to be replicated. Note that it is conventional to use the third person when describing the method employed.

METHOD (Design and Overview): This sub-section concisely outlines the logical structure of the investigation. Normally it includes information about the number of conditions, the independent and dependent variables and, where appropriate, the experimental design used. Some indication of the major features of control and the comparisons to be made can also be included here.

METHOD (Participants and Experimenters): This sub-section provides details about the participants involved in the investigation. A sensible balance in terms of detail should be struck here. Thus the reader needs to know more than just the number of participants, but would not need biographical details of each! Sex, age range, and social and/or educational background are usually included, as is the method by which the participants were sampled. Where special requirements for participants are necessary (such as native language), these should also be mentioned. The experimenters (or researchers if the investigation is not an experiment) involved should also be briefly mentioned.

METHOD (Apparatus): The apparatus and materials used, such as questionnaires, should be described here. With complex apparatus, a schematic diagram would be informative. Again it is important to strike a sensible balance. The reader needs to be able to reconstruct or otherwise reproduce the apparatus, but does not need to know the brand name of the pen used to record data! The actual stimulus material should not be presented here but should be included in an Appendix, and reference to the Appendix made.

seconds than when it is delayed by 10 seconds. The null hypothesis for this experimental hypothesis is that there will be no difference in the recall of verbal material, and that any difference observed will be due to the operation of chance factors.

For each experimental hypothesis, the 5% significance level has been selected as the critical probability level. If the result of a statistical test indicates that the likelihood of obtaining the observed results under the null hypothesis (i.e. that chance factors alone are operating) is less than 1 in 20, then that hypothesis will be rejected in favour of the experimental hypothesis. Otherwise, the null hypothesis will be retained.

METHOD

(a) Design and Overview: There are three conditions in this experiment, delaying recall by 0, 10, and 30 seconds respectively. The length of time by which recall is delayed constitutes the independent variable. Performance is measured in terms of the participants' ability to recall lists of four consonants in their correct order. This constitutes the dependent variable. Since each participant appears in all three conditions, the experimental design is a repeated measures design. To rule out the possibility of order effects confounding the results, counterbalancing is used. Comparisons of 0 versus 10 seconds delay, 0 versus 30 seconds delay, and 10 versus 30 seconds delay will be made using an appropriate inferential statistical test.

(b) Participants and Experimenters: 13 participants (six male, seven female) were selected using the opportunity method of sampling. The participants were full-time students at a local College of Further Education and ranged in age from 16–21 years. Participants were required to be familiar with the English alphabet and to have normal hearing. Each participant was tested by an experimenter who was a second year student studying A-level Psychology at the same College of Further Education.

(c) Apparatus: The stimulus material for this experiment can be found in Appendix 1. Appendix 1 consists of four columns headed 'Stimulus', 'Delay (in secs.)', 'Interpolated Task' and 'Score'. The 'Stimulus' column contains the lists of four consonants such as XMPT and YNWB. The 'Delay' column gives the number of seconds (0, 10, 30) by which recall of the consonant list is delayed. The 'Interpolated Task' column indicates the three digit number from which the participant is required to count out loud backwards in threes. Note that for trials on which recall is delayed by 0 seconds, no three digit number appears. The only other apparatus used consisted of Standardized Instructions (see Procedure), a stopwatch (to time delay intervals) and a pen (to record the participant's responses in the Score column).

(d) Procedure: Participants were tested individually by each experimenter. Prior to the participant's arrival at the testing room (an empty classroom), the experimenter ensured that all the necessary apparatus was available. Having ascertained that the participant was familiar with the English alphabet, and had normal hearing, the procedure began. The experimenter, who was seated at a table opposite the participant, read out the following standardized instructions:

> This is a study of memory. In a short while, I will read out to you a list of four consonants. When I have done that you will hear me say either 'Recall', or a three digit number such as 'two hundred and ninety four'. If you hear me say 'Recall' you should immediately try

METHOD (Procedure): The procedure sub-section describes what the participants and experimenters did (note the verb tense) with the apparatus. The procedure needs to describe clearly what was done so that the reader could replicate the investigation just by reading your report of it.

METHOD (Procedure continued): Details of important controls (such as single or double blind control) and, if appropriate, a verbatim transcript of standardized instructions, need to be presented as well. Note that participants should be thanked for being involved and debriefed as to the purpose of the investigation. This should be mentioned. The procedure by which the data were collated for summary purposes can also be described here.

and recall the four consonants you heard. Please recall these out loud.

➤ If you hear me say a three digit number, you should immediately begin to count backwards in threes as fast as you can from that number. It does not matter if you make mistakes in doing this, but it is vitally important that you count out loud. After a period of time you will hear me say 'Recall', at which point you should try to recall the consonants you heard. Please recall these out loud.

In all, there will be 18 trials. Do not try to rehearse the consonants on those trials on which you are required to count backwards in threes. By rehearsal, I mean repeating the consonants in order to make their recall easier. Before we begin, do you have any questions?

Both standardized instructions and experimental procedures were used to try to prevent experimenter effects (that is, differential behaviour towards participants on the part of the experimenter). However, since the participant was ➤ informed that he or she was taking part in a study of memory, the possibility of demand characteristics (participants actively influencing their own responses) cannot be ruled out entirely.

When the experimenter had answered any questions asked by the participant the experiment began. In all there were 18 trials, six each for recall delays of 0, 10 and 30 seconds. The delay intervals were timed as accurately as possible, and the participant's responses were recorded after each trial. The entire session lasted for approximately five minutes. At the end of the experiment the participant was thanked and debriefed as to the purpose of the study. Participants were requested not to divulge any details of the experiment to others.

Participants were awarded one point for each consonant correctly recalled in its correct place. Any letter not recalled in its correct place scored zero. Thus, if the consonant list was XMPT, and XMPT was recalled, four points were scored. X—T was awarded two points, PJXT was awarded one point (since only T was in the correct position), and TXMP was awarded no points (since no consonants were in their correct position).

In Peterson and Peterson's original experiment, participants recalled sets of three consonants, and the number of consonant sets recalled in their entirety was scored. In this experiment, however, participants were required to recall lists of four consonants, and the scoring method was, as indicated above, different. This experiment's use of a slightly more difficult task and a different method of scoring recall has the effect of reducing the number of trials necessary.

When the score obtained on each trial had been calculated, the six trials on which recall was delayed by 0 seconds were totalled. This value was then divided by 6 to produce a mean score for 0 seconds delay, and the procedure repeated for the 10 and 30 second delay trials. The experimenters then pooled the data each of them had obtained in order to test the experimental hypotheses.

RESULTS

Since the data (scores) have been collected at the interval/ratio level of measurement, the most appropriate measure of central tendency to describe them is the mean. (Note, however, that with interval/ratio level data other measures such as the median and mode could also be used to describe central tendency.) The measure of dispersion which complements the mean as a measure of central tendency is the standard deviation. This gives an indication of the distribution of

RESULTS: This section is meant to be descriptive only. You should talk the reader through both this section and the one which follows. Clarity is all important, so you should try to find concise and informative modes of presentation. This can be achieved by presenting a summary table (or tables) of the results in terms of appropriate measures of central tendency and dispersion, and a pictorial illustration (or illustrations) such as a graph, of the investigation's findings. Tables and figures should be consecutively numbered in two separate sequences, and have titles. Take great care to label them clearly, bearing in mind that tables and figures should be self-explanatory: the reader should not have to refer to the text to understand your tables and figures. Large amounts of raw data do not belong in this section, but should be placed in a separate Appendix. The reader may wish to examine the raw data and should be informed of where they can be found.

scores around the mean: if the standard deviation is large, then there is considerable variation in the data, and if it is small, then there is little variation. Note again, that with interval/ratio level data, the range and variation ratio could also be used to describe the dispersion of the data. The raw data from this experiment can be found in Appendix 2.

Table 1. Means and standard deviations of the number of consonants correctly recalled in the three experimental conditions

	MEAN SCORE (Max. = 4)	STANDARD DEVIATION
0 secs. delay	3.92	0.14
10 secs. delay	1.27	0.78
30 secs. delay	0.74	0.61

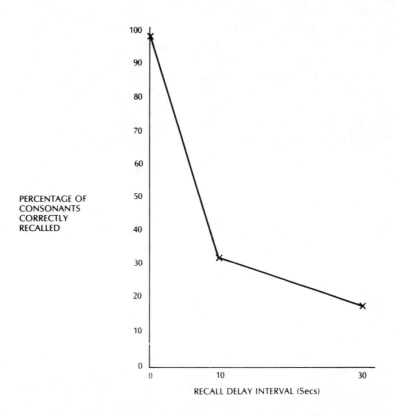

PERCENTAGE OF CONSONANTS CORRECTLY RECALLED

RECALL DELAY INTERVAL (Secs)

Figure 1. Graph illustrating how recall is affected when it is delayed by 0, 10, and 30 seconds and rehearsal is prevented.

Table 1 shows the mean scores obtained by participants in each condition. The maximum score in each case is four. Figure 1 provides a visual impression of the results of the experiment. Table 1 also shows the standard deviations associated with each condition. In the 0 seconds delay there is very little deviation from the mean value. The other two conditions do, however, show some variation.

ANALYSIS OF RESULTS: The Results section will have made some suggestions about the outcome of the investigation. In this section the outcome of inferential statistical testing is described. Explanations of what is going to be analysed, and how it is intended to carry out the analysis, should be provided. The choice of statistical test must be justified in terms of whether a difference or relationship is being looked for, the number of conditions, level of measurement, and type of experimental design.

ANALYSIS OF RESULTS (Cont.): If an inferential test has been used, the value of the test statistic, degrees of freedom (or number of participants), and the critical value at a given level for a one- or two-tailed test must be presented. The reader should be told what rejection of a null or experimental hypothesis means.

ANALYSIS OF RESULTS(Cont.): Finally in this section, the results of the test(s) conducted should be summarized in a clearly labelled table. In an experiment, the table would include the comparison(s) made, relevant means, calculated statistic, critical value of the test statistic, degrees of freedom (or number of participants), and the probability level at which the outcome of the test is (or is not) significant. Calculations of the test(s) should not be presented here but in an Appendix. Remember to indicate this to the reader.

On first inspection the means in Table 1 seem to lend some support to the Passive Decay theory of forgetting from STM. Thus, poor recall is associated with longer recall delays. The pattern of means is not, however, sufficient to allow the claim to be made that the experiment has successfully replicated Peterson and Peterson's (1959) findings. In order to determine whether the differences between the conditions are statistically significant, an inferential statistical test for a difference must be conducted.

ANALYSIS OF RESULTS

All of the experimental hypotheses predicted a difference (rather than a relationship) between two conditions (0 versus 10 seconds, 0 versus 30 seconds, and 10 versus 30 seconds). Since a difference between conditions has been predicted, a repeated measures design should be employed, and given that interval/ratio level data have been collected, the related 't' test is the most appropriate to use in these circumstances. However, the related 't' is a parametric test, and makes assumptions about the nature of the data and the underlying population. The first assumption, that the data is at the interval/ratio level, is clearly satisfied. The second assumption, that the data has been collected from an underlying population which is normally distributed is, in this instance, reasonable to make. The dependent 't' test has therefore been used.

Comparison of 0 versus 10 seconds delay yielded a 't' value of 12.16 with 12 degrees of freedom. For a one-tailed test at the 0.0005 level, the critical value of 't' is 4.32. Since the obtained value of 't' is greater than the tabled value, the null hypothesis may be confidently rejected: there is a less than 1 in 2000 probability that the results are due to chance. Thus recall is highly significantly impaired when delayed by 10 seconds as compared with 0 seconds.

Comparison of 0 versus 30 seconds delay yielded a 't' value of 17.93 with 12 degrees of freedom. Since the critical value of 4.32 for a one-tailed test at the 0.0005 level has been exceeded, the null hypothesis may be rejected: there is a less than 1 in 2000 probability that the results are due to chance. Thus recall is highly significantly impaired when delayed by 30 seconds as compared with 0 seconds.

Comparison of 10 versus 30 seconds delay yielded a 't' value of 1.84. With 12 degrees of freedom, the critical value of the test statistic for a one-tailed test at the 0.05 level is 1.78. Since the critical value has been exceeded, the null hypothesis may be rejected: there is a less than 1 in 20 probability that the results are due to chance. Thus recall is significantly impaired when delayed by 30 seconds as compared with 10 seconds.

The results of the statistical tests are summarized in Table 2. The calculations can be found in Appendix 3.

Table 2. Summary of statistical analyses conducted

	MEAN	MEAN	't' VALUE	CRITICAL VALUE	d.f.	p (one-tailed)
0 vs. 10 secs	3.92	1.27	12.16	4.32	12	<.0005
0 vs. 30 secs	3.92	0.74	17.93	4.32	12	<.0005
10 vs. 30 secs	1.27	0.74	1.84	1.78	12	<.05

DISCUSSION: Begin by briefly mentioning your results and whether or not they support the hypothesis or hypotheses under test. There is no point in presenting a thorough Results section unless you comment on what the results indicate!

DISCUSSION(Cont.): You should then go on to discuss the results in light of the relevant background research and/or theory which started off the investigation. Where does the theory/research stand in the light of your findings? Can your data be interpreted in alternative theoretical terms? Are there other explanations for the study's outcome which are more or less plausible than the theory you were examining?

DISCUSSION(Cont.): Take a critical look at the way the investigation was conducted (even if the hypothesis or hypotheses were supported) by discussing shortcomings and possible limitations. Criticism should always be constructive, so avoid making trivial points. If some aspect of the investigation could realistically have affected the outcome (such as a serious omission in control), it should be mentioned; otherwise not.

DISCUSSION

In this experiment, it was predicted that the ability to recall consonants from STM would be poorer the longer the recall delay when rehearsal was prevented. This general prediction was based on the earlier findings of Peterson and Peterson (1959) whose study this experiment conceptually replicated. As a result, the findings may be taken as further support for the Passive Decay theory of forgetting from STM.

The claim that Passive Decay offers the best explanation for STM forgetting must, however, be treated cautiously, since two other alternative theories of STM forgetting have been suggested. Some researchers have proposed that Peterson and Peterson's data can be interpreted in terms of Interference theory. It has been suggested that recall decreases with the passage of time because the interpolated task interferes with the previous learning of the consonants. However, this 'Retroactive Inhibition' (RI) explanation is unlikely to be true, since both the Petersons' study and the present experiment used an interpolated task designed to minimize the possibility of an RI effect (the task itself involved consonants, and the interpolated task involved numbers).

An alternative explanation based on Interference theory suggests that 'Proactive Inhibition' (PI) may be at work. Keppel and Underwood (1962) have reported that the very first sequence of consonants produces little forgetting but, thereafter, forgetting does take place. They argue that learning a subsequent item involves unlearning the previous item. As time elapses, the prior item spontaneously recovers and causes forgetting by interfering with the items to be recalled. The longer the delay the greater the recovery of the prior item, and hence the greater the amount of forgetting.

This account is, however, also unlikely to be true. As Baddeley (1976) has noted, PI generally reaches a maximum within three trials and does not build up gradually as in LTM (Loess, 1964). Additionally, Conrad (1967) has shown that phonemically similar intrusion errors are more likely to occur after short, rather than long, delays. Interference theory would predict that similar items should produce maximial unlearning, be the last to recover, and hence should produce such intrusions after long, rather than short, delays. Inspection of the data generated in this experiment also supports Conrad's findings and argues against a RI explanation.

Displacement theory has also been proposed as a better explanation for STM forgetting than Passive Decay theory. Evidence in support of this proposal comes from Waugh and Norman (1965). Whilst they would not dispute that the data from this experiment are consistent with Passive Decay theory, their 'Serial Probe' task seems to suggest that the displacement of items does take place in STM. However, it should be noted that the data they reported does not completely rule out Passive Decay theory. Quite possibly, both displacement and decay are at work in STM forgetting, and therefore the two theories could be seen as complementary rather than competitive. Certainly, the data for the present experiment are consistent with a Passive Decay account.

Despite the present experiment's support for Passive Decay theory, there are some shortcomings and limitations. For example, using 13 different experimenters may have resulted in errors due to inaccuracy in timing the delay intervals. Experimenters may also have used different experimental settings, some of which may have been more distracting than others. Additionally, demand characteristics and experimenter effects might have played a role despite attempts to minimize them. The relatively small sample size and the nature of the

DISCUSSION(Cont.): Having mentioned some of the shortcomings and limitations of the investigation, you should then suggest ways in which these could be modified so that the investigation could reach higher standards.

DISCUSSION(Cont.): A very important part of the discussion section concerns the implications that the investigation's findings have for theory and further research. You should try to suggest some avenues of research for other investigators. If the investigation has practical applications these should be mentioned too.

DISCUSSION(Cont.): Finally, if the statistical treatment could have affected the outcome of the investigation, this should also be discussed.

CONCLUSION: The conclusion should be a brief summary of the investigation expressed in both words and statistics, and be no more than a single paragraph in length.

REFERENCES: It is important to provide references for every author whose name is cited in the write-up. Some teachers insist on full references which should be presented using the style illustrated in Version 1. Other teachers insist only that 'primary sources' are fully referenced. A primary source is any book or article that you have consulted during your write-up. Occasionally, a write-up may use material derived from the primary source. This is called a 'secondary source' and is placed with other secondary sources in a list after the primary source, as illustrated in Version 2.

population from which the sample was drawn (that is, college students) could also have had confounding effects.

The experimental procedure could, however, be easily modified in order to overcome some of these limitations. Accurate timing devices, constancy in experimental setting, and a single experimenter would all be simple remedies. The use of an experimenter blind to the hypotheses of the experiment (double blind control) could also be used, as could visually, rather than verbally, presented standardized instructions.

Much more difficult to control for are acoustic confusion errors (Conrad, 1964). An examination of the means indicates that recall after 0 seconds delay was not perfect (3.92 out of 4). This could be due to forgetting but might also be the result of acoustic confusion errors. Conrad showed that when participants wrongly recalled individual letters, the wrongly recalled letter sounded similar to the presented letter (for example, B for T). An examination of the data from this experiment reveals similar sorts of errors, and it would seem necessary to distinguish these errors from genuine forgetting.

The present experiment could be extended in several ways. For example, acoustic confusion errors could be eliminated by using different stimulus material. Participants could, for example, be tested with sequences of digits and, perhaps, be required to read a passage from a book as the interpolated task. Future researchers could also look at forgetting from STM when more meaningful material is used. It could be argued that the stimulus material used in this experiment lacks ecological validity since most people do not attempt to memorize lists of four consonants in everyday life. Craik and Tulving (1975) have suggested that information is processed at different levels – structural, phonetic and semantic. The influence of depth of processing could be revealing in terms of assessing the plausibility of theories of forgetting.

Finally, some mention should be made of the statistical treatment of this experiment's data. Conducting a series of independent 't' tests can result in what Neher (1967) has called 'probability pyramiding', in which the probability of making a type one error (rejecting the null hypothesis when it is true) increases as the number of tests conducted increases. An alternative test, such as analysis of variance, is probably a better choice of test when three conditions are used in an experiment.

CONCLUSION

This experiment tested hypotheses deriving from the Passive Decay theory of forgetting. Analysis of the results showed that recall was significantly poorer when delayed by 10 seconds as compared with 0 seconds ($p < 0.0005$), significantly poorer when delayed by 30 seconds as compared with 0 seconds ($p < 0.0005$), and significantly poorer when delayed by 30 seconds as compared with 10 seconds ($p < 0.05$). On the basis of these results, which replicate earlier findings reported by Peterson and Peterson (1959), it was concluded that the Passive Decay theory does offer a reasonable account of forgetting from STM.

References (Version 1)

BADDELEY, A.D. (1976) *The Psychology of Memory*. London: Harper and Row.

CLIFFORD, B. (1991) Memory. In J. RADFORD and E. GOVIER (Eds) *A Textbook of Psychology*, 2nd edn. London: Routledge.

CONRAD, R. (1964) Acoustic confusion in immediate memory. *British Journal of Psychology*, 55, 75–84.

REFERENCES (Cont.): Note that for journal articles the conventional style to use is:
author(s), year of publication, title of article, journal title, volume number and page number(s).

For books, the conventional style to use is:
author(s), year of publication, title of book, place of publication and publisher. References are in alphabetical order.

REFERENCES (Cont.): Primary sources are placed in alphabetical order and follow the style outlined above.

Secondary sources, also placed in alphabetical order, are listed under the primary source from which they came.

CONRAD, R. (1967) Interference or decay over short retention intervals. *Journal of Verbal Learning and Verbal Behaviour, 6,* 49–54.

CRAIK, F.I.M. and TULVING, E. (1975) Depth of processing and the retention of words in episodic memory. *Journal of Experimental Psychology General, 104,* 268–294.

DUNCAN, C. (1949) The retroactive effect of electro-shock on learning. *Journal of Comparative Physiology, 42,* 32–44.

GLANZER, M. and CUNITZ, A.R. (1966) Two storage mechanisms in free recall. *Journal of Verbal Learning and Verbal Behaviour, 5,* 351–360.

HEBB, D. (1949) *The Organization of Behaviour.* New York: Wiley.

JAMES, W. (1890) *The Principles of Psychology.* New York: Holt.

KEPPEL, G. and UNDERWOOD, B.J. (1962) Proactive inhibition in short-term retention of single items. *Journal of Verbal Learning and Verbal Behaviour, 1,* 153–161.

LOESS, H. (1964) Proactive inhibition in short-term memory. *Journal of Verbal Learning and Verbal Behaviour, 3,* 362–368.

MURDOCK, B.B. (1962) The serial position effect in free recall. *Journal of Experimental Psychology, 64,* 482–488.

NEHER, A. (1967) Probability pyramiding, research error and the need for independent replication. *Psychological Record, 17,* 257–262.

PETERSON, L.R. and PETERSON, M.J. (1959) Short-term retention of individual items. *Journal of Experimental Psychology, 58,* 193–198.

SHALLICE, T. and WARRINGTON, E.K. (1970) Independent functioning of verbal memory stores: a neuropsychological study. *Quarterly Journal of Experimental Psychology, 22,* 261–273.

WAUGH, N.C. and NORMAN, D.A. (1965) Primary memory. *Psychological Review, 72,* 89–104.

REFERENCES (Version 2)

BADDELEY, A.D. (1976) *The Psychology of Memory.* London: Harper and Row.

The following references were obtained from Baddeley (1976):
Conrad (1964; 1967)
Glanzer and Cunitz (1966)
Keppel and Underwood (1962)
Loess (1964)
Murdock (1962)
Peterson and Peterson (1959)
Waugh and Norman (1965)

CLIFFORD, B. (1991) Memory. In J. RADFORD and E. GOVIER (Eds), *A Textbook of Psychology.* London: Routledge.

The following references were obtained from Clifford (1991):
Craik and Tulving (1973)
Duncan (1949)
Hebb (1949)
James (1890)
Shallice and Warrington (1970)

NEHER, A. (1967) Probability pyramiding, research error and the need for independent replication. *Psychological Record, 17,* 257–262.

APPENDICES: Any additional information such as raw data, statistical calculations, stimulus material and so on should be placed here. Each Appendix should be numbered, have a full title, and be referred to somewhere in the main body of the write-up.

⟶

APPENDICES

Appendix 1: Stimulus material

Appendix 2: Raw data

Appendix 3: Calculations of statistical tests